Barcelona

WHAT'S NEW | WHAT'S ON | WHAT'S BEST

www.timeout.com/barcelona

Contents

Don't Miss

Itineraries

Barcelona by Area

Essentials

Published by Time Out Guides Ltd
Universal House
251 Tottenham Court Road
London W1T 7AB
Tel: + 44 (0)20 7813 3000
Fax: + 44 (0)20 7813 6001
Email: guides@timeout.com
www.timeout.com

Managing Director Peter Fiennes
Editorial Director Ruth Jarvis
Business Manager Daniel Allen
Editorial Manager Holly Pick
Management Accountants Margaret Wright, Clare Turner

Time Out Guides is a wholly owned subsidiary of Time Out Group Ltd.

© **Time Out Group Ltd**
Chairman & Founder Tony Elliott
Chief Executive Officer David King
Chief Operating Officer Aksel Van der Wal
Group Financial Director Paul Rakkar
Group General Manager/Director Nichola Coulthard
Time Out Communications Ltd MD David Pepper
Time Out International Ltd MD Cathy Runciman
Time Out Magazine Ltd Publisher/Managing Director Mark Elliott
Group Commercial Director Graeme Tottle
Group IT Director Simon Chappell
Group Marketing Director Andrew Booth

Time Out and the Time Out logo are trademarks of Time Out Group Ltd.

This edition first published in Great Britain in 2011 by Ebury Publishing
A Random House Group Company
Company information can be found on www.randomhouse.co.uk
Random House UK Limited Reg. No. 954009
10 9 8 7 6 5 4 3 2 1

Distributed in the US and Latin America by Publishers Group West (1-510-809-3700)
Distributed in Canada by Publishers Group Canada (1-800-747-8147)

For further distribution details, see www.timeout.com

ISBN: 978-1-84670-235-8

A CIP catalogue record for this book is available from the British Library.

Printed and bound in Germany by Appl.

The Random House Group Limited supports the Forest Stewardship Council® (FSC®),
the leading international forest certification organisation. All our titles that are printed on
Greenpeace approved FSC® certified paper carry the FSC® logo. Our paper procurement
policy can be found at www.randomhouse.co.uk/environment.

Time Out carbon-offsets all its flights with Trees for Cities (www.treesforcities.org).

Barcelona Shortlist

The **Time Out Barcelona Shortlist** is one of a series of guides that draws on Time Out's background as a magazine publisher to keep you current with everything that's going on in town. As well as Barcelona's key sights and the best of its eating, drinking and leisure options, it picks out the most exciting venues to have recently opened and gives a full calendar of annual events. It also includes features on the important news, trends and openings, all compiled by locally based editors and writers. Whether you're visiting for the first time in your life or you're a regular, you'll find the *Time Out Barcelona Shortlist* contains all you need to know, in a portable and easy-to-use format.

The guide divides central Barcelona into seven areas, each containing listings for Sights & Museums, Eating & Drinking, Shopping, Nightlife and Arts & Leisure, and maps pinpointing their locations. At the front of the book are chapters rounding up these scenes citywide, and giving a shortlist of our overall picks. We also include itineraries for days out, plus essentials such as transport information and hotels.

Our listings give phone numbers as dialled within Barcelona. From abroad, use your country's exit code followed by 34 (the country code for Spain) and the number given.

We have noted price categories by using one to four euro signs (**€-€€€€**), representing budget, moderate, expensive and luxury. Major credit cards are accepted unless otherwise stated. We also indicate when a venue is NEW , and give Event highlights.

All our listings are double-checked, but places do sometimes close or change their hours or prices, so it's a good idea to call a venue before visiting. While every effort has been made to ensure accuracy, the publishers cannot accept responsibility for any errors that this guide may contain.

Venues are marked on the maps using symbols numbered according to their order within the chapter and colour-coded as follows:

- ❶ Sights & Museums
- ❶ Eating & Drinking
- ❶ Shopping
- ❶ Nightlife
- ❶ Arts & Leisure

Map Key	
Major sight or landmark	
Hospital or college	
Railway station	
Park	
River	
Carretera	
Main road	
Main road tunnel	
Pedestrian road	
Airport	✈
Church	✚
Metro station, FGC station	Ⓜ

Time Out **Barcelona** Shortlist

EDITORIAL
Editor Sally Davies
Deputy Editor Ros Sales
Proofreader Kieron Corless

DESIGN
Art Director Scott Moore
Art Editor Pinelope Kourmouzoglou
Senior Designer Kei Ishimaru
Group Commercial Designer Jodi Sher

Picture Editor Jael Marschner
Acting Deputy Picture Editor Liz Leahy
Picture Desk Assistant/Researcher
  Ben Rowe

ADVERTISING
New Business & Commercial Director
  Mark Phillips
International Advertising Manager
  Kasimir Berger

International Sales Executive
  Charlie Sokol
Advertising Sales (Barcelona)
  Hazel Walker

MARKETING
**Sales & Marketing Director, North
  America & Latin America** Lisa Levinson
Senior Publishing Brand Manager
  Luthfa Begum
Guides Marketing Manager
  Colette Whitehouse
Group Commercial Art Director
  Anthony Huggins
Marketing Co-ordinator Alana Benton

PRODUCTION
Group Production Manager
  Brendan McKeown
Production Controller Katie Mulhern

CONTRIBUTORS
This guide was researched and written by Sally Davies, with additional contributions
by Stephen Burgen, Nadia Feddo, Mary Ann Gallagher, Ruth Jarvis and Alx Phillips.

PHOTOGRAPHY
Photography by pages 9, 28 (top), 38, 92, 96, 106, 126, 163 Marc Goodwin; pages 11,
52, 115 Natalie Pecht; pages 12, 19, 20, 27, 42, 44, 45, 47, 55, 64, 69, 78, 84, 111,
119, 170 Elan Fleisher; pages 13, 157 Scott Chasserot; pages 14, 18, 22, 23, 24, 31,
66, 75, 103, 108 (top), 123, 130, 149, 150, 169 Greg Gladman; pages 17, 26, 28 (bottom), 30, 32, 41, 49, 51, 58, 62, 81, 108 (bottom), 139, 144, 147, 166, 174 Olivia
Rutherford; page 71 Istvan Csak; page 89 Cesar Casellas; page 133 Ivan Gimenez; page
152 Mariano Herrera/MCNB.

The following images were provided by the featured establishments/artists :
pages 7, 35, 36, 116, 136, 161, 168, 172, 175.

Cover photograph: Casa Batlló. Credit: Isidoro Ruiz Haro/Photolibrary.com.

MAPS
JS Graphics (john@jsgraphics.co.uk).

About **Time Out**

Founded in 1968, Time Out has expanded from humble London beginnings into the
leading resource for those wanting to know what's happening in the world's greatest
cities. As well as our influential what's-on weeklies in London, New York and Chicago,
we publish nearly 30 other listings magazines in cities as varied as Beijing and
Mumbai. The magazines established Time Out's trademark style: sharp writing,
informed reviewing and bang up-to-date inside knowledge of every scene.

Time Out made the natural leap into travel guides in the 1980s with the City Guide
series, which now extends to over 50 destinations around the world. Written and
researched by expert local writers and generously illustrated with original photography,
the full-size guides cover a larger area than our Shortlist guides and include many more
venue reviews, along with additional background features and a full set of maps.

Throughout this rapid growth, the company has remained proudly independent,
still owned by Tony Elliott four decades after he started Time Out London as a single
fold-out sheet of A5 paper. This independence extends to the editorial content of all
our publications, this Shortlist included. No establishment has been featured because
it has advertised, and no payment has influenced any of our reviews. And, for our critics,
there's definitely no such thing as a free lunch: all restaurants and bars are visited
and reviewed anonymously, and Time Out always picks up the bill.
For more about the company, see www.timeout.com.

Don't Miss

CosmoCaixa p154

Sights & Museums

Barcelona has not had an easy time of it in these economically troubled times, with tourism dropping by about 20 per cent in the last couple of years. As the state tightens its belt, the most interesting new openings have been private endeavours or those run by foundations, such as the fabulous collection of art and furniture at the Museu del Modernisme Català (see p125). One exception is the new Museu Blau (see p158), which incorporates and expands the collections from the former zoology and geology museums.

Pressure to pull in tourists has, however, prompted existing museums and galleries to revamp their collections, and the Fundació Tàpies (see p122) and the MNAC (see p110) have both invested in several new pieces to bolster their holdings.

The Arts Santa Mònica (see p54) and the MACBA (see p86) both have new directors appointed to cast a fresh eye, and others, such as the Museu Frederic Marès (see p57), are undergoing huge renovation. Other centres have added strings to their bows, such as the guided tours at Casa Amatller (see p122).

Many projects, though, have been put on hold until the current climate improves. Norman Foster's spectacular Gaudí-inspired overhaul of the Camp Nou stadium is one of these, along with Frank Gehry's makeover of La Sagrera station and creation of a new transport museum, and Richard Rogers' reworking of the Les Arenes bullring into a leisure and office complex.

Plans for a grand Museu del Disseny (Design Museum) in the Plaça de les Glòries have also been stalled, though there has been some movement. The idea is that it will incorporate the clothing, ceramics and decorative arts museums, along with several smaller collections. For the meantime, the Museu Tèxtil has moved from its longstanding home in a Born mansion to the Palau Reial de Pedralbes, which it shares with the Museu de Ceràmica and the Museu de les Arts Decoratives. These are now collectively known as DHUB Barcelona (see p154).

Barrio by barrio

The medieval Barri Gòtic, with the cathedral at its heart, is the starting point for most visitors. A stroll through its narrow alleyways and secluded squares is the best possible introduction to the city, combined, of course, with a wander down La Rambla, frenetic and commercial, but with a certain charm.

The last decade or so has been very kind to the districts of the Born and Sant Pere, and where monied Catalans once feared to tread, they now covet property. The two areas are divided by C/Princesa, which runs from metro Jaume I to the verdant Parc de la Ciutadella. The Born's main artery, the wide, pedestrianised Passeig del Born, is a former jousting ground and one of Barcelona's prettiest thoroughfares, bookended by the magnificent wrought-iron 19th-century market building and the glorious 14th-century Santa Maria del Mar church.

Once considered a no-go area for tourists, the Raval is undergoing a dramatic transformation, which began in 1995 with the addition of Richard Meier's monumental white MACBA, housing the city's principal collection of modern art. Then, in 2008, the five-star, futuristic Barceló hotel was erected smack in the centre of this

SHORTLIST

Best newcomers
- Museu Blau (see p158)
- Museu del Modernisme Català (see p125)

Best revamps
- DHUB Barcelona (see p154)
- Fundació Antoni Tàpies (see p122)
- Museu Frederic Marès (see p57)

Neat transport
- Catamaran Orsom (see p105)
- Telefèric de Montjuïc (see p113)
- Tramvia Blau (see p155)

Best churches
- Cathedral (see p54)
- Sagrada Família (see p127)
- Sant Pau del Camp (see p87)

Quirky collections
- Museu de Carrosses Fúnebres (see p125)
- Museu del Calçat (see p56)
- Museu del Perfum (see p125)

Picnic spots
- Parc de la Ciutadella (see p74)
- Park Güell (see p142)

Kids' stuff
- L'Aquàrium (see p104)
- CosmoCaixa (see p154)
- Zoo de Barcelona (see p74)

Glorious Gaudí
- Casa Batlló (see p122)
- Palau Güell (see p87)
- Sagrada Família (see p127)

Best for free
- Arts Santa Mònica (see p54)
- CaixaForum (see p109)
- Fundació Joan Brossa (see p124)
- Palau Güell (see p87)

previously rundown area. Some of its gems have been around for much longer – Gaudí's medievalist Palau Güell was an early, brave attempt towards gentrification.

The city's seafront was famously ignored until the 1992 Olympic Games, when the makeshift restaurants and illegal dwellings were controversially swept aside and thousands of tons of sand laid down; the city now has seven kilometres of golden sands running from the bustling Port Vell to the upscale Port Olímpic and beyond. The former fishermen's district of Barceloneta still retains its local feel and is home to some of the city's best seafood restaurants.

It's often left off visitors' itineraries, but the hill of Montjuïc merits at least a day's wander. The Fundació Joan Miró is as impressive for its Corbusier-influenced building as its collection, while Montjuïc's lesser-known museums are a varied bunch, dedicated to themes as diverse as archaeology and sport.

The Eixample (literally 'the expansion'), with its grid layout, was created in 1854 and became a Modernista showcase. Its buildings include the Sagrada Família and La Pedrera. Bisecting the area is the Passeig de Gràcia; to its right is the fashionable Dreta area, while to the left is the more down-at-heel Esquerra.

Beyond the Eixample lies the low-rise, studenty *barrio* of Gràcia, which, like workaday Sants and well-heeled Sarrià, was once an independent town swallowed up as Barcelona spread; each area retains a distinct and separate identity. Above Gràcia is Gaudí's Park Güell. Other notable places outside the centre include the former industrial area of Poblenou, touted by many as the city's answer to the Meatpacking District, though this transformation is very much a work in progress.

Casa Batlló p122

Getting around

Barcelona is a breeze to navigate.
Many major sights are within
walking distance of each other, and
the natural enclosure formed by the
sea and the mountains means it's
hard to get too lost. Remember that
uphill is *muntanya* (mountain) and
downhill is *mar* (sea) – locals often
give directions with these terms.
As well as using your feet or the
cheap, user-friendly metro and
bus systems (for a map of the
metro, see the back flap; the
subterranean tourist information
office in Plaça Catalunya provides
a very good bus map), you can also
choose to get around in a variety of
increasingly bizarre contraptions
(see box p101).

The city council runs walking
tours on various themes (from
Picasso to Modernisme, gourmet to
Gothic) at weekends and occasional
other days. These tours start in the
Plaça Catalunya tourist office, and

Casa Amatller p122

take 90 minutes to two hours,
excluding the museum trip.
For more information, see
www.barcelonaturisme.com.

There are two tourist buses
seen all over town: the orange
Barcelona Tours (93 261 56 79,
www.barcelonacitytours.cat) and
the white Bus Turístic (93 285 38
32, www.tmb.net). The former is
less frequent but less popular, so
you won't have to queue, while the
latter gives a book of discounts for
various attractions. Both visit many
of the same sights and cost much
the same.

Discounted passes

The Articket (www.articketbcn.org,
€22) gives free entry to seven major
museums and galleries (one
visit per venue over six months):
Fundació Miró, MACBA, the
MNAC, La Pedrera, Fundació
Tàpies, the CCCB and the Museu
Picasso. The Barcelona Card
(www.barcelonacard.com) allows
unlimited transport on metro and
buses, and gives discounts on sights,
cable cars and on the airport bus.
It costs €27 for a two-day pass,
€33 for three days, €34 for four
and €40.50 for five.

A word of warning

While the situation has improved
of late, Barcelona's reputation for
muggings is not completely without
justification. You are very unlikely
to be physically assaulted, but bag-
snatching and pickpocketing are
rife, especially in the Old City, on
the beach and on public transport.
Leave whatever you can in your
hotel, keep your wallet in your front
pocket, wear backpacks on the front
and be wary of anyone trying to
clean something off your shoulder,
sell you a posy or get you to point
something out on a map.

Bar del Pla p76

WHAT'S BEST
Eating & Drinking

Thus far, Barcelona's dining scene has proved itself remarkably resilient to recession, and despite the drop in tourism, it's as difficult as it ever was to bag an unreserved table at a good restaurant on a Friday night. Bars and cafés also seem to be weathering the crisis, with few closures and no perceptible slowdown in business.

This is partly explained by local habits. Catalans tend not to entertain at home, so the bar is as crucial a meeting place as ever, while restaurants are kept afloat by the continuing brisk trade in lunchtime *menús del dia* for the workers – the sandwich habit has never really caught on in Spain.

At the luxury end of the spectrum, many of Barcelona's top chefs have responded to the situation by creating diffusion lines – some are now offering catering for people to eat at home, and others have opened lower-key, more affordable eateries. As ever, superchef Ferran Adrià leads the way with his new tapas bar Tickets (see p117), while Michelin-starred chef Carles Abellan's tapas place, Tapaç24 (see p131) is also popular. Also, renowned chefs Carlos Gaig and Fermi Puig have opened what they term 'bistros' – Fonda Gaig (see p129) and Petit Comité (Ptge de la Concepció 13, Eixample, 93 550 06 20, www.petitcomite.cat) – though neither is especially cheap.

Elsewhere, the expats have it, with the excellent new Australian-run café Federal (see p129); En Petit Comité (see p79) adding a little French savoir faire to the

Tapaç24 p13

Plaça Sant Pere in the Born, and the excellent Routa (see p131) flying the flag for New Nordic.

Drink up

If you want draught beer, ask for a *caña*, which is a small measure; tourists invariably request *cerveza*, which is a bottled beer. Recently there has been a welcome comeback for Moritz beer, brewed in Barcelona and preferred by many to the ubiquitous Estrella. Shandy (*clara*) is also popular, here made with bitter lemon and very refreshing in summer. Sangría is rarely offered outside tourist traps.

Catalan wines are becoming better known internationally as they improve, and it's worth looking out for the local DOs Priorat, Montsant, Toro and Costers del Segre, as well as the commonplace Penedès. Most wine drunk here is red (*negre/tinto*), apart from the many cavas, which run from *semi-sec* ('half-dry', but actually pretty sweet) to *brut nature* (very dry). Freixenet is the best known, but there are better cavas, including Parxet and Albet i Noya.

Coffee in Barcelona is mostly strong and mostly good. The three basic types are *solo* (also known simply as *café*), a small strong black coffee; *cortado*, the same but with a little milk; and *café con leche*, the same with more milk. An *americano* is black coffee diluted with more water and *carajillo* is a short, black coffee with a liberal dash of brandy. Decaffeinated coffee (*descafeinado*) is popular and widely available, but specify *de máquina* (from the machine) unless you want instant (*de sobre*).

Tea is pretty poor and generally best avoided. If you can't live without it, ask for cold milk on the side ('*leche fría aparte*') or run the risk of getting a glass of hot milk and a teabag.

SHORTLIST

Best new restaurants
- Bacoa (see p76)
- En Petit Comité (see p79)
- Picnic (see p80)
- The Tatami Room (see p117)
- Tintoreria Dontell (see p132)

Best cafés
- Bar del Convent (see p76)
- Drac Café (see p77)
- Federal (see p129)
- Olivia (see p91)

Best tapas bars
- Bar del Pla (see p76)
- Tapaç24 (see p131)
- La Taverna del Clínic (see p131)
- Tickets (see p117)

Best for kids
- Bar Kasparo (see p87)
- El Jardí (see p91)
- La Nena (see p145)

Best vegetarian
- La Báscula (see p76)
- Buenas Migas (see p88)
- Juicy Jones (see p91)

Best for tea and cake
- Caj Chai (see p60)
- La Granja (see p61)
- La Nena (see p145)

Best for seafood
- Cal Pep (see p77)
- Can Majó (see p100)
- Kaiku (see p102)
- La Paradeta (see p79)

Best for winos
- Ginger (see p60)
- La Vinateria del Call (see p64)
- La Vinya del Senyor (see p80)

DON'T MISS

Picnic restaurant

On a bright corner near the Parc de Cuitadella you'll find Picnic, a casually chic restaurant/bar offering a diverse international tapas menu, extensive wine list and exciting cocktails, and of course their famous brunch.

Chef and owners Jaime and Andrew offer a mix of homemade family dishes boasting flavours they've learned to love whilst abroad. American, Chilean and Australian roots blended with Catalan influences offer a lovely mix of tapas using recipes passed down through the family with added gourmet touches. Service is a big deal for us, so we promise to always do our best to make you feel at home.

Open all week for lunch & dinner as well as brunch on Saturdays & Sundays.

**Calle Comerç 1, Barcelona 08003, España
T. 93 511 6661 www.picnic-restaurant.com**

Tapas tips

Tapas are not especially popular in Barcelona, though there are some excellent options, the new Tickets (see p117), Tapaç24 (see p131) and Quimet i Quimet (p114) among them. The custom of giving a free tapa with a drink is almost unheard of in Catalonia.

Slightly different from the archetypal Spanish tapas bars are *pintxo* bars – their Basque origin means that the word is always given in Euskera – such as Euskal Etxea (see p79). A *pintxo* (be careful not to confuse it with the Spanish term *pincho*, which refers to a very small tapa) consists of some ingenious culinary combination on a small slice of bread. Platters of them are usually brought out at particular times, often around 1pm and again at 8pm. *Pintxos* come impaled on toothpicks, which you keep on your plate so that the barman can tally them up at the end.

Sadly, Brits hold the worst reputation for abusing this eminently civilised system by 'forgetting' to hand over all their toothpicks.

Without a decent grasp of the language, tapas bars can be quite intimidating unless you know exactly what you want. Don't be afraid to seek guidance, but some of the more standard offerings will include *tortilla* (potato omelette), *patatas bravas* (fried potatoes in a spicy red sauce and garlic mayonnaise), *ensaladilla* (Russian salad), *pinchos morunos* (small pork skewers), *champiñones al ajillo* (mushrooms fried in garlic), *gambas al ajillo* (prawns and garlic), *mejillones a la marinera* (mussels in a tomato and onion sauce), *chocos* (squid fried in batter), *almejas al vapor* (steamed clams with garlic and parsley), *pulpo* (octopus) and *pimientos del padrón* (little green peppers, one or two of which will kick like an angry mule, in a vegetable Russian roulette).

Caj Chai p60

Order, order

The concept of 'rounds' is unknown here; instead, drinks are tallied up and paid for when you leave. There are some exceptions, mostly in tourist-oriented or very busy places, where you may be asked to pay as you order, particularly if you sit out on the terrace. To attract a waiter's attention, a loud but polite '*oiga*' or, in Catalan, '*escolti*' is acceptable. On the vexed question of throwing detritus on the floor (cigarette ends, olive pits and so on), it's safest to keep an eye on what the locals are doing.

Kitchens usually open around 1.30 or 2pm and go on until roughly 3.30 or 4pm; dinner is served from about 9 until 11.30pm or midnight. Some restaurants open earlier in the evening, but arriving before 9.30 or 10pm generally means you'll be dining alone or in the company of other foreigners. Reserving a table is generally a good idea: not only on Friday and Saturday nights, but also on Sunday evenings and Monday lunchtimes, when few restaurants are open. Many also close for holidays, including about a week over Easter, and the month of August. We have listed closures of more than a week wherever we can, but restaurants are fickle.

Costs

For US and UK visitors particularly, eating out in Barcelona is not as cheap as it used to be, but low mark-ups on wines keep the cost relatively reasonable. The majority of restaurants serve an economical, fixed-price *menú del dia* at lunchtime; this usually consists of a starter, main course, dessert, bread and something to drink.

Laws governing the issue of prices are often flouted, but, legally, menus must declare if the seven per cent IVA (VAT) is included in prices or not (it rarely is), and also if there is a cover charge (generally expressed as a charge for bread).

Kaiku p102

Arlequí Mascares p65

Shopping

Strolling down the golden retail belts of Portal de l'Angel, Rambla de Catalunya or Passeig de Gràcia you would never know there was a recession. Down the sidestreets, however, owners of small shops have had to adapt to survive, with creative measures such as that at MTX Barcelona (see p82), a designer clothes store that now plays host to a different artist every month. Small designers have sought safety in numbers, forming collectives and making their clothes in workshops attached to the storefront. Vintage stores are also growing steadily in popularity, particularly in the Raval and Gràcia, with many stocking repurposed and recycled garments on the side.

Large malls continue to thrive and multiply: most notably in 2011, when the Richard Rogers-designed Les Arenes opened in the former bullring on Plaça Espanya.

Depêche mode

To widespread consternation, Bread & Butter, the titan of Barcelona fashion fairs, upped sticks and returned to its roots in Berlin, but an ever-expanding cast of one-day markets, pop-up shops and other niche shopping events keep Barcelona's fickle fashion scene on the move. Pulgas Mix (www.pulgas mix.net) combines indie designer clothes stalls with music and urban art three times a year at the Convent Sant Agustí in the Born; the international Fashion Freak Festival www.fashionfreak.es) is more of a roving nightclub event with clothes stalls and DJs late into the night;

Maremàgnum

while the biannual Changing Room (www.changing room.org) takes place at the Chic & Basic Hotel, where 25 designers take over rooms with their designs.

Wining ways

Everybody and his dog seem to be taking evening classes in wine tasting these days, and entering a wine shop has become a statement about your lifestyle choice rather than a quick foray to grab a bottle of plonk. Wine shops are no longer fusty old *bodegas* where customers have to poke about and rely on guesswork: shops such as Vila Viniteca (see p83), Torres (C/Nou del a Rambla 25, Raval, 93 317 32 34, www.vinosencasa.com) and Vinus & Brindis (C/Torrent de l'Olla 147, Gràcia, 93 218 30 37, www.vinus brindis.com) have expanded and reinvented themselves to offer taster spaces, designer tapas to complement the wines, wine courses, vineyard tours and gourmet food products. Inverting the paradigm, many gourmet food shops now offer wines to complement their products – try a combination of fine Iberian ham and wine at Jamonisimo (C/Provença 85, Eixample, 93 439 08 47, www.jamonisimo.com).

Small is beautiful

It is Barcelona's wealth of tiny independent shops that really make it unique as a shopping destination, although it can be hard to see how the shops devoted to a single obscure speciality such as felt dolls or retro vinyl can survive. Look out for the dressmakers and one-off fashion boutiques in the Born; the indie art galleries of the upper Raval; the traditional artisans, antique shops and speciality food stores of the Barri Gòtic and the

SHORTLIST

Best newcomers
- Les Arenes (see p19)
- Discos Juandó (see p82)
- Ivo & Co (see p82)

Best for books
- Altaïr (see p132)
- Casa del Llibre (see p134)
- FNAC (see p135)

Best for street chic
- Capricho de Muñeca (see p80)
- Free (see p94)
- Hatquarters (see p82)

Best malls
- Barcelona Glòries (see p158)
- Diagonal Mar (see p158)
- Maremàgnum (see p102)

Best foot forward
- Camper (see p134)
- Mango (see p135)
- Muxart (see p135)

Best for arts and crafts
- Almacenes del Pilar (see p65)
- Arlequí Mascares (see p65)
- El Ingenio (see p67)

Best emblematic design
- Camper (see p134)
- Custo Barcelona (see p81)
- Vinçon (see p137)

Best local chains
- Camper (see p134)
- Mango (see p135)

Best for kids
- Du Pareil au Même (see p134)
- Imaginarium (see p135)
- El Ingenio (see p67)

Best historical
- Caelum (see p65)
- Cereria Subirà (see p67)
- Formatgeria La Seu (see p67)
- Herboristeria del Rei (see p67)

Capricho de Muñeca p80

quirky jewellery workshops or vintage clothes shops of Gràcia. These shops are also among the most photogenic in the city, often holding treasures such as the ancient butter-making machinery in Formatgeria La Seu (see p67), the old toasting ovens at Casa Gispert (C/Sombrerers 23, Born, 93 319 75 35) or the medieval Jewish baths at Caelum (see p65).

Market forces

In the Ajuntament's book, a revamped local market is the first step on the road to urban regeneration. This was true for the Mercat Santa Caterina in Sant Pere and the Mercat de la Barceloneta, both spectacular pieces of architecture in their own right and the catalysts for reinventing previously downtrodden neighbourhoods. In an attempt to fuse modern and traditional approaches to shopping, the new markets tend to hold far fewer actual stalls than before, with more space turned over to supermarkets and restaurants. The largest current project is the complete overhaul of the Mercat Sant Antoni, set to include three new subterranean floors and provide a new home for the traditional Els Encants flea market, while retaining its spectacular iron Modernista shell. While building work takes place, the market stalls and Els Encants have been moved to provisional buildings on the Ronda de Sant Antoni between C/Casanova and C/Urgell.

Finding an outlet

One of Barcelona's hotspots for bargain clothes shopping is C/Girona. In particular, the two blocks between C/Ausiàs Marc and Gran Via de les Corts Catalanes are crammed with remainder stores and factory outlets of varying quality. By far the most popular is the Mango Outlet (C/Girona 37, 93 412 29 35). See also box p136.

Dedicated bargain hunters also make the 30-minute pilgrimage outside Barcelona to La Roca Village (93 842 39 39, www.larocavillage.com), with more than 50 discount outlets of designer brands.

Shop tactics

Most small independent stores still open 10am-2pm and 5-8pm Monday to Saturday, but high-street shops tend to stay open through the siesta period. Markets mostly open only until 2 or 3pm, though some stay open into the evening from Thursday to Saturday. Sales (*rebaixes* or *rebajas*) usually run from 7 January to late February, and again during July and August.

Tourist offices stock free *Shopping Guide* booklets, with a map and advice on everything from how to get your VAT refund to using the Barcelona Shopping Line bus.

Caelum p65

Sidecar Factory Club p70

Nightlife

There's an energy and creativity in Barcelona's nightlife that's hard to find anywhere else, demonstrated by the anything-goes mix of people in bars, the willingness to experiment with sound and art, and the continued devotion to innovation in interior bar design. But a night out in Barcelona is greater than the sum of these parts; it's a spiritual matter. It's a vibe, created and fostered by a population who party well, knowing when to go for it and when to call it quits, when to clap and when to soft-shoe… but most of all understanding that going out – like eating – is a necessary (and pleasurable) part of life that should be done right.

While battles between club owners and the town hall continue to inspire an apocalyptic image in local media, the exaggerated rumours of the death of the city's music scene are gradually fading. In a long-awaited move, officials have simplified the convoluted licencing laws and offered financial support to owners who are willing to soundproof their spaces.

Millions of words have already been spent lamenting the victims of the government's anti-noise campaign, with the future of several beloved bars and clubs (mostly notably the Raval's elegant dancehall, La Paloma) still hanging in the balance. The good news is that there are venues and nights springing up to fill the void, such as den of soul, funk and rare groove, Marula Café (see p70), Jazzy

Down Floor, located in the downstairs of El Foro restaurant (C/Princesa 53, Born, 93 310 10 20), and the recent reopening of the much-missed Café Royale (C/Nou de Zurbano 3, Barri Gòtic 93 412 14 33).

Live acts

There is further evidence that all is not as bad as it seems: local acts continue to pop up like toast, their success and profligacy attesting to Barcelona's tenacious relevancy on the wider Spanish music scene. Live electro group Love of Lesbian, folk popsters Manel, Cineplexx & the Odeons and the chirpy Pinker Tones are some names to look out for. There are also more active metal-core bands than you can shake a death rattle at, if that's your thing, and a slew of internationally minded musicians drawing from a blend of rock, flamenco, rai, hip hop and various South American, Asian and African styles – the best known among them are Ojos de Brujo, Raval's 08001 and CaboSanRoque, all of them favourites at Barcelona's various music festivals.

The main venue for international names (as well as hotly tipped unknowns) is the multi-faceted industrial space Razzmatazz (see p158), which has recently hosted bands from M.I.A., Caribou and MGMT to where-are-they-now bands like Sonic Youth or Crowded House. Moving into fallback position, the mall-like Bikini (see p151) still nets some top-notch international names (recent appearances include Adele and Gil Scott-Heron) and plenty of local stars.

For less well-known acts, the old dancehalls Sala Apolo (see p118)

SHORTLIST

Best for big-time bands
- Bikini (see p151)
- Luz de Gas (see p156)
- Razzmatazz (see p158)
- Sala Apolo (see p118)

Best for intimate gigs
- Harlem Jazz Club (see p68)
- Heliogabal (see p148)
- El Paraigua (see p70)
- Sala Monasterio (see p104)
- Sidecar Factory Club (see p70)

Best under the stars
- La Caseta del Migdia (see p114)
- Elephant (see p156)
- La Terrrazza (see p118)

Best for bohemians
- Bar Marsella (see p88)
- Bar Pastis (see p94)
- Tinta Roja (see p117)

Best for boys' stuff
- Arena (see p137)
- D-Boy (see p137)

Best hands-in-the-air action
- City Hall (see p137)
- La Terrrazza (see p118)

Best for rare groove
- Diobar (see p83)
- Jazzy Down Floor (see left)
- Marula Café (see p70)

Best for a bit of glam
- CDLC (see p104)
- Eclipse at the W Hotel (see p171)
- Mondo (see p104)

Best for a late drink
- Barcelona Pipa Club (see p68)
- Big Bang (see p95)
- La Concha (see p95)

and Luz de Gas (see p156) host several concerts a week. Global superstars perform in Montjuïc's sports stadiums or at the sprawling Fòrum, where even 44,000 people at Primavera Sound can't seem to fill the space.

Times & tickets

Going out happens late here, with people rarely meeting for a drink much before 11pm – if they do, it's a pre-dinner thing. Bars tend to close around 2am, or 3am at weekends, and it's only after this that the clubs get going, so many offer reduced entrance fees or free drinks to those willing to be seen inside before 1am. And if you're still raring to go at 6am, just ask around – more often than not there'll be an after-party catering to the truly brave.

For concert information, see the weekly listings magazine *Time Out Barcelona* or the Friday papers, which usually include listings supplements. Look in bars and music shops for free magazines such as *Go*, *AB*, *Mondo Sonoro* (all mostly independent pop/rock/electronica) and *Batonga!* (which covers world music). *Punto H* and *Suite* are good for keeping up to date on the club scene.

Also try the following listings websites for information:
www.infoconcerts.cat
www.atiza.com
www.salirenbarcelona.com
www.barcelonarocks.com
www.clubbing spain.com.

For music festivals, try www.festivales.com and www.whatsonwhen.com.

You can also get information and tickets from Tel-entrada and Servi-Caixa, and FNAC. Record shops are good for info and flyers.

Elephant p156

La Pedrera p127

Arts & Leisure

A steady stream of new performing arts venues such as the Fabra i Coats centre for theatre and dance studies, and the recently inaugurated Auditori in La Pedrera, show that despite hard economic times, there is always enthusiasm and funding for the arts in Barcelona. Major projects in the pipeline are the Illa Philips, an enormous new dance space due to open in late 2012; the 12-million euro Filmoteca projected to open in the Raval, also in 2012; a circus centre at the Fòrum, and La Seca – a space for theatre, dance, puppetry and cabaret created in an old coin factory in the Born, and projected to open in 2014.

The most warmly received new arts festival in recent times has been Montjuïc de Nit, a night of over 50 free cultural activities ranging from cinema to circus; inspired by similar nights in other European cities, Barcelona characteristically took a good idea and improved on it, concentrating all events on the magic mountain of Montjuïc and boosting its image as a cultural hotspot.

Film

Dubbing is a huge industry in Barcelona and although it is generally very well done, recent legislation means that 50 per cent of dubbing must be in Catalan rather than Spanish, a move that cinemas mostly object to for economic reasons (there are far fewer takers for the Catalan versions). A sense of linguistic regional pride combined with an increasing mastery of English

CosmoCaixa

has greatly encouraged the local trend for subtitles over dubbing, even in large commercial cineplexes such as the Yelmo Icària. This is all good news for the foreign filmgoer and additions in recent years to the cinemas that show films in *versió original* (VO) include the Cinema Maldà (C/Pi 5, Barri Gòtic, 93 317 85 29) and the Casablanca-Kaplan (see p138). Subtitled indie flicks are also shown at occasional outdoor cinema cycles, such as the Sala Montjuïc (www.salamontjuic.com) or Gandules in the patio of the CCCB (see p86), both in July and August.

Classical music

In recent years there has been a huge increase in the range of classical music on offer, thanks to the opening of facilities such as the Auditori in Gaudí's landmark La Pedrera (see p127), the subterranean Conservatori at the Liceu opera house (see p70) and the modern extension to the Modernista Palau de la Música Catalana (see p72). All of these spaces offer an alternative to the classical canon with dynamic and sometimes surprisingly daring programmes of chamber opera, recitals and contemporary compositions.

An injection of state funding for local projects, known as the Plan Zapatero, has also paid for a new four-floor extension to the ever-expanding Auditori (see p138), providing concert and rehearsal space for the Banda Municipal de Barcelona and other Auditori residents such as the Quartet Casals, the classical ensemble BCN 216, the Capella Reial de Catalunya and the Orquestra Àrab.

Performing Arts

Showcasing Barcelona's knack for appropriating unlikely spaces for

---

SHORTLIST

Best for indie flicks
- Cinemes Méliès (see p138)
- La FilmoTeca (see p138)
- Renoir-Floridablanca (see p138)

Best dance venues
- Fabra i Coats (see below)
- Mercat de les Flors (see p118)
- Teatre Nacional (see p138)

Best for kids
- L'Aquàrium (see p104)
- CosmoCaixa (see p154)
- Camp Nou (see p151)

Best cultural freebies
- Festes de la Mercè (see p39)
- Montjuïc de Nit (see p36)

Best classical music venues
- L'Auditori (see p138)
- Gran Teatre del Liceu (see p70)
- Palau de la Música Catalana (see p72)

DON'T MISS

---

innovative purposes is the disused Fabra i Coats textile factory (C/Sant Adrià 18-24) in the outlying neighbourhood of Sant Andreu, which has been sleekly reinvented as a space for performing arts. The dance and theatre programmes are particularly strong with a much-needed emphasis on children's productions. The next project to redress the city's current lack of major dance venues is the 600sq m Illa Philips, based in Zona Franca, which is currently being transformed into the Centre de Creació de la Dansa and is due to open in 2012. Other major performing art venues include the Teatre Nacional (see p138), for large-scale pieces by big names such as Sol Pico or Nacho Duato, and the Mercat de les Flors (see p118), with its concentration on the kookier end of the scale with plenty of offbeat and experimental performances.

Kids

In Barcelona, children are never too young to get their first taste of opera or classical music and L'Auditori, the Liceu and the Palau de la Música all offer very popular family sessions that might include anything from percussion for under-twos to a specially adapted version of Stravinsky's 'Firebird'. Other fun educational treats include learning about anything from geckos to gravity at CosmoCaixa (see p154), a trip to the Zoo (see p74) or L'Aquàrium (see p104), or even making chocolate figures at the Museu de la Xocolata (see p72). To let off steam, there's always fun to be had at the beach, the Parc de la Ciutadella (see p74), or a day at the Tibidabo Funfair (see p153).

Sports

The city's excellent Olympic facilities attract a steady stream of events throughout the year, but the main focus of local sporting life is undoubtedly football, and there are plans to make the Camp Nou stadium, already the biggest in Europe, even bigger. A project for a controversial €250m facelift by Norman Foster, which would increase its capacity from 98,000 to 106,000 and coat it with an outer Gaudiesque shell of multicoloured screens, seems to have been shelved for the duration of the recession, but is still in the pipeline.

Another major draw is the Formula One Spanish Grand Prix; the big new name is local (and frighteningly young) driver Dani Clos.

L'Auditori p138

Calendar

Festival del Grec p36

The festivals story in 2011 was of yet more foldings and few openings, so check these events before you set off. Information and exact dates can be found nearer the time from the *Time Out Barcelona* magazine (www. timeout.cat), along with flyers and seasonal guides available from tourist offices (see p185). For gay and lesbian events, look out for free magazines such as *Nois* and *Shanguide*.

Dates highlighted in **bold** are public holidays.

January

Ongoing Drap Art (see Dec)

1 Any Nou (New Year's Day)

5 Cavalcada dels Reis
All over Barcelona
www.bcn.cat/nadal
The three kings (Melchior, Gaspar and Balthasar) head a grand parade around town from 5pm to 9pm.

6 Reis Mags (Three Kings)

Around 17 **Festa dels Tres Tombs**
Around Mercat Sant Antoni & Raval
www.xarxantoni.net/festamajor
Festival celebrating St Anthony's day.

Around 29-30 **Sa Pobla a Gràcia**
Gràcia, around Plaça Diamant
www.bcn.cat
Two days of festivities drawn from Mallorcan folk culture.

February

Festival Internacional de Percussió
L'Auditori (p138)
www.auditori.org
International and local percussion acts.

Week of 12 Feb **Santa Eulàlia**
All over Barcelona
www.bcn.cat/santaeulalia
Blowout winter festival in honour of Santa Eulàlia, co-patron saint of the city and a particular favourite of children. Expect many kids' activities.

Santa Eulàlia p31

Shrove Tuesday & Ash Wednesday
Carnival
All over Barcelona
www.bcn.cat/carnaval
King Carnestoltes leads the fancy dress parades and street parties before being burned on Ash Wednesday.

Mid Feb **Barcelona Visual Sound**
Various venues
www.bcnvisualsound.org
Ten-day showcase for untried film talent covering shorts, documentaries, animation and web design.

Late Feb **Minifestival de Música Independent de Barcelona**
La [2] (p117) & Convent de Sant Agustí, Born
www.minifestival.net
Two-day indie and folk festival.

March

3 **Festes de Sant Medir de Gràcia**
Gràcia
www.santmedir.org
People riding horse-drawn carts shower the crowds with blessed sweets.

Week of 17 March **El Feile**
Various venues
www.elfeile.com
Irish festival of music, dance and comedy for Saint Patrick's day.

25 (2012) **Marató Barcelona**
Starts & finishes at Plaça de Espanya
www.maratobarcelona.com
City marathon.

Late March **Kosmopolis**
CCCB (see p86)
www.cccb.org/kosmopolis
Three-day festival of literature.

April

Apr-May **Festival Guitarra**
Various venues
www.theproject.cat
Guitar festival spanning everything from flamenco to jazz.

Early April **La Cursa el Corte Inglés**
All over Barcelona
www.cursaelcorteingles.com
Over 50,000 participants attempt the seven-mile race.

Early Apr **Festival de Música Antiga**
L'Auditori (p138)
www.auditori.org
Two-week cycle of ancient music.

2-8 (2012) **Setmana Santa (Holy Week)**
Palm fronds are blessed at the cathedral on Palm Sunday at the start of Holy Week, and children receive elaborate chocolate creations.

6 (2012) **Divendres Sant (Good Friday)**

9 (2012) **Dilluns de Pasqua (Easter Monday)**

23 **Sant Jordi**
La Rambla & all over Barcelona
Feast day of Sant Jordi (St George), the patron saint of Catalonia. Couples exchange gifts of red roses and books.

Late Apr **Dia de la Terra**
Passeig Lluis Companys, Born
www.diadelaterra.org
One-day eco-festival.

Late Apr
Feria de Abril de Catalunya
Fòrum area
www.fecac.org
Satellite of Seville's famous fair with decorated marquees, flamenco and manzanilla sherry, over a week.

May

Ongoing Festival Guitarra (see Apr)

1 **Dia del Treball (May Day)**
Various venues
A day of demonstrations and marches take place across the city, led by trade unionists.

Loop Festival

11 Sant Ponç
C/Hospital, Raval
www.bcn.cat
Street market of herbs, honey and candied fruit to celebrate the day of Saint Ponç, patron saint of herbalists.

Mid May
Festival Internacional de Poesia
All over Barcelona
www.bcn.cat/barcelonapoesia
Week-long city-wide poetry festival, with readings in English.

Mid May
Festa Major de Nou Barris
Nou Barris
www.bcn.cat
Neighbourhood festival famous for outstanding flamenco.

Mid May **Loop Festival**
Various venues
www.loop-barcelona.com
Experimental video art festival.

Mid May
Festival de Flamenco de Ciutat Vella
CCCB (p86)
www.flamencociutatvella.com
A four-day flamenco festival, with concerts, films and activities for children.

Mid May **Nit dels Museus**
All over Barcelona
www.museus2012.cat
Museums open late – and they're free.

18 Dia Internacional dels Museus
All over Barcelona
www.museus2012.cat
Free entrance to the city's museums during the daytime.

Late May **La Tamborinada**
Parc de la Ciutadella, Born
www.fundaciolaroda.cat
A vibrant one-day festival of concerts, workshops and circus performances, aimed at children.

Montjuïc de Nit p36

Late May **Primavera Sound**
Fòrum area
www.primaverasound.com
A big-name indie music festival, taking
place over three days.

28 (2012) **Segona Pasqua
(Whitsun)**

June

June-Aug **Música als Parcs**
Various venues
www.bcn.cat/parcsijardins
Free alfresco music in Barcelona's
parks: jazz on Wednesday and Friday
nights, and classical music on
Thursday and Sunday.

Early June **Festa dels Cors
de la Barceloneta**
Barceloneta
www.bcn.cat
Choirs sing and parade on Saturday
morning and Monday afternoon.

7-9 (2012) **L'Ou com Balla**
Cathedral cloisters & other venues
www.bcn.cat/icub
Corpus Christi processions and the
L'Ou Com Balla – hollowed-out eggs
dancing on decorated fountains.

Mid June **Sónar**
Various venues
www.sonar.es
Four-day festival of electronic music,
urban art and media technologies.

Mid June **Festa de la Música**
All over Barcelona
www.bcn.cat/festadelamusica
Free international music festival with
amateur musicians from 100 countries.

Late June **Gran Trobada
d'Havaneres**
Passeig Joan de Borbó, Barceloneta
www.bcn.cat/icub
Sea shanties with fireworks and cremat
(flaming spiced rum) over a few days.

23-24 Sant Joan
All over Barcelona
Summer solstice means cava, all-night bonfires and fireworks.

Late June-Aug **Festival del Grec**
Various venues
www.bcn.cat/grec
Two-month spree of dance, music and theatre all over the city.

July

Ongoing Música als Parcs (see June), Festival del Grec (see June)

Early July **Dies de Dansa**
Various venues
www.marato.com
Several days of dance performances in public spaces dotted around the city.

Early July **Hipnotik**
CCCB (p86)
www.cccb.org or *www.hipnotikfestival.com*
A one-day festival of all things hip hop.

Early July **Montjuïc de Nit**
Montjuïc
www.bcn.cat/cultura/montjuicnit

Theatre, dance, cinema and art up on the hill, with a live music in unlikely venues and museums staying open until around 3am.

Mid July
Festa Major del Raval
Raval
www.bcn.cat/icub
Over three days, entertainment includes giants, a fleamarket, children's workshops, free concerts and ethnic food stalls on the Rambla del Raval.

Mid July **Cruïlla BCN**
Parc del Fòrum
www.cruillabarcelona.com
A two-day festival of Spanish and world music.

August

Ongoing Música als Parcs (see June), Festival del Grec (see June)

Mas i Mas Festival
Various venues
www.masimas.com

Europes p40

European Commissions

New festival Europes aspires to build cultural bridges.

Launched in autumn 2010 and set to become a regular feature on the city's calendar, Europes, 'Festival of Contemporary Culture', has as its wildly ambitious but very laudable aim an exploration of the continent's latest trends in art, architecture, theatre, dance, film, food, music, literature and – for any miscellanea that might have dropped through the cracks – 'cultural thought'.

Held over 25 days in October and November, it involved over 250 activities, held in 200 different locations. Nothing if not multidisciplinary, these ranged from the soundscapes of the Orchestra of Chaos at the Museu Picasso (see p72) to Booker Prize-winning author John Banville giving a talk in a local library to the north of the city. A surprise hit was the talk given by Eugen Gomringer, considered to be one of the creators of 'concrete' or

'shape' poetry, while a double bill of Romanian cinema pulled an equally impressive crowd.

There were three days of debates on cultural themes, and a abundance of performances in different genres, most notably held at the Liceu opera house (see p70), the Mercat de les Flors (see p118) and the CaixaForum (see p109).

The showcasing of young art students from across Europe is considered to be one of the pillars of the festival, and organisers La Fábrica (www.lafabrica.com) created a well-intentioned, if slightly unfortunately named, scheme: Bed Sharing. This involved Catalan students supplying accommodation to their counterparts from the rest of Europe for the run of the festival, on the understanding this would be reciprocated in the future.
■ www.europes-festival.eu

Festes de la Mercè

Wildly varied festival, with acts from Latin to chamber music.

Every Wed **Summer Nights at CaixaForum**
CaixaForum (see p109)
www.fundacio.lacaixa.es
All exhibitions are open until midnight with music, films and other activities.

Every Tue-Thur **Gandules**
CCCB (see p86)
www.cccb.org
A series of outdoor film screenings held on the deckchair-strewn patio of the CCCB.

15 L'Assumpció (Assumption Day)

Week of 16 Aug **Festa de Sant Roc**
Barri Gòtic
www.bcn.cat
The Barri Gòtic's party with parades, fireworks, traditional street games and fire-running.

Late Aug **Festa Major de Gràcia**
Gràcia
www.festamajordegracia.cat
A best-dressed street competition for the Gràcia neighbourhood; it also features giants and human castles.

Late Aug **Festa Major de Sants**
Sants
www.festamajordesants.cat
A neighbourhood festival consisting of a series of street parties, along with concerts and fire-running.

September

Festival L'Hora del Jazz
Various venues
www.amjm.org
Month-long festival of local jazz acts, with free daytime concerts.

11 Diada Nacional de Catalunya
All over Barcelona
Flags and marches affirm cultural identity on Catalan National Day.

Late Sept **Festival Asia**
Various venues
www.festivalasia.es
Two weeks of shows, music and stalls.

Week of 24 Sept **Festes de la Mercè**
All over Barcelona
www.bcn.cat/merce
Barcelona's biggest and brightest festival has human castles, giants, concerts, an airshow and fireworks on the beach.

24 La Mercè

During Festes de la Mercè **Mostra de Vins i Caves de Catalunya**
Moll de la Fusta, Port Vell
An outdoor tasting fair of local wines and cavas.

During Festes de la Mercè **Barcelona Acció Musical (BAM)**
Various venues
www.bcn.cat/bam/2011/index.htm
Around 40 concerts, mostly from local acts, and many of which are free.

Late Sept **L'Alternativa**
CCCB (see p86)
http://alternativa.cccb.org/2011
Indie film festival.

End Sept **Festa Major de la Barceloneta**
All over Barceloneta
www.cascantic.net
Festival fever fills the fishing quarter, with fireworks, acrobats, music and parades.

October

LEM Festival
Various venues, Gràcia
www.gracia-territori.com
Month-long festival of multimedia art and experimental electronica.

Early-mid Oct **Festival de Músiques del Món**
L'Auditori (see p138)
www.auditori.cat

Two-week world music festival featuring 20 concerts and related exhibitions.

Oct-Nov **Europes**
All over Barcelona
See box p37.

12 Dia de la Hispanitat

15-16 (2012) **Caminada Internacional de Barcelona**
www.euro-senders.com/internacional
The International Walk is conducted along different routes of varying lengths.

Mid Oct **Festival de Tardor Ribermúsica**
Various venues, Born
www.ribermusica.org
Over 100 free music performances, held in squares, churches, bars and shops.

Mid Oct **Open House BCN**
Various venues, Born
www.48openhousebarcelona.org
Over 150 architecturally or historically significant buildings open to the public.

Late Oct-early Nov **In-Edit Beefeater Festival**
Various venues, Eixample
www.in-edit.beefeater.es
A film festival devoted to international musical documentaries.

31-**1** Nov
La Castanyada
All over Barcelona
All Saints' Day and the evening before are celebrated with piles of roast chestnuts and floral tributes at cemeteries.

Late Oct-Nov
Festival Internacional de Jazz de Barcelona
Various venues
www.barcelonajazzfestival.com
Jazz from bebop to big band.

November

Ongoing La Castanyada (see Oct), Europes (see Oct), In-Edit Beefeater Festival (see Oct),

Festival Internacional de Jazz de Barcelona (see Oct)

Art Futura
Arts Santa Mònica (p54)
www.artfutura.org
Digital and cyber art festival.

1 Tots Sants (All Saints' Day)

December

Els Grans del Gospel
Various venues
www.theproject.cat
A three-week festival of gospel music.

1-24 Fair of Sant Eloi
C/Argenteria, Born
www.acar.cat
A Christmas street fair with artisans selling their wares. Live music is performed from 6pm to 8pm.

3-23 (2012) Fira de Santa Llúcia
Pla de la Seu & Avda de la Catedral, Barri Gòtic
www.bcn.cat/nadal
Fira de Santa Llúcia is a Christmas market with trees, decorations and nativity-scene figures.

6 Día de la Constitución

8 La Immaculada

Mid Dec-mid Jan **Drap-Art**
CCCB (p86)
www.drapart.org
A creative recycling fest, with concerts, workshops and a Christmas market.

25 Nadal (Christmas Day)

26 Sant Esteve (Boxing Day)

28 Día dels Inocents
Local version of April Fool's Day, with paper figures attached to the backs of unsuspecting victims.

31 Cap d'Any (New Year's Eve)
Swill cava and eat a grape for every chime of the clock at midnight. Wear red underwear for good luck.

Itineraries

Sagrada Família p44

Tales of the City

From cathedral confession boxes to brothels, from medieval alleyways to modern industrial parks, Barcelona in all its glory and its grimness has been immortalised in numerous novels and books. An exhaustive literary tour of the city would take weeks, but this full-day itinerary covers a few of the highlights, travelling uptown from the Born to the neighbourhood of Gràcia.

The tour starts in the Born district at the basilica of **Santa Maria del Mar** (see p74), focus of Ildefonso Falcones' recent bestseller, *Cathedral of the Sea*. Set in medieval times, the thriller follows the fortunes of Arnau Estanyol and is dominated by the construction of Santa Maria del Mar. Young Arnau joins the stonemasons' guild and helps to build the church, while his adopted brother Joan studies to become a priest and eventually joins the Inquisition. When Arnau falls in love with a forbidden Jewish woman (cunningly also named Mar), he is hauled before none other than his own brother, facing execution just as his beloved Cathedral of the Sea is finally completed.

Turn down C/Canvis Vells and on to Pla de Palau to catch the 59, 64 or 157 bus to the bottom of **La Rambla**. Standing with your back to the sea, the **Barri Xinès** (Barrio Chino) lies to the left. This seedy downtown district retains a little of its edge from the 1930s, when Jean Genet prowled its streets as a rent boy among the 'whores, thieves, pimps and beggars' that populate his memoir, *The Thief's Journal*. From La Rambla, walk along to the end of the narrow C/Arc del Teatre to what is now the **Plaça Jean Genet**, where Genet shared a bed in a *pensión* with 'six other vagrants', including his lover Salvador and a one-armed pimp named Stilitano.

While you're in the area, you could pick a worse guide than

Pepe Carvalho, the gourmet sleuth of Manuel Vázquez Montalbán's famous series of detective novels. Carvalho's wanderings through the Chino neighbourhood take him past familiar local bars, shops and characters, such as his prostitute girlfriend, Charo, and his informant, Bromide the shoeshine man – replaced in the later books by El Mohammed, marking the new wave of North African immigrants in the area.

Walk up from Plaça Jean Genet along Avda Drassanes to the **Rambla del Raval** to see the square named in Montalbán's honour, inaugurated in February 2009. The square is located a few steps from the apartment where he was born and grew up, although we can hardly imagine that the staunchly socialist Montalbán would appreciate today's side view of the luxurious new Barceló hotel. Even Barcelona's Mayor, Jordi Hereu, acknowledged that the writer would be less than delighted, particularly given his dislike of what are known as Barcelona's 'hard squares'. A more appropriate way to commemorate the great writer would be to nip next door for a slap-up fish lunch in Carvalho's favourite restaurant, **Casa Leopoldo** (C/Sant Rafael 24, 93 441 30 14).

At the top of the Rambla de Raval, turn right on to C/Hospital and when you hit La Rambla again, turn left. Here, in his *Homage to Catalonia*, George Orwell famously documented his part in the Civil War and his time spent fighting for the Trotskyist POUM party, entrenched on the Raval side of La Rambla. In May 1937, Orwell spent three days on the roof of the **Teatre Poliorama** (no.115) with its high observatory and twin domes, defending the POUM headquarters from the Guardia

Civil barricaded inside the Café Moka, an ersatz version of which still stands opposite at no.126. 'I think few experiences could be more sickening, more disillusioning or, finally, more nerve-racking than those evil days of street warfare,' wrote Orwell of his time in Barcelona.

Turn off La Rambla on to C/Canuda, turn right at Portal del Angel and continue to the Gothic **Cathedral** (see p54). A confession box surrounded by tourists is the unlikely setting for one of the funniest sex scenes in Quim Monzó's *The Enormity of the Tragedy*. Probably Catalonia's most prominent contemporary writer, Monzó has written the Catalan answer to *Portnoy's Complaint*, telling the story of Ramón Maria, a middle-aged trumpet player who wakes up one day with a permanent erection.

Exit the cathedral through the cloisters and head down C/Sant Sever, turning right into **Plaça Sant Felip Neri**. This quiet, melancholy square is the setting for a key scene in Carlos Ruiz Zafón's blockbuster thriller *The Shadow of the Wind*. Here, young Daniel Sempere meets and falls for Núria Monfort, daughter of the keeper of the Cemetery of Forgotten Books and 'the typical woman that I think we all fall in love with', as she is sitting and reading by the walls of the Baroque church to escape the damp oppressiveness of her nearby apartment. If you need a caffeine fix at this point, backtrack to C/Canuda for a quick coffee at the delightful first-floor café of the Ateneu library, another pivotal *Shadow of the Wind* spot, where Daniel meets Gustavo Barceló.

Continue back past the cathedral and turn right on to Via Laietana to catch the metro from Plaça de Sant

Cathedral p43

Jaume. Take line 4 to Passeig de Gràcia, change on to line 2 and get off at **Sagrada Família** (see p127), Gaudí's iconic temple is the setting for the latest *Da Vinci Code* clone: *The Gaudí Key* by local boys Esteban Martin and Andreu Carranza. The preposterous premise is that Gaudí was one of the mysterious Knights of Moriah, who guard a fabulous pre-Christian relic. Generations after Gaudí was fatally pushed under a tram by members of an evil sect, doctoral candidate María Givell and her boyfriend Miguel (a mathematician and dashing swordsman, naturally) dodge baddie bullets and hunt for clues to Gaudí's symbolic message to the Catholic world hidden within the architectural fabric of his Sagrada Família.

Back on the metro again, take line 2 to Diagonal and change over to line 3; get off at Fontana and walk along C/Astúries until you arrive at **Plaça del Diamant**, on the right. This square is the setting for several pivotal scenes in Mercè Rodoreda's *The Time of the Doves* (in Catalan, *La Plaça del Diamant*), one of the most acclaimed Catalan novels of all time. Here, Natalia and Quimet meet and fall in love just before the Civil War breaks out; the commemorative bronze statue of **La Colometa** ('Little Dove', Quimet's nickname for Natalia) depicts her fleeing Quimet's pet doves, which have become symbols of her suffering. The Bar Monumental where they eat and drink vermouth together in the novel is long gone, but the quiet **Bar Diamant** on the corner (C/Astúries 67, 93 237 25 98) is as good a place as any to curl up with a copy of the book that put the neighbourhood of Gràcia, and indeed all of Barcelona, firmly on the literary map.

The Jewish Quarter

Barcelona is a seriously *goyische* place these days. The current lack of Jewish presence on the streets makes it hard to believe that Jews thrived here for over a thousand years and, before the 14th-century pogroms, made up over 15 per cent of Barcelona's population. The city is now enjoying some of the first signs of Hebraic regeneration in over 500 years, with a recent influx of Ashkenazi Jews from Argentina, newly established synagogues, study centres such as the Chabad Lubavitch (www.chabadbarcelona.org) and even the Jewish Film Festival (www.fcjbarcelona.org).

The best place to start a half-day tour of Jewish Barcelona is the **Call** (from the Hebrew word *kahal*, which means community or congregation), a tiny patch of narrow medieval streets to the west of the cathedral. Despite heavy taxes and few civil rights, the Jews prospered here; by the 13th century, the Call held over 4,000 inhabitants and was regarded as one of the most religious and learned Sephardic Jewish communities. Beginning at Plaça Sant Jaume, head west down C/Call, once the Call's main street and where the ghetto gates at either end were locked at night. The first street to your right is C/Sant Honorat, where the water fountains were located; the second is C/Sant Domènec del Call, once the religious heart of the Call, and home to the main synagogue, kosher slaughter-houses and schools; the third street is the Call's western boundary of C/Arc de Sant Ramon, where there was once a Jewish women's school.

The Christianised street names are the result of the vicious pogrom of 1391, when the Call passed into the hands of the king, inhabitants were murdered or forced to convert to Catholicism and emblematic buildings were decorated with Catholic effigies.

Double back to C/Sant Domènec del Call, and walk halfway up to C/Marlet, where at No.5 part of the main synagogue still survives (see p59). With foundations dating back to the first century AD, it is one of the oldest synagogues in Europe, but after the pogrom it fell into obscurity. These two small, semi-subterranean rooms were being used as an electrical supplies warehouse when a chance investigation revealed their identity. The Call Association of Barcelona restored the space and it reopened in 2002 as a museum and working synagogue, and was finally consecrated in 2006. The main room, to the left of the entrance, has a Max Iaffa stained-glass window featuring the Star of David and 12 stones to commemorate the tribes of Israel, a large collection of Judaic pewter and the huge iron menorah by Mallorcan artist Ferran Aguiló.

Coming out of the synagogue, head a few steps west towards C/Arc de Sant Ramon, where an eye-level engraving in Hebrew renders homage to Rabbi Samuel Ha-Sardi who lived here in the seventh century. In a bid to draw more attention to the area's history, the Ajuntament has renovated various buildings and created a series of information plaques in Catalan, Spanish and English. The publication of Ildefonso Falcones' bestselling *Cathedral of the Sea* has also boosted interest in the area.

Head left, back down on to C/Call and turn right on to C/Banys Nous (New Baths street), where there are two hidden *mikvot* (Jewish ritual baths). The men's *mikveh* is at the back of S'Oliver furniture shop (at No.10), where the well-preserved arches are dramatically lit in sulphurous yellow tones and tower over the bed frames and wooden coffee tables below. Where C/Banys Nous meets C/Palla is the café **Caelum** (see p65) with the women's *mikveh* in its basement; descend to enjoy some sticky traditional treats of ironic provenance: the Catholic monasteries of Spain.

Walk back down C/Banys Nous to C/Ferran; at No.30 is the church of Sant Jaume, once the synagogue of the Call Menor, an extension of the overflowing Jewish quarter. The only visible traces of this neighbourhood's Jewish past are a few faint niches over the doorways where *mezuzot* once hung, containing a rolled-up prayer.

Follow C/Ferran past Plaça Sant Jaume and down C/Llibreteria, turning left onto C/Verguer to reach the Plaça del Rei. Here, in the **Museu d'Història de Barcelona** (see p57), are Jewish tombstones, most of which were unceremoniously recycled as building materials after the pogrom: near the exit of the subterranean walk, Hebrew inscriptions are visible on the foundations of the 15th-century Palau del Lloctinent.

The Jewish necropolis itself lies across town on **Montjuïc** ('Jewish mountain'), named after one of the oldest and largest Jewish cemeteries in Europe, dating from the ninth century. To get there, head back down C/Ferran to La Rambla and take the metro from Liceu to Paral·lel followed by the funicular and the cable car.

Some of the tombstones are housed in the neighbouring **Castell de Montjuïc** (see p106) but in 2001, over 500 more were discovered during construction on the mountain. Despite lobbying from local Jewish communities, there is no monument commemorating the site's historic importance and the Ajuntament is about to build visitor facilities directly over the burial grounds.

Port Olímpic p48

Lay of the Sand

Barcelona never had much of a beach culture until the 1992 Olympics opened the city's eyes to the commercial potential of its location. What little sand there was before then was grey and clogged with private swimming baths and *xiringuitos* (beach restaurants) that served seafood on trestle tables set up on the sand; the rest was given over to heavy industry and waste dumps, cut off from the rest of the city by a strip of rail track, warehouses and factories. For the grand Olympic makeover, the beaches were swiftly cleared and filled with tons of golden sand, imported palm trees and landscaped promenades, and nowadays the city's seven kilometres of sand pulls in millions of visitors every year.

For a day at the beach that involves more than just soaking up the rays, take bus no.14 or 41 from Plaça Catalunya to the **Platja Mar Bella** (*'platja'* means beach in Catalan). This is one of the more lively beaches, with basketball nets, volleyball courts, table-tennis tables and a half-pipe for BMXers and skaters. A focal point is the **Base Nàutica de la Mar Bella** (Avda Litoral, 93 221 04 32, www.basenautica.org) at the southerly end of this beach, where you can hire a kayak for an hour or so of messing about in boats. Experienced surfers can also hire boards, subject to a proficiency test. For pleasures of a more cerebral sort, an alternative is the **Cementiri de Poblenou**, a short walk back from the beach. The cemetery contains some impressive examples of funerary art, many of which were built at the height of the romantic-Gothic craze at the end of the 19th century. A leaflet or larger guide sold at the entrance suggests a route around 30 of the more interesting monuments.

Back on the shoreline, the next beach along is the **Platja de Bogatell**, which really comes into its own after dark, when its *xiringuitos* light torches among the loungers and pump out the latest beats from their soundsystems. This beach leads to the broader stretch of sand at **Nova Icària** and, beyond, the flashy marina of the **Port Olímpic**. The port and the Vila Olímpica neighbourhood behind it were created to house the athletes during the 1992 Games, and these days draw a curious mix of well-heeled Catalan residents of the area and drunk, scantily clad tourists attracted to the tawdry bars around the port.

Behind the port rise the landmark twin towers of the Mapfre insurance building and the luxurious **Hotel Arts** (see p171), while just in front of the Arts you'll see Frank Gehry's vast, glittering **Fish** sculpture. By now it should be lunchtime, so drop down to the beach just below *Fish*, and after a hundred metres or so you'll find **Agua** (see p100), a relaxed restaurant with globally influenced dishes and tables on a terrace giving on to the beach. If Agua is full, backtrack to Italian sister restaurant **Bestial** (see p100) or, for more old-fashioned fish dishes and paella, head to one of any number of restaurants in Barceloneta.

After lunch comes the most relaxing part of the day. Just along from Agua on the sheltered walkway running alongside the beach, you'll find the **Centre de la Platja** (Passeig Maritim s/n, 93 224 75 71), a beach centre with a small library that lends books, magazines and papers (some in English) along with buckets and spades and beach toys from June to September. Take a passport to borrow some reading material and repair to the beach for some late afternoon sun.

This area has been the beneficiary of a staggering amount of sculpture,

mostly as part of the drive to prettify it for the Olympics; the most obvious (and therefore the beach meeting point of choice) is Rebecca Horn's tower of rusty cubes, **Estel Ferit** (*Wounded Star*), which pays homage to the much-missed *xiringuitos* that lined the sands in pre-Olympic days. Stroll past this to the end of the Platja Barceloneta to Juan Muñoz's disturbing sculpture of five caged figures known as **Una habitació on sempre plou (A Room Where It Always Rains)** at the top of **Passeig Joan de Borbó**. This maritime promenade separates the Port Vell from the tight-knit seaside community of **Barceloneta**, which is slowly metamorphosing from a working-class neighbourhood dependent on fishing and heavy industry into a node of leisured bucket-and-spade tourism, with ever greater numbers of bars, restaurants and holiday flats.

The district was created in the 18th century to rehouse workers left homeless when the area now occupied by the Ciutadella park was razed to make way for the hated citadel. Narrow rows of cheap housing were set around a central square (now home to the recently redesigned Mercat de la Barceloneta) and the two-storey houses became home to fishermen, sailors and dockers. With the arrival of factories and shipbuilding yards in the 19th century, the area soon became so overcrowded with workers that the houses were split in half and later quartered. The infamous '*quarts de casa*' typically measured no more than 30 square metres (320 square feet), had no running water until the 1960s and often held families of ten or so. Most were later built up to six or more storeys, but even today, many of the flats remain cramped and in bad condition, despite their brightly painted façades.

Back on Passeig Joan de Borbó, walk down the broad portside esplanade looking down for Mario Merz's **Crescendo Appare** (*Growing in Appearance*) halfway down. These neon numbers set below glass represent the Fibonacci sequence, and were part of the 1992 sculptural bonanza, as was, further along, Lothar Baumgarten's **Rosa dels Vents** (*Wind Rose*), which features the names of Catalan sea winds embedded in the pavement. For a better view of it, take the lift to the rooftop café of the **Museu d'Història de Catalunya** (see p97; admission to the café is free) in the Palau de Mar, the only remaining warehouse from the area's industrial past, which has been converted into offices, restaurants and the museum.

From here you also get a great panorama that takes in the Port Vell leisure marina (heralded with Roy Lichtenstein's pop art *Barcelona Head*), the hill of Montjuïc and across the city. Just over the grassy slopes in front is the **Ictineo II**, a replica of the world's first combustion-powered submarine, created by Narcis Monturiol and launched from Barcelona port in 1862. The Virgin in the foreground as you look to Montjuïc tops the Mercè church in the Barri Gòtic, and the towering column to its left is the **Monument a Colom** (see p97). Pull up a seat for a restorative *caña* (draught beer) while admiring the view, and there should just be time to head back into town to shower off the sand before dinner.

World Class

Perfect places to stay, eat and explore.

TIME OUT GUIDES
WRITTEN BY
LOCAL EXPERTS
visit timeout.com/shop

Barcelona by Area

La Rambla

Barri Gòtic & La Rambla

At the centre of the Gothic Quarter is the **cathedral**, surrounded by a knot of medieval streets and small, shady squares. A triumvirate of more imposing squares nearby comprises the Plaça Sant Jaume, which now hosts the city council (**Ajuntament**) and the Catalan regional government (Generalitat) buildings, the well-preserved Plaça del Rei – which houses the **Museu d'Història de Barcelona**, the Escheresque 16th-century watchtower (Mirador del Rei Martí) and the Capella de Santa Àgata – and, finally, the arcaded Plaça Reial, known for its bars, cheap backpacker hostels and rather scuzzy atmosphere at night. The *plaça* has the Tres Gràcies fountain in the centre, and lamp-posts designed by the young Gaudí.

The Barri Gòtic is flanked by the east by **La Rambla**, the famed, mile-long boulevard that leads from Plaça Catalunya to the sea. In the absence of any truly great buildings or museums, it's the people who provide the spectacle: from flower sellers to living statues, opera-goers to clubbers, all human life is here. On its west side is the Palau de la Virreina exhibition and cultural information centre, and the superb **Boqueria** market. A little further down is the pavement mosaic created in 1976 by Joan Miró and recently restored to its original glory. On the left is the extraordinary Bruno Quadros building (1883); a former umbrella shop, it is decorated with roundels of open parasols and a Chinese dragon carrying a Peking lantern.

Sights & museums

Ajuntament (City Hall)
Plaça Sant Jaume (93 402 73 64, www.bcn.cat). Metro Jaume I or Liceu. **Open** *Office* 8.30am-2.30pm

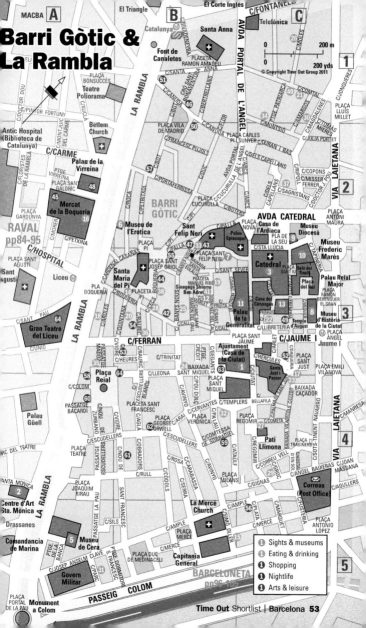

Barri Gòtic & La Rambla

MACBA **A**

B El Triangle · El Corte Inglés · C/FONTANELL **C**

Teléfonica

Catalunya

Santa Anna

Font de Canaletes

Antic Hospital (Biblioteca de Catalunya)

Palau de la Virreina

Betlem Church

Mercat de la Boqueria

RAVAL
pp84-95

Museu de l'Eròtica

BARRI GÒTIC

Sant Felip Neri

Santa Maria del Pi

Liceu

Gran Teatre del Liceu

AVDA CATEDRAL

Casa de l'Ardiaca

Museu Diocesà

Museu Frederic Marès

Catedral

Palau Reial Major

Palau de la Generalitat

Museu d'Història de la Ciutat

PLAÇA SANT JAUME

C/FERRAN

Ajuntament (Casa de la Ciutat)

C/JAUME I

Plaça Reial

Palau Güell

Pati Llimona

Correus (Post Office)

Centre d'Art Sta. Mònica

Museu de Cera

La Mercè Church

Comandancia de Marina

Govern Militar

Capitania General

Monument a Colom

PASSEIG COLOM

BARCELONETA
pp96-105

❶ Sights & museums
❶ Eating & drinking
❶ Shopping
❶ Nightlife
❶ Arts & leisure

© Copyright Time Out Group 2011

Barna by bike

Fancy the bit on the side?

Of the latest crop of quirky tours to hit Barcelona, the most fun might be this sidecar tour from BrightSide, offering tours of varying lengths for sidecar and pillion passengers.

The bikes are classic green Ural motorbikes, which themselves hold quite a story. During World War II five of these were smuggled from Germany, via neutral Sweden, into Russia and, under Stalin's orders, were painstakingly replicated; eventually 10,000 of these gleaming beasts were ridden into battle.

Those used by BrightSide are modern versions, comfortable and safety-checked with sidecars legally approved even to carry children, and helmets are provided. One passenger can ride pillion and a second can go in the sidecar – the driver doubles as guide.

Prices start at €45 per person, for the 90-minute 'Time Machine' jaunt, which comprises a whistle-stop tour of the Old City and the Passeig de Gràcia, taking in the cathedral, the MACBA, Casa Batlló and La Rambla, among other sights. Other tours include Barcelooona, which lasts a half-or full day, and also covers the uptown districts, the Camp Nou stadium, Montjuïc and Park Güell, and starts at €125 per person.

There's also a night-time tour; a romantic trip up to the hills of Tibidabo and the Collserola range, and tailor-made tours to celebrate special occasions.

■ www.ridebrightside.com

Mon-Fri. *Visits* 10.30am-1.30pm Sun. **Admission** free. **Map** p53 C3 ❶
The Ajuntament's centrepiece is the famous Saló de Cent, where the Consell de Cent ruled the city between 1372 and 1714. The Saló de Cròniques is filled with Josep Maria Sert's immense black-and-gold mural (1928), depicting the early 14th-century Catalan campaign in Byzantium and Greece. Full of art and sculptures by the great Catalan masters from Clarà to Subirachs, the interior of the city hall is open on Sundays, and certain holidays, such as the Mercè (24 Sept), Santa Eulàlia (12 Feb) and Sant Jordi (23 Apr).

Arts Santa Mònica
La Rambla 7 (93 576 11 10, www.artssantamonica.net). Metro Drassanes. **Open** 11am-9pm Tue-Sat; 11am-3pm Sun. **Admission** free. **Map** p53 A4 ❷
In a controversial move, the Generalitat has appointed new director Vicenç Altaió to pump up the lacklustre visitor numbers for this contemporary art space. Altaió vowed to create 'a multi-disciplinary centre for art, science, thought and communication', although detractors fear that the governmental hijacking of the management will mean diluted programming. After remodelling, the museum reopened in 2009. There are plans to move the CASM to a new contemporary art centre, the Canòdrom in La Sagrera, at an as yet unspecified date.

Catedral
Pla de la Seu (93 342 82 60, www.catedralbcn.org). Metro Jaume I. **Open** *Combined ticket* 1-5pm Mon-Fri; 2-5pm Sat, Sun. *Church & Cloister* 8am-12.45pm, 5-7.30pm daily. *Museum* 10am-12.30pm, 5.15-7pm daily. **Admission** *Combined ticket* €5. *Church & cloister* free. *Museum* €2. *Lift to roof* €2.50. *Choir* €2.20. **No credit cards**. **Map** p53 C3 ❸
Construction on Barcelona's Gothic cathedral began in 1298, but, although

La Rambla p52

the architects remained faithful to the vertical Nordic lines of the 15th-century plans, the façade and central spire were not finished until 1913. Inside, it is a cavernous and slightly forbidding place, but many paintings, sculptures and an intricately carved central choir from the 1390s shine through the gloom. The cathedral is dedicated to Saint Eulàlia, whose remains lie in the dramatically lit crypt, in an alabaster tomb carved with torture scenes from her martyrdom. The cloister is famous for its 13 geese and half-erased floor engravings. The cathedral museum, which is housed in the 17th-century chapterhouse, includes paintings and sculptures by local Gothic masters. A combined ticket (*visita especial*) has a timetable that's intended to keep tourists and worshippers from bothering one another. From 1-4.30pm, the entry fee is obligatory; however, ticket-holders have the run of the cloister, church, choir and lift, and can enter some chapels and take photos (normally prohibited).

Dalí Barcelona Real Cercle Artístic

C/Arcs 5 (93 318 17 74, www.dali barcelona.com). Metro Jaume I or Liceu. **Open** 10am-10pm daily. **Admission** €10; €7 reductions; free under-7s. **Map** p53 C2 ❹

This private collection of Dalí sculptures looks right at home amid the red velvet curtains and high Gothic arches of the Palau Pignatelli. In his later years, Dalí signed his name to almost anything, but these 44 pieces were moulded by his own hands in wax by the pool at his house in Port Lligat and show he was just as accomplished at sculpting as painting. Broadly divided into themes such as eroticism, Don Quixote and mythology, they include such gems as a small bronze that's simultaneously a swan, a dragon and an elephant, and an erotic vision of Dulcinea, Quixote's reluctant lady.

Museu de Cera

Ptge de la Banca 7 (93 317 26 49, www.museoceracbn.com). Metro Drassanes. **Open** *Mid July-mid Sept* 10am-10pm daily. *Mid Sept-mid July* 10am-1.30pm, 4-7.30pm Mon-Fri; 11am-2pm, 4.30-8.30pm Sat, Sun. **Admission** €12; €7 reductions; free under-5s. **Map** p53 A5 ❺

A fun but somewhat shabby wax museum, featuring all the usual characters: Frankenstein, Luke Skywalker and Princess Diana (here holding hands with Mother Teresa while Charles and Camilla look smug). Children who've been to Madame Tussauds are unlikely to be impressed.

Museu de l'Eròtica

La Rambla 96 bis (93 318 98 65, www.erotica-museum.com). Metro Liceu. **Open** *June-Sept* 10am-9pm daily. *Oct-May* 10am-8pm daily. **Admission** €9; €7-€8 reductions; under-15s free. **Map** p53 B2 ❻

The Erotic Museum is a surprisingly limp affair. Expect plenty of filler in the form of Kama Sutra illustrations and airbrushed paintings of naked maidens, with the odd fascinating item such as studded chastity belts or a Victorian walking stick topped with an ivory vagina. Genuine rarities include Japanese drawings, a painful-looking 'pleasure chair' and compelling photos of brothels in the city's Barrio Chino in the decadent 1930s.

Museu del Calçat (Shoe Museum)

Plaça Sant Felip Neri 5 (93 301 45 33). Metro Jaume I. **Open** 11am-2pm Tue-Sun. **Admission** €2.50; free under-10s. No credit cards. **Map** p53 B2 ❼

Housed in what was once part of the medieval shoemakers' guild, this quirky little museum details the cobbler's craft from practical Roman sandals to tottering 1970s platform boots. The earlier examples are reproductions, although those from the 17th century to the present day are originals, including clogs, swagged musketeers' boots and even celebrity footwear such as the tiny shoes of diminutive cellist, Pau Casals.

Museu d'Història de Barcelona (MUHBA)

Plaça del Rei 1 (93 256 21 00, www.museuhistoria.bcn.cat). Metro Jaume I. **Open** *Apr-Sept* 10am-8pm Tue-Sun. *Oct-Mar* 10am-2pm, 4-7pm Tue-Sat; 10am-8pm Sun. **Admission** *All exhibitions* €7; €5 reductions; free under-16s. Free to all 3-8pm Sun. *Temporary exhibitions* vary. No credit cards. **Map** p53 C3 ❽

Stretching from the Plaça del Rei to the cathedral are four sq km (1.5sq miles) of subterranean Roman ruins, including streets, villas and storage vats for oil and wine. The labyrinth is reached via the Casa Padellàs, a merchant's palace dating from 1498. Admission also allows access to the Capella de Santa Àgata – with its 15th-century altarpiece by Jaume Huguet – and the Saló del Tinell. This majestic room began life in 1370 as the seat of the Catalan parliament and was converted in the 18th century into a Baroque church, which was dismantled in 1934. The Rei Martí watchtower is still closed to the public while it awaits reinforcement. Tickets for the museum are also valid for the convent at Pedralbes.

Museu Diocesà

Avda de la Catedral 4 (93 315 22 13, www.cultura.arqbcn.cat). Metro Jaume I. **Open** 10am-2pm, 5-8pm Tue-Sat; 11am-2pm Sun. **Admission** €6; €3 reductions; free under-8s. No credit cards. **Map** p53 C2 ❾

A hotchpotch of religious art, including 14th-century alabaster virgins, altarpieces by Bernat Martorell and wonderful Romanesque murals. The building itself is also something of a mishmash; it includes the Gothic Pia Almoina, an almshouse and soup kitchen founded in 1009 and stuck on to a Renaissance canon's residence complete with Tuscan columns, which

in turn was built inside an octagonal Roman defence tower. The museum has space for two temporary exhibitions, usually dedicated to local artists, photographers and architects.

Museu Frederic Marès

Plaça Sant Iu 5-6 (93 310 58 00, www.museumares.bcn.cat). Metro Jaume I. **Open** closed at time of writing; phone or check website for times. **Map** p53 C3 ❿

Kleptomaniac and magpie Frederic Marès (1893-1991) 'collected' everything he laid his hands on, from hairbrushes to opera glasses and gargoyles. His collection is divide into three main sections. The basement, ground floor and first floor are devoted to sculpture dating from the pre-Roman era to the 20th century, including a vast array of polychromatic religious carvings, tombs, capitals and entire church portals, all exquisitely carved. On the second floor sits the Sentimental Museum, with objects from everyday life; look out for the Ladies' Room, filled with fans, sewing scissors and perfume flasks, and the Entertainment Room, with mechanical toys, puppets and a room dedicated to smoking paraphernalia. Also on the second floor, comprising the third main collection, is a room devoted to photography, as well as Marès' study and library, filled with sculptures. Closed at the time of writing, reopening was scheduled for 14 May 2011.

Palau de la Generalitat

Plaça Sant Jaume (93 402 46 17, www.gencat.cat/generalitat/eng/guia/ palau). Metro Jaume I or Liceu. **Guided tours** every 30-40mins approx, 10am-1pm, 2nd & 4th weekend of mth. **Admission** free. **Map** p53 C3 ⓫

The home of Catalan government has a Gothic side entrance on C/Bisbe with a beautiful relief of St George, patron saint of Catalonia, made by Pere Johan in 1418. Inside the building, the finest features are the first-floor Pati de

BARCELONA BY AREA

Temple Romà d'August

Tarongers (Orange Tree Patio), and a magnificent 15th-century chapel. The Generalitat is open to the public on Sant Jordi (23 April), La Diada (11 September) and La Mercè (24 September). Guided tours are generally in Spanish or Catalan, so it's best to call ahead for an English-speaking guide.

Sinagoga Shlomo Ben Adret

C/Marlet 7 (93 317 07 90, www.call debarcelona.org). Metro Jaume I or Liceu. **Open** June-Oct 10.30am-7pm Mon-Fri; 10.30am-3pm Sat, Sun. Nov-May 10.30am-6pm; 10.30am-3pm Sat, Sun. **Admission** €2; under-15s free. **Map** p53 B3 ⑫

The main synagogue of the Call until the pogrom in 1391, this tiny basement space lay abandoned for many years until its rediscovery in recent times. Once again a working synagogue, one of the two rooms is a place of worship with several interesting artefacts, the other holds the 14th-century dyeing vats used by the family that lived here until their status as crypto-Jews was discovered. The façade of the building, slightly skewing the street, fulfils religious requirements by which the synagogue has to face Jerusalem; the two windows at knee height allow light to enter from that direction.

Temple Romà d'August

C/Paradís 10 (93 315 11 11). Metro Jaume I. **Open** 10am-8pm Tue-Sat; 10am-3pm Sun. **Admission** free. **Map** p53 C3 ⑬

Four stunning fluted Corinthian columns dating from the first century BC soar out of their podium in the most unlikely of places: a back patio of the Mountaineering Centre of Catalonia. Part of the rear corner of the temple devoted to the Roman emperor Augustus (who after his death was elevated to the pantheon), the columns were discovered and isolated from the structure of a medieval building in 1835.

Eating & drinking

Ácoma

C/Boqueria 21 (93 301 75 97, www.acomacafe.com). Metro Liceu. **Open** 9am-midnight daily. **Café**. **Map** p53 B3 ⑭

A regular enough looking bar from the street, Ácoma is almost unique in the Old City for its sheltered patio at the back. Here there are tables in the shade of an orange tree and the rear of the Santa Maria del Pi church, and a small pond from which bemused fish and turtles can observe singer-songwriters and small groups perform for a young and merry foreign crowd. Salads, burgers, burritos and the like are served from midday to 11.30pm.

Bar Celta

C/Mercè 16 (93 315 00 06). Metro Drassanes. **Open** noon-midnight Tue-Sun. **€**. **Tapas**. **Map** p53 C5 ⑮

Celta's unapologetically 1960s interior is fiercely lit, noisy and not recommended for anyone feeling a bit rough. For all this, it is, however, one of the more authentic experiences to be had in the Gòtic. A Galician tapas bar, it specialises in food from the region, such as lacón con grelos (boiled gammon with turnip tops) and good seafood, accompanied by crisp Albariño wine served in traditional white ceramic bowls.

Bar Pinotxo

La Boqueria 466-467, La Rambla 89 (mobile 647 869 821). Metro Liceu. **Open** 6am-4pm Mon-Sat. No credit cards. **Bar**. **Map** p53 A2 ⑯

Just inside the entrance of the Boqueria, on the right-hand side, is this essential market bar, run by Juanito, one of the city's best-loved figures. In the early morning the place is popular with ravenous night owls on their way home and, at lunchtime, foodies in the know. Various tapas are available, along with excellent specials such as tuna casserole or scrambled eggs with clams.

Cafè de l'Acadèmia

C/Lledó 1 (93 319 82 53). Metro Jaume I. **Open** 1.30-4pm, 8.30-11.30pm Mon-Fri. Closed Aug. €€. **Catalan**. Map p53 C3 ⑰

An assured approach to the classics of Catalan cuisine, combined with the sunny terrace tables on the pretty Plaça Sant Just, make this one of the best-value restaurants around. The set lunch changes daily, but eat à la carte for quail stuffed with duck's liver and botifarra with wild mushroom sauce, or duck confit with poached onion and orange sauce.

Cafè de l'Opera

La Rambla 74 (93 317 75 85, www.cafeoperabcn.com). Metro Liceu. **Open** 8am-2.30am Mon-Fri, Sun; 8am-3am Sat. **Café**. Map p53 A3 ⑱

Cast-iron pillars, etched mirrors and bucolic murals create an air of fading grandeur at Café de l'Opera, which now seems incongruous among the fast-food joints and tawdry souvenir shops. Coffee, pastries and a handful of tapas are served by attentive bow-tied waiters to a largely tourist clientele, but given the atmosphere (and the opposition), there's no better place for a coffee on La Rambla.

Caj Chai

C/Sant Domènec del Call 12 (93 301 95 92). Metro Jaume I. **Open** 3-10pm Mon; 10.30am-10.30pm Tue-Sun. No credit cards. **Tea house**. Map p53 B3 ⑲

A cosy tearoom, where first-flush Darjeeling is approached with the reverence afforded to a Château d'Yquem. A range of leaves comes with tasting notes describing not only the origins, but giving suggestions for maximum enjoyment. It has recently begun serving bocadillos and breakfasts.

Can Culleretes

C/Quintana 5 (93 317 30 22, www.culleretes.com). Metro Liceu. **Open** 1.30-4pm, 9-11pm Tue-Sat; 1.30-4pm Sun. Closed mid July-mid Aug. €. **Catalan**. Map p53 B3 ⑳

The rambling dining rooms at the 'house of teaspoons' have been packing 'em in since 1786, making this the second oldest restaurant in Spain. The secret to Can Culleretes' longevity is a straightforward one: honest, hearty cooking and decent wine served at the lowest possible prices. Under huge oil paintings and a thousand signed black-and-white photos, diners munch sticky boar stew, tender pork with prunes and dates, goose with apples, partridge escabeche and some superbly fresh seafood.

Cerveceria Taller de Tapas

C/Comtal 28 (93 481 62 33, www.tallerdetapas.com). Metro Catalunya. **Open** 9am-2am Mon-Sat; 10am-midnight Sun. €€. **Tapas**. Map p53 C1 ㉑

Although strictly speaking a tapas bar, with a wide range and a useful menu in English, the Cerveceria has tried to fill a gap in the market by providing a reasonable selection of beers from around the world. The list provides a refreshing alternative to the ubiquitous Estrella, with Argentine Quilmes, Brazilian Brahma (this one, admittedly, via Luton), Bass Pale Ale, Leffe and Hoegaarden, among others.

Gelaaati!

C/Llibreteria 7 (93 310 50 45). Metro Jaume I. **Open** 9.30am-midnight daily. Closed mid Jan-mid Feb. No credit cards. **Ice-cream**. Map p53 C3 ㉒

One of the more recent wave of gelateries, Gelaaati! has built up a loyal following quickly, and with good reason. All its flavours are made on the premises every day, using natural ingredients – no colourings, no preservatives. Especially good are the hazelnut, pistachio and raspberry ice-creams; unusual flavours include soya bean, celery, and avocado.

Ginger

C/Palma de Sant Just 1 (93 310 53 09, www.ginger.cat). Metro Jaume I. **Open**

7pm-2.30am Tue-Thur; 7pm-3am Fri, Sat. Closed 3wks Aug. **Bar**. Map p53 C4 ㉓

Ginger manages to be all things to all punters: art deco cocktail bar with comfortable buttercup yellow banquettes; purveyor of fine tapas and wines; and, above all, a superbly relaxed place to chat and listen to music. The foreigner quotient is high, but it would be shortsighted to dismiss this little gem for that.

El Gran Café

C/Avinyó 9 (93 318 79 86, www. restaurantelgrancafe.com). Metro Liceu. **Open** 1-4.30pm, 7.30pm-midnight daily. €€. **Mediterranean**. **Map** p53 B3 ㉔

The fluted columns, bronze nymphs, suspended globe lamps and wood panelling help El Gran replicate a classic Parisian vibe. The cornerstones of brasserie cuisine – onion soup, duck magret, tarte tatin and even crêpes suzette – are all present and correct. The imaginative Catalan dishes spliced into the menu also work, but the distinctly non-Gallic attitude towards the hastily assembled set lunch is less convincing.

La Granja

C/Banys Nous 4 (93 302 69 75). Metro Liceu. **Open** May-July, Sept 9.30am-1.30pm, 5-9.30pm Mon-Sat. Oct-Apr 9.30am-1.30pm, 5-9.30pm Mon-Sat; 5-9pm Sun. Closed Aug. No credit cards. **Café**. Map p53 B3 ㉕

La Granja is an old-fashioned café filled with yellowing photos and antiques, which has its very own section of Roman wall. You can stand your spoon in the tarry-thick hot chocolate, which won't be to all tastes; but the xocolata amb café, a mocha espresso, or the xocolata picant, chocolate with chilli, pack a mid-afternoon energy punch.

Machiroku

C/Moles 21 (93 412 60 82). Metro Catalunya or Urquinaona. **Open** 1.30-3.30pm, 8.30-11.30pm Mon-Fri; 8.30-11.30pm Sat. Closed Aug. €€. No credit cards. **Japanese**. Map p53 C1 ㉖

A cosy, modest space decorated with Japanese wall hangings and prints. Service is charming and friendly and the various set menus at lunchtime offer good value, featuring rice and miso soup and then a choice of sushi, teriyaki, yakinuku (chargrilled beef) or a bento box with prawn tempura.

Matsuri

Plaça Regomir 1 (93 268 15 35). Metro Jaume I. **Open** 8pm-midnight daily. €€. **Asian**. Map p53 C4 ㉗

A welcoming space painted in tasteful shades of ochre and terracotta, with the obligatory trickling fountain, wooden carvings and wall-hung candles, but saved from eastern cliché by some thoroughly occidental jazz in the background. Reasonably priced tom yam soup and pad thai feature, while the less predictable choices include pho bo, a Vietnamese broth with meat and spices, and sake niku, a delicious beef dish with wok-fried broccoli and a lightly perfumed soy sauce.

Mesón Jesús

C/Cecs de la Boqueria 4 (93 317 46 98). Metro Jaume I or Liceu. **Open** 1-4pm, 8-11pm Mon-Fri. Closed Aug. €. **Spanish**. Map p53 B3 ㉘

Old-school Castilian, with gingham tablecloths, oak barrels and cartwheels aplenty. The menu is limited and never changes, but the dishes are reliably good and inexpensive to boot – try the sautéed green beans with ham to start, then the superb grilled prawns or a tasty zarzuela (fish stew). The waitresses are incessantly cheerful with a largely non-Spanish-speaking clientele.

Milk

C/Gignas 21 (93 268 09 22, www. milkbarcelona.com). Metro Jaume I. **Open** 6pm-3am Mon-Wed; 10am-3pm Thur-Sun. €€. **Fusion/cocktails**. Map p53 C4 ㉙

Still unchallenged in the Old City in its provision of a decent brunch, Milk's fry-ups, pancakes and smoothies are sadly

Els Quatre Gats

only available at weekends (until 4pm). Its candlelit, low-key baroque look, charming service and cheap prices make it a good bet at any time, however, with solid homemade bistro grub from Caesar salad to fish and chips.

Onofre

C/Magdalenes 19 (93 317 69 37, www.onofre.net). Metro Urquinaona. **Open** 10am-5pm, 7.30pm-midnight Mon-Sat. Closed Aug. **€€**. **Tapas**. **Map** p53 C1 ㉚

It's tiny and not especially well known, but Onofre has a merited following among local gourmands for its impeccably sourced wines, cured meats, pâtés, hams and artisanal cheeses from around the country. Increasingly, it provides more elaborate dishes too, such as a scallop gratin with caramelised onion, or a pear tatin with melted goat's cheese and Mallorcan *sobrassada* sausage.

El Paraguayo

C/Parc 1 (93 302 14 41). Metro Drassanes. **Open** 1-4pm, 8pm-midnight Tue-Sun. **€€€**. **Paraguayan**. **Map** p345 A5 ㉛

The only way to go at El Paraguayo is to order a fat juicy steak, a bottle of good cheap house Rioja and a bowl of piping hot yucca chips. The rest is largely menu filler. As to which steak, a helpful chart walks you through the various cuts, but a *bife de chorizo* should satisfy the ravenous. The place itself is cosy and wood-panelled, with Botero-esque paintings of buxom madams and their admirers.

Peimong

C/Templers 6-10 (93 318 28 73). Metro Jaume I. **Open** 1-4pm, 8-11.30pm Tue-Sat; 1-4pm Sun. Closed 2wks Aug. **€**. **Peruvian**. **Map** p53 B4 ㉜

Not, perhaps, the fanciest-looking restaurant around (think Peruvian gimcracks, strip lighting and tapestries of Macchu Pichu) or indeed the fanciest-looking food, but it sure tastes like the real thing. Start with a pisco sour and a dish of yucca chips or maybe some spicy corn tamales, and then move on to ceviche or the satisfying *lomo saltado* – pork fried with onions, tomatoes and coriander. There are two types of Peruvian beer and even – for the very nostalgic or the hypoglycaemic – Inca Kola.

El Portalón

C/Banys Nous 20 (93 302 11 87). Metro Liceu. **Open** 8.45am-11.30pm Mon-Sat. Closed Aug. **€**. **Tapas**. **Map** p53 B3 ㉝

A rare pocket of authenticity in the increasingly touristy Barri Gòtic, this traditional tapas bar is located in what were once medieval stables, and it doesn't seem to worry too much about inheriting the ancient dust. The tapas list is long, but the *torrades* are also good: toasted bread topped with red peppers and anchovy, cheese, ham or whatever takes your fancy. House wine comes in terracotta jugs.

Els Quatre Gats

C/Montsió 3 bis (93 302 41 40, www.4gats.com). Metro Catalunya. **Open** 1pm-1am daily. **€€€**. **Café/Catalan**. **Map** p53 C1 ㉞

The essence of fin-de-siècle Barcelona, the 'Four Cats' was designed by Modernista heavyweight Puig i Cadafalch and patronised by the cultural glitterati of the era, most notably Picasso, who hung out here with Modernista painters Santiago Rusiñol and Ramon Casas. These days it's mostly frequented by tourists, but is nonetheless an essential stop for a coffee or a reasonable set lunch.

Les Quinze Nits

Plaça Reial 6 (93 317 30 75, www.quinzenits.com). Metro Liceu. **Open** 1-3.45pm, 8.30-11.30pm daily. **€**. **Spanish**. **Map** p53 A3 ㉟

The staggering success of the Quinze Nits enterprise (there are countless branches here in Barcelona and now in Madrid too, along with a handful of hotels) is down to one simple concept: style on a budget. All the restaurants have a certain Manhattan chic, yet you'll struggle to pay much more than €20 a head. The food plays second fiddle and is a hit-and-miss affair, but order simple dishes and at these prices you can't go far wrong.

Schilling

C/Ferran 23 (93 317 67 87, www.cafeschilling.com). Metro Liceu. **Open** 11am-2am Mon-Thur; 10am-2.30am Fri, Sat; noon-midnight Sun. **Café**. **Map** p53 B3 ❸

Schilling's large windows that face on to the main thoroughfare connecting La Rambla with the Plaça Sant Jaume were once the spot to see and be seen, and although the place has lost some of its cachet, it's still undeniably elegant – the high ceilings, bookshelves and traditional air contrasting with the fiercely modern young waiting staff. Weave through to the back for more intimate seating.

Shunka

C/Sagristans 5 (93 412 49 91). Metro Jaume I. **Open** 1.30-3.15pm, 8.30-11.15pm Tue-Sun. Closed Aug & 10 days at Christmas. **€€€**. **Japanese**. **Map** p53 C2 ❸

The speciality here is prime-grade *toro*: fatty and deliciously creamy tuna belly. It's expensive as a main, but you can sample it as nigiri-zushi. The house salad with raw fish makes for a zingy starter; then you'll find all the usual sushi, along with heartier options like udon *kakiage* – a broth of langoustine tempura, vegetables and noodles.

Taller de Tapas

Plaça Sant Josep Oriol 9 (93 301 80 20, www.tallerdetapas.com). Metro Liceu. **Open** noon-midnight Mon-Thur, Sun; noon-1am Fri, Sat. **€€**. **Tapas**. **Map** p53 B3 ❸

At its best, Taller de Tapas is an easy, multilingual environment in which to try tapas from razor clams to local wild mushrooms. At busy periods, however, service can be hurried and unhelpful,

Café de l'Opera p60

with dishes prepared in haste and orders confused, so it pays to avoid the lunchtime and evening rush hours. Plentiful outdoor seating is a big draw.

Tokyo

C/Comtal 20 (93 317 61 80). Metro Catalunya. **Open** 1.30-4pm, 8-11pm Mon-Sat. Closed Aug. **€€€**. **Japanese**. **Map** p53 C1 ❹

A small and simple space, where suspended beams, plastic plants and slatted wooden partitions are used to clever effect and the walls are lined with photos and drawings from grateful clients. The speciality is *edomae* (hand-rolled nigiri-zushi), but the meat and vegetable sukiyaki, which is cooked at your table, is also good, while the *menú* of sushi and tempura is great value. The red bean and green tea mochi rolls to finish are something of an acquired taste.

La Vinateria del Call

C/Sant Domènec del Call 9 (93 302 60 92). Metro Jaume I or Liceu. **Open** 8pm-midnight daily. **€€€**. **Tapas**. **Map** p53 B3 ❹

An atmospheric little bar, which places a high priority on the sourcing of its wine, hams and cheeses, and which has excellent homemade dishes, like a delicious fig ice-cream. Despite the antique fittings and dusty bottles, the staff are

– like the music they play – young and lively, and some speak English.

Shopping

Almacenes del Pilar

C/Boqueria 43 (93 317 79 84, www.almacenesdelpilar.com). Metro Liceu. **Open** 10am-2pm, 4-8pm Mon-Sat. Closed 2wks Aug. **Map** p53 B3 ㊷
An array of traditional Spanish fabrics and accessories is on display in this colourful, shambolic interior, dating all the way back to 1886. You'll find the richly hued brocades used for Valencian *fallera* outfits and other rudiments of folkloric dress from various parts of the country. Lace mantillas, and the high combs over which they are worn, are stocked, along with fringed, hand-embroidered pure silk shawls and colourful wooden fans.

L'Arca de l'Àvia

C/Banys Nous 20 (93 302 15 98, www.larcadelavia.com). Metro Liceu. **Open** 10.30am-2pm, 5-8.30pm Mon-Fri; 11am-2pm Sat. Closed 1wk Aug. **Map** p53 B3 ㊸
Specialising in antique textiles, the 'Grandmother's Ark' smells of cloves and freshly ironed linen and is bursting with both antique and reproduction curtains, bedlinen, table cloths, clothes and a snowstorm of handmade lace. It's particularly popular with brides seeking original veils, and is also the perfect place for a lace mantilla (headdress) or lavishly embroidered *mantones* (fringed silk shawls).

Arlequí Mascares

Plaça Sant Josep Oriol 8 (93 317 24 29, www.arlequimask.com). Metro Liceu. **Open** 10.30am-8.30pm Mon-Sat; 10.30am-4.30pm Sun. **Map** p53 B3 ㊹
The walls here are dripping with masks, crafted from papier mâché and leather. Whether gilt-laden or in feathered commedia dell'arte style, simple Greek tragi-comedy styles or traditional Japanese or Catalan varieties, they make striking

fancy dress or decorative staples. Other trinkets and toys include finger puppets, mirrors and ornamental boxes.

La Boqueria

La Rambla 89, Raval (93 318 25 84, www.boqueria.info). Metro Liceu. **Open** 8am-8pm Mon-Sat. **Map** p53 A3 ㊺
Thronged with tourists searching for a little bit of Barcelona's gastro magic, and usually ending up with a pre-sliced quarter of overpriced pineapple, Europe's biggest food market is still an essential stop. Admire the orderly stacks of ridged Montserrat tomatoes, the wet sacks of snails and the oozing razor clams on the fish stalls. If you can't or don't want to cook it all yourself, you can eat instead at several market tapas bars.

Visit in the morning for the best produce, including the smallholders' fruit and veg stalls in the little square attached to the C/Carme side of the market, where prices tend to be cheaper. But if you come only to ogle, remember that this is where locals come to shop. Don't touch what you don't want to buy, ask before taking photos and watch out for vicious old ladies with ankle-destroying wheeled shopping bags.

Le Boudoir

C/Canuda 21 (93 302 52 81, www.leboudoir.net). Metro Catalunya. **Open** 11am-8.30pm Mon-Fri; 11am-9pm Sat. **Map** p53 B1 ㊻
Make like Dita Von Teese with feather boas, stockings, masks, gloves and, of course, racks of sexy bras, knickers, basques and suspender belts. To show you how to use it all, the shop runs monthly striptease classes.

Caelum

C/Palla 8 (93 302 69 93, www.caelum barcelona.com). Metro Liceu. **Open** 10.30am-8.30pm Mon-Thur; 10.30am-11pm Fri, Sat; 11.30am-9pm Sun. Closed 2wks Aug. **Map** p53 B2 ㊼
Spain's monks and nuns have a naughty sideline in traditional sweets including *'pets de monja'* (little chocolate biscuits

Top ten Boqueria picks

Bacallà salat

Dried, salted cod has been a staple in Catalonia for centuries, and entire stalls in the Boqueria are given over to this simple foodstuff. Try it in *esqueixada*, a salad of tomatoes, onions and black olives topped with *bacallà*.

Bolets

Catalans are mad for mushrooms, and Bolets Petràs (stall Nos.867 and 870) is a mecca for fresh and dried funghi of all kinds, including meaty *rovellons*, slender *camagrocs* and succulent *llenegues*.

Bull

Catalans take pride in their *embotits* (charcuterie), and the curiously misshapen, roundish *bull* is a beloved local speciality. Some recipes call for head and tongue to be used.

Calçots

Midway between a leek and an onion in both appearance and taste, calçots are traditionally eaten at mass barbecues called *calçotades*. Shuck off the charred skin and dunk the stem in *romesco* sauce.

Cargols

The humble Catalan snail is a traditional component of several country dishes, particularly *cargols a la llauna* (oven-baked snails). Delicious dipped in *alioli* or *romesco* sauce.

Codonyat

Dense, reddish slabs of tart quince jelly are usually found alongside cheese at market stalls, and are the ideal accompaniment to the Catalan curd cheese, *mató*, or a hunk of manchego.

Montserrat tomatoes

These giant, bulging tomatoes may not look very pretty, but they are beloved by local foodies for their intense flavour and dense flesh.

Percebes

There are plenty of strange aquatic creatures to gawp at in the Boqueria, but *percebes* – knobbly goose-neck barnacles scraped from Galician cliffs – might be the strangest of all.

Peus de porc

No part of the pig goes to waste in Catalunya, and you'll see the chunky trotters (alongside snouts and offal) at most butchers' stalls. Try them stewed with snails or tripe, or even *rebossat* (tossed in breadcrumbs and fried), then dusted with sugar.

Tripas

Those long, greyish-white, frilly things displayed at butchers' stalls are tripe (pigs' intestines), a traditional ingredient of the classic Catalan dish *cap i pota* ('head and foot').

known as 'nuns' farts'), candied saints' bones, and drinkable goodies such as eucalyptus and orange liqueur, all beautifully packaged. If you'd like to sample before committing to a whole box of Santa Teresa's sugared egg yolks, there's a café downstairs on the site of the medieval Jewish thermal baths.

Casa Beethoven

La Rambla 97 (93 301 48 26, www.casabeethoven.com). Metro Liceu. **Open** 9am-2pm, 4-8pm Mon-Fri; 9am-1.30pm, 5-8pm Sat. Closed 3wks Aug. **Map** p53 A2 ㊽

The sheet music and songbooks on sale in this old shop run the gamut from Wagner to the White Stripes, with a focus on opera. Books cover music history and theory, while CDs are particularly strong on both modern and classical Spanish music.

Cereria Subirà

Baixada de Llibreteria 7 (93 315 26 06). Metro Jaume I. **Open** 9am-1.30pm, 4-7.30pm Mon-Fri; 9am-1.30pm Sat. **Map** p53 C3 ㊾

With a staircase fit for a full swish from Scarlett O'Hara, this exquisite candle shop dates back to the pre-electric days of 1716 when candles were an everyday necessity at home and in church. These days, the votive candles sit next to novelties such as After Eight-scented candles and candles in the shape of the Sagrada Família.

Decathlon

C/Canuda 20 (93 342 61 61, www.decathlon.es). Metro Catalunya. **Open** 9.30am-9.30pm Mon-Sat. **Map** p53 B2 ㊿

Whether you need boxing gloves or a bivouac, a beach volleyball or a bicycle lock, this multi-storey French chain will probably be able to see you right. Additional services include bike repair and hire, and team-kit stamping.

Flora Albaicín

C/Canuda 3 (93 302 10 35). Metro Catalunya. **Open** 10.30am-1pm, 5-8pm Mon-Sat. **Map** p53 B1 (51)

This tiny boutique is bursting at the seams with brightly coloured flamenco frocks, polka-dotted shoes, head combs, bangles, shawls and everything else you need to dance the sevillanas in style.

Formatgeria La Seu

C/Dagueria 16 (93 412 65 48, www.formatgerialaseu.com). Metro Jaume I. **Open** 10am-2pm, 5-8pm Tue-Thur; 10am-3.30pm, 5-8pm Fri, Sat. Closed Aug. No credit cards. **Map** p53 C3 (52)

This is the only shop in the country to specialise in Spanish-only farmhouse cheeses. Scottish owner Katherine McLaughlin hand-picks her wares, such as a manchego that knocks the socks off anything you'll find in the market, or the truly strange Catalan tupí. She also stocks six varieties of cheese ice-cream and some excellent-value olive oils.

Herboristeria del Rei

C/Vidre 1 (93 318 05 12). Metro Liceu. **Open** 4-8pm Tue-Fri; 10am-8pm Sat. Closed 2wks Aug. **Map** p53 B3 (53)

Designed by a theatre set designer in the 1860s, this atmospheric shop hides myriad herbs, infusions, ointments and unguents for health and beauty. More up-to-date stock includes vegetarian foods, organic olive oils and organic mueslis; it's also a good place to buy saffron.

El Ingenio

C/Rauric 6 (93 317 71 38, www.elingenio.com). Metro Liceu. **Open** 10am-1.30pm, 4.15-8pm Mon-Fri; 11am-2pm, 5-8.30pm Sat. **Map** p53 B3 (54)

At once enchanting and disturbing, El Ingenio's handcrafted toys, tricks and costumes are reminders of a pre-digital world where people made their own entertainment. Its cabinets are full of practical jokes and curious toys; its fascinating workshop produces the oversized heads and garish costumes used in Barcelona's traditional festivities.

Joguines Monforte

Plaça Sant Josep Oriol 3 (93 318 22 85, www.joguinesmonforte.com). Metro Liceu. **Open** 9.30am-1.30pm, 4-8pm Mon-Fri; 10am-2pm, 4.30-8.30pm Sat. **Map** p53 B3 ⑤⑤

This venerable toy shop has been selling traditional toys, board games and everything you need for a game of billiards since 1840. Try the Spanish version of snakes and ladders (*el juego de la oca*, or the 'goose game') and ludo (*parchís*) along with chess, jigsaws, painted tin toys and outdoor games such as croquet and skittles.

Papabubble

C/Ample 28 (93 268 86 25, www.papabubble.com). Metro Barceloneta or Drassanes. **Open** 10am-2pm, 4-8.30pm Mon-Fri; 10am-8.30pm Sat. Closed 2wks Aug. **Map** p53 C5 ⑤⑥

Push through the crowds to watch Papabubble's sweet-makers stretch, roll and chop their kaleidoscopic rock candy into lollies, sticks, humbugs and novelty sculptures. The goodies come in any flavour from strawberry to lavender or passion fruit, and there's a bespoke service for special occasions.

Women's Secret

C/Portaferrissa 7-9 (93 318 92 42, www.womensecret.com). Metro Liceu. **Open** 10am-9pm Mon-Sat. **Map** p53 B2 ⑤⑦

There are some sexy pieces at Women's Secret, but the stock is mostly versatile strap bras, brightly printed cotton PJs and a funky line of under-/outerwear in cartoonish stylings: skimpy shorts, miniskirts and vest tops.

Nightlife

Barcelona Pipa Club

Plaça Reial 3, pral (93 301 11 65, www.bpipaclub.com). Metro Liceu. **Open** 11pm-3am daily. **Admission** free. No credit cards. **Map** p53 A3 ⑤⑧

A converted flat on Plaça Reial, decorated with oak, velvet, Sherlock Holmes-style memorabilia and a bar that's often impossible to get anywhere near, despite the high prices. For all its genteel decor, it has a semi-underground quality and is mostly rammed with young Americans and their Catalan friends. Ring the bell to get in.

Harlem Jazz Club

C/Comtessa de Sobradiel 8 (972 864 561m www.harlemjazzclub.es). Metro Jaume I. **Open** *July-Sept* 8pm-4am Tue-Thur; 8pm-5am Fri, Sat. *Oct-June* 8pm-4am Tue-Thur, Sun; 8pm-5am Fri, Sat. *Gigs* vary. Closed 2wks Aug. **Admission** €5.50 (incl 1 drink) Tue-Thur; €5.50 Fri-Sun. No credit cards. **Map** p53 B4 ⑤⑨

Despite the DJ booth, live music is what the Harlem Jazz Club does best, and it's a regular hangout for not-so-cashed-up musicians, buffs and students. A lot of local musical history's gone down at Harlem, and some of the city's greatest talents have emerged from here. Not only jazz, but styles ranging from klezmer and funk to flamenco get a run.

Jamboree/Los Tarantos

Plaça Reial 17 (93 319 17 89, www.masimas.com). Metro Liceu. **Open** 1-5am Mon-Thur, Sun; 1-6am Fri, Sat. **Shows** *Jamboree* 9pm, 11pm daily. *Los Tarantos* 8.30pm, 9.30pm, 10.30pm daily. **Admission** *Shows* €13. *Club* €8. **Map** p53 A4 ⑥⓪

The cave-like Jamboree hosts jazz, Latin or blues gigs by mainly Spanish groups – on Mondays, in particular, the outrageously popular WTF jazz jam session is crammed with a young crowd. Upstairs, slicker sister venue Los Tarantos stages flamenco performances, then joins forces with Jamboree to become one big, fun club later on.

La Macarena

C/Nou de Sant Francesc 5 (no phone, www.macarenaclub.com). Metro Drassanes. **Open** midnight-4.30am Mon-Thur, Sun; midnight-5am Fri, Sat. **Admission** free before

Gran Teatre del Liceu p70

1.30am; €6 afterwards (but can vary). No credit cards. **Map** p53 B4 ⑥①

La Macarena is smaller than your apartment but has big-club pretensions in the best possible sense: for one thing, the musical selection is generally excellent – minimal electro selected by resident DJs and the occasional big-name guest (who usually appear the day before or after a bigger gig elsewhere) – and is complemented by a kicking sound system. Watch your bag and your drink, however.

Marula Café

C/Escudellers 49 (93 318 76 90, www.marulacafe.com). **Open** 11pm-5am Mon-Thur, Sun; 11.30pm-6am Fri; 9.30pm-6am Sat. **Admission** free-€10 (incl 1 drink). **Map** p53 B4 ⑥②

Grown-up clubbers were thrilled when the popular Marula Café in Madrid announced it was opening a sister club in Barcelona, and it hasn't disappointed. The musical policy is what is known in Spain, somewhat uncomfortably, as *música negra* – a fairly useless label that in this case ranges from Sly and the Family Stone to Michael Jackson via Fela Kuti, but is a byword for quality and danceability. On Saturday nights there's live music.

El Paraigua

C/Pas de l'Ensenyança 2 (93 302 11 31, www.elparaigua.com). Metro Jaume I or Liceu. **Open** 9.30am-midnight Mon-Thur; 9.30am-3am Fri; 11am-3am Sat; noon-midnight Sun. **Admission** free. **Map** p53 B3 ⑥③

Upstairs is a beautifully elegant Modernista cocktail bar, mirrored and wood-panelled, while downstairs is a cosy vaulted space with bare-brick walls, which sees some of Barcelona's most promising new bands performing on Friday and Saturday nights. It seems to hold a special appeal for expat musicians, and any given month might include an Irish soul singer, a British funk band and a mixed-nationality a cappella group.

Sidecar Factory Club

Plaça Reial 7 (93 302 15 86, www.sidecar.es). Metro Liceu. **Open** 7pm-5am Mon-Thur; 7pm-6am Fri, Sat. **Admission** (incl 1 drink) €5-€9. *Gigs* €6-€20. No credit cards. **Map** p53 B3 ⑥④

Sidecar still has all the ballsy attitude of the spit 'n' sawdust rock club that it once was and programming that includes breakbeat, indie and electro continues to pack in the local indie kids and Interrailers. Sidecar also hosts some great concerts in its bare-bricked cosy basement space.

Arts & leisure

Gran Teatre del Liceu

La Rambla 51-59 (93 485 99 13, www.liceubarcelona.cat). Metro Liceu. **Open** *Information* 11am-2pm, 3-8pm Mon-Fri. *Box office* 1.30-8pm Mon-Fri; 1hr before performance Sat, Sun. Closed 2 wks Aug. **Map** p53 A3 ⑥⑤

Since it opened in 1847, two fires, a bombing and a financial crisis have failed to quash the spirit and splendour of the Gran Teatre del Liceu. A restrained façade opens into an elegant 2,292-seat auditorium of red plush, gold leaf and ornate carvings. The latest mod cons include seat-back subtitles in various languages that complement the Catalan subtitles above the stage. Under the stewardship of artistic director Joan Matabosch and musical director Sebastian Weigle, the Liceu has consolidated its programming policy, mixing co-productions with leading international opera houses with its own in-house productions. Classical, full-length opera is the staple. Its adjoining Conservatori (C/Nou de la Rambla 82-88, 93 327 12 00, www.conservatori-liceu.es) lends its 400-seater basement auditorium to classical and contemporary concerts, small-scale operas and even jazz.

Event highlights *La Bohème* (27 Feb-19 Mar 2012); *Aïda* (21-30 July 2012).

Parc de la Ciutadella p74

Born & Sant Pere

Label-happy coolhunters throng the Born's pedestrian streets, where museums, restored 13th-century mansions and churches alternate with cafés, galleries and boutiques. Regeneration has come more slowly for the neighbouring area of Sant Pere, north of C/Princesa, which maintains a slightly grungier feel despite the municipal money-pumping. Still, there have been recent large-scale improvements, such as the long Plaça Pou de la Figuera and the spectacularly reinvented Santa Caterina market. The area is demarcated to the east by the glorious Parc de la Ciutadella and to the west by Via Laietana. In 2012, work is due to start on turning over some of the latter's car lanes to pedestrians.

'Born' originally meant 'joust' or 'list', and in the Middle Ages, and for many centuries thereafter, the neighbourhood's main artery, the Passeig del Born, was the focal point of the city's festivals, processions, tournaments, carnivals and the burning of heretics by the Inquisition. At one end of the road is the old Born market, a magnificent 1870s wrought-iron structure, which is to be turned into a cultural centre and museum, although progress is painfully slow. Leading off the Passeig del Born is C/Montcada, lined with a succession of 15th-century merchants' mansions.

Sights & museums

Museu Barbier-Mueller d'Art Precolombí
C/Montcada 14 (93 310 45 16, www. barbier-mueller.ch). Metro Jaume I. **Open** 11am-7pm Tue-Fri; 11am-8pm Sat, Sun. **Admission** €3.50; €1.70 reductions; free under-16s, 3-8pm Sun & 1st Sun of mth. **Map** p73 B4 ❶

Located in the 15th-century Palau Nadal, this world-class collection of pre-Columbian art was ceded to Barcelona in 1996 by the Barbier-Mueller Museum in Geneva. The holdings focus solely on the Americas, representing most of the styles from the ancient cultures of Meso-America, Andean America and the Amazon region. The frequently changing selection of masks, textiles, jewellery and sculpture includes pieces dating from as far back as the second millennium BC running through to the early 16th-century (demonstrating just how loosely the term 'pre-Columbian' can be used).

Museu de la Xocolata

Chocolate Museum
C/Comerç 36 (93 268 78 78, www. museudelaxocolata.cat). Metro Arc de Triomf or Jaume I. **Open** 10am-7pm Mon-Sat; 10am-3pm Sun. **Admission** €4.30; €3.65 reductions; free under-7s. **Map** p73 C3 ❷

The best-smelling museum in town draws chocoholics of all ages to view its collection of chocolate sculptures made by Barcelona's master *pastissers* for the Easter competition. These range from multicoloured models of Gaudí's Casa Batlló to characters from *Chicken Run*, while audio-visual shows and touch-screen computers help lead children through what would otherwise be the dry history of the cocoa bean.

Museu Picasso

C/Montcada 15-23 (93 256 30 00, www.museupicasso.bcn.cat). Metro Jaume I. **Open** (last ticket 30mins before closing) 10am-8pm Tue-Sun. **Admission** All exhibitions €10; €6 reductions. *Temporary exhibition only* €6; €3 reductions; free under-16s. Free (permanent exhibition only) 3-8pm Sun, & all day 1st Sun of mth. **Map** p73 B4 ❸

The Picasso Museum takes up a row of medieval mansions, with the main entrance now at the Palau Meca. By no means an overview of the artist's work, it's a record of the vital formative years that the young Picasso spent nearby at La Llotja art school, and later hanging out with the fin-de-siècle avant-garde.

The presentation of Picasso's development from 1890 to 1904, from deft pre-adolescent portraits to sketchy landscapes to the intense innovations of his Blue Period, is seamless and unbeatable; the collection then leaps to a gallery of mature Cubist paintings from 1917. The pièce de résistance, however, is the complete series of 57 canvases based on Velázquez's famous *Las Meninas*, stretching through three rooms. The display ends with a wonderful collection of ceramics. Temporary exhibitions are held under the magnificent coffered ceiling of the Palau Finestres. An annual pass is excellent value and allows the visitor to skip the interminable queues.

Palau de la Música Catalana

C/Sant Francesc de Paula 2 (93 295 72 00, www.palaumusica.org). Metro Urquinaona. **Open** Box office 10am-9pm Mon-Sat. *Guided tours* Sept-July 10am-3.30pm daily. Aug 10am-6pm daily. **Admission** €12; €10 reductions; free under-12s. **Map** p73 A2 ❹

Commissioned by the nationalistic Orfeó Català choral society, this jaw-dropping concert hall was intended as a paean to the Catalan *renaixença* and a showcase for the most outstanding Modernista workmanship available. Domènech i Montaner's façade is a frenzy of colour and detail, including a large allegorical mosaic representing the members of the Orfeó Català, and floral tiled columns topped with the busts of Bach, Beethoven and Palestrina on the main façade and Wagner on the side. Indoors, decoration erupts everywhere. The ceiling is an inverted bell of stained glass

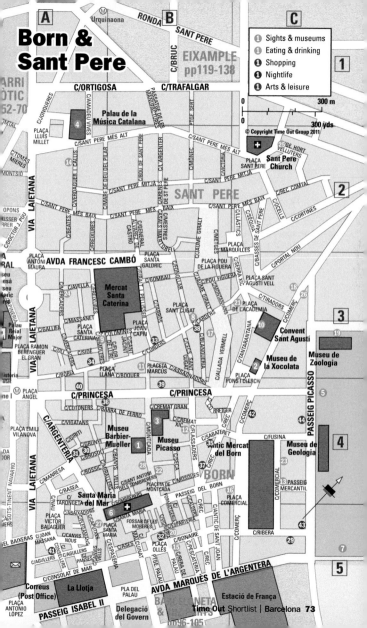

Born & Sant Pere

A   Urquinaona   RONDA   **B**   SANT PERE

C

1. Sights & museums
1. Eating & drinking
1. Shopping
1. Nightlife
1. Arts & leisure

EIXAMPLE pp119-138

1

C/ORTIGOSA   C/TRAFALGAR

0   300 m
0   300 yds

© Copyright Time Out Group 2011

4   Palau de la Música Catalana

PLAÇA LLUÍS MILLET

Sant Pere Church

PLAÇA SANT PERE

SANT PERE

2

AVDA FRANCESC CAMBÓ

PLAÇA ANTONI MAURA

PLAÇA SANTA GALDRIC

Mercat Santa Caterina

PLAÇA POU DE LA FIGUERA

PLAÇA SANT AGUSTÍ VELL

18

26

3

PLAÇA SANT CUGAT

PLAÇA DE L'ACADEMIA

21

10   Convent Sant Agustí

Museu de Zoologia **19**

2   Museu de la Xocolata

PLAÇA PONS I CLERCH

5

PLAÇA RAMON BERENGUER EL GRAN

PLAÇA LLANA

PLAÇETA MARCUS

39

40

C/PRINCESA   C/PRINCESA

PLAÇA EMILI VILANOVA

36

PLAÇA ANGEL

42

44

Museu de Geologia

23

3

Museu Barbier-Mueller **1**

Museu Picasso

Antic Mercat del Born

BORN

4

28

22

PLAÇA COMERCIAL

16

PASSEIG MERCANTIL

13

Santa Maria del Mar **6**

PLAÇA VÍCTOR BALAGUER

PLAÇA SANTA MARIA

Fossar de les Moreres

43

29

PLAÇA OLLES

7

5

Correus (Post Office)

La Llotja

PLAÇA ANTONIO LÓPEZ

PLA DEL PALAU

Delegació del Govern

Estació de França

AVDA MARQUÈS DE L'ARGENTERA

PASSEIG ISABEL II

depicting the sun bursting out of a blue sky; 18 half-mosaic, half-relief Muses appear from the back of the stage; winged horses fly over the upper balcony, and Wagnerian Valkyries ride over a bust of Beethoven.

Guided tours are available in English every hour and start with a short film of the Palau's history.

Parc de la Ciutadella

Passeig Picasso (93 413 2400). Metro Arc de Triomf or Barceloneta. **Open** 9am-sunset daily. **Admission** free.
Map p73 C4 ❺

Named after the hated Bourbon citadel – the largest in Europe – that occupied this site from 1716 to 1869, this elegant park contains a host of attractions, including the city zoo (see below), the Natural History Museum, a boating lake and more than 30 pieces of imaginative statuary. The giant mammoth statue at the far side of the boating lake is a huge hit with kids, as is the trio of prancing deer by the zoo dedicated to Walt Disney. In the north-east corner is the Cascade, an ornamental fountain topped with Aurora's chariot, on which a young Gaudí worked as assistant to Josep Fontseré, the architect of the park. Not to be missed are Fontseré's slatted wooden Umbracle (literally, 'shade house'), which provides a pocket of tropical forest within the city, and the elegant Hivernacle ('winter garden') designed by Josep Amargós in 1884. Outside, on the Passeig Picasso, is Antoni Tàpies's *A Picasso*, which is a giant Cubist monument to the artist.

Santa Maria del Mar

Plaça de Santa Maria (93 310 23 90). Metro Jaume I. **Open** 9am-1.30pm, 4.30-8pm Mon-Sat; 10am-1.30pm, 4.30-8pm Sun. **Admission** free.
Map p73 B5 ❻

One of the most perfect surviving examples of the Catalan Gothic style, this graceful basilica stands out for its characteristic horizontal lines, plain surfaces, square buttresses and flat-topped octagonal towers. Its superb unity of style is down to the fact that it was built relatively quickly, with construction taking just 55 years (from 1329 to 1384). In the broad, single-nave interior, two rows of perfectly proportioned columns soar up to fan vaults, creating an atmosphere of space around the light-flooded altar. There's also superb stained glass, especially the great 15th-century rose window above the main door. The original window fell down during an earthquake, killing 25 people. The incongruous modern window at the other end was a 1997 addition, belatedly celebrating the Olympics.

It's perhaps thanks to the group of anti-clerical anarchists who set the church ablaze for 11 days in 1936 that its superb features can be appreciated today – without the wooden Baroque furniture that clutters so many Spanish churches, the simplicity of its lines can emerge.

Event highlights Handel's *Messiah* (Christmas 2011 & 2012); Mozart's *Requiem* (Easter 2012).

Zoo

Parc de la Ciutadella (93 225 67 80, www.zoobarcelona.com). Metro Barceloneta or Ciutadella-Vila Olímpica. **Open** *Jan-Mar, Oct-Dec* 10am-5.30pm daily. *Apr-mid May, mid Sept-Oct* 10am-7pm daily. *Nov-mid Mar* 10am-5pm daily. *Mid May-mid Sept* 10am-8pm daily. **Admission** €16.50; €9.90 3-12s; free under-3s.
Map p73 C5 ❼

The dolphin shows are the big draw, but the decently sized zoo has plenty of other animals in its collection, all of whom look happy enough in reasonably spacious enclosures. Favourites include giant hippos, the prehistoric-looking rhino, sea lions, elephants, giraffes, lions and tigers. Child-friendly features include a farmyard zoo, pony rides, picnic areas and two excellent playgrounds.

Zoo

El Atril

C/Carders 23 (93 310 12 20, www.
atrilbarcelona.com). Metro Jaume I.
Open 1.30-4.30pm, 7.30-12.30pm
Tue; 1pm-midnight Wed-Sun. €€.
Global.Map p73 B3 ❽
El Atril's handful of tables require a
reservation on most nights of the
week thanks to some reliably good
cooking traversing a broad range of
cuisines. On the tapas menu fried
green plantains with coriander and
lime mayonnaise sit alongside *boti-*
farra with caramelised onions, while
a catholic selection of main courses
includes a bowl of Belgian-style mussels and chips.

Bacoa

NEW *C/Colomines 2 (93 268 95 48).*
Metro Jaume I. **Open** 1-11pm Tue-
Thur; 1pm-midnight Fri, Sat. **No**
credit cards. Map p73 A3 ❾
This gourmet burger bar opened in
2010 and set off a wave of similar
places, none of which is quite as good.
Succulent chargrilled half-pounders
are loaded up with manchego cheese,
caramelised onions and a whole load
of more outré toppings (try the Swiss,
with rösti and gruyere, or the Japanese
with teriyaki sauce).

Bar del Convent

Plaça de l'Acadèmia (93 256 50 17,
www.bardelconvent.com). Metro Arc
de Triomf or Jaume I. **Open** 10am-
10pm Mon-Thur; 10am-11pm Fri;
1pm-11pm Sat. No credit cards.
Café. Map p73 C3 ❿
The 14th-century Convent de Sant
Agustí has had a new lease of life in
recent years – first with James
Turrell's fabulous 'light sculpture'
surrounding the C/Comerç entrance,
and then with the opening of a
dynamic civic centre. And now this
secluded little café has opened in the
cloister. There are croissants, pastries
and light dishes available all day, as

well as live music, DJs, storytelling
and other performances on Friday and
Saturday nights.

Bar del Pla

C/Montcada 2 (93 268 30 03).
Metro Jaume I. **Open** noon-11pm
Tue-Thur, Sun; noon-midnight Fri,
Sat. €€€. **Tapas**. Map p73 B3 ⓫
The look at the Bar del Pla is halfway
between a French bistro and tapas
joint, complete with a long marble bar.
You can get three small dishes and a
pudding for €10; otherwise, there are
tapas or *raciones* (such as divine pig's
trotters with foie, and outstanding *pa*
amb tomàquet). Drinks include Mahou
on tap, and there are some good wines
by the glass.

La Báscula

C/Flassaders 30 (93 319 98 66).
Metro Jaume I. **Open** 1pm-11.30pm
Wed-Sun. €. No credit cards.
Vegetarian. Map p73 B4 ⓬
After a sustained campaign, the threat
of demolition has been lifted from this
former chocolate factory turned café.
Just as well, since it's a real find, with
good vegetarian food and a large dining room situated out back. An impressive list of drinks runs from chai to
Glühwein, taking in cocktails, milkshakes, smoothies and iced tea, and the
pasta and cakes are as good as you'll
find anywhere.

Big Fish

C/Comercial 9 (93 268 17 28,
www.bigfish.cat). Metro Jaume I.
Open 1.30-4pm, 8.30pm-midnight
Tue-Sun. €€€. **Fish**. Map p73 C4 ⓭
Sumptuously designed in a Manhattan
style, with leather Chesterfields, cas-
cading lampshades and a gilt-edged
fireplace, Big Fish doubles as a
Mediterranean fish restaurant and
sushi bar. The food is good to excellent
and the experience is hard to fault –
except, perhaps, for the noise levels.
Tables are very close together and the
music is jacked up to club volume by

about 11pm, at which point the waiting staff give up straining to hear you and bring you what they feel you'd probably like.

El Bitxo

C/Verdaguer i Callis 9 (93 268 17 08). Metro Urquinaona. **Open** 1pm-1am Tue-Thur; 1pm-2am Fri, Sat; 7.30pm-1am Sun. No credit cards. **€€. Tapas. Map** p73 A2 ⑭

A small, lively tapas bar specialising in excellent cheese and charcuterie from the small Catalan village of Oix, along with more outré fare such as salmon sashimi with a coffee reduction. The wine list is steadily increasing and now has around 30 suggestions, all of them good. Being so close to the Palau de la Música, the bar can get packed in the early evening before concerts.

Cal Pep

Plaça de les Olles 8 (93 310 79 61, www.calpep.com). Metro Barceloneta. **Open** 7.30-11.30pm Mon; 1-3.45pm, 7.30-11.30pm Tue-Fri; 1-3.45pm Sat. Closed Aug and Easter wk. **€€€. Seafood. Map** p73 B5 ⑮

As much tapas bar as restaurant, Cal Pep is always packed: get here early for the coveted front seats. The affable Pep will take the order, steering the neophytes towards the *trifásico* – a mélange of fried whitebait, squid rings and shrimp. Other faves are the exquisite little *tallarines* (wedge clams), and *botifarra* sausage with beans.

Casa Delfín

Passeig del Born 36 (93 319 50 88). Metro Barceloneta or Jaume I. **Open** 8am-1am daily. **€€. Catalan. Map** p73 B4 ⑯

Locals were heartbroken when the old, beloved Casa Delfin served its last plate of fried sardines, but the place has scrubbed up very nicely indeed in its new incarnation. Meticulous attention has been paid to respecting traditional Catalan recipes, with a rich and sticky *suquet* (fish stew) and excellent

'mountain' lamb with wild mushrooms. Brit owner Kate has left her imprint, however, and you'll also find the best Eton mess this side of Windsor.

Casa Paco

C/Allada-Vermell 10 (93 295 51 18). Metro Arc de Triomf or Jaume I. **Open** *May-Oct* 9am-2am Mon-Thur; 9am-3am Fri; 1pm-3am Sat; *Nov-Apr* 6pm-2am Tue-Thur; 6pm-3am Fri, Sat. No credit cards. **Bar. Map** p73 B3 ⑰

Not much more than a hole-in-the-wall with a handful of zinc tables outside, Casa Paco is the improbable nerve centre for a young and thrusting scene that attracts DJs from the higher echelons of cool. In the daytime, it's just a nice place for parents to have a cheeky beer on the terrace while the children amuse themselves in the playground just in front.

Comerç 24

C/Comerç 24 (93 319 21 02, www.comerc24.com). Metro Arc de Triomf. **Open** 1.30-3.30pm, 8.30pm-11pm Tue-Sat. **€€€€. Modern tapas. Map** p73 C3 ⑱

Carles Abellan trained under Ferran Adrià but now ploughs his own very successful furrow in this sexy restaurant. A selection of tiny playful dishes changes seasonally, but normally includes the ever popular 'Kinder egg' (lined with truffle) and the tuna sashimi and seaweed on a wafer-thin pizza crust. Adrià's latest discoveries continue to affect Abellan's menu, so recently he's been embracing Eastern cuisine.

Drac Café

Parc de la Ciutadella, Passeig Lluís Companys entrance (93 310 76 06, www.draccafe.com). Metro Arc de Triomf. **Open** *Mar-Nov* 9am-9pm Tue-Sun. **€.** No credit cards. **Café. Map** p73 C3 ⑲

With this alfresco terrace café, the Parc de la Ciutadella finally has a healthy alternative to the *kioskos* serving overpriced beer and bags of rainbow

Market routes

Walking tour for shopaholics.

Mercat de Santa Caterina

One of the great and unintended tourist attractions of Barcelona is the **Boqueria food market** on La Rambla. More than 35 years since Les Halles and Covent Garden markets were shunted out to the Paris and London suburbs, the Boqueria remains in the city centre, serving its populace and restaurants for miles around. But the Boqueria is only one of many traditional markets in the city and, in celebration of this fact, the council has devised a series of DIY tours, collectively known as the **Ruta dels Mercats**. Tourist offices have leaflets detailing the routes, or they can be printed out from www.mercatsbcn.com.

The most appealing and accessible is the Ruta dels Mercats Emblemàtics, which takes in six of the most famous, starting with the Boqueria. From there it takes you across to **Santa Caterina**, the city's oldest, rebuilt by the architect Enric Miralles (who was born next door), and reopened in 2005. The city

is running a rolling programme of refurbishing the historic markets; **Barceloneta**, next on the tour, was rebuilt from scratch, although with less architectural finesse than Santa Caterina. The building is entirely powered by solar panels, but somewhere in the process the place lost its neighbourhood ambience. This is not the case, however, with the **Mercat de Sant Antoní**, which lies just outside the line of the old city walls, on the edge of the Raval. Sant Antoní has a truly proletarian feel, selling not just food but cheap clothes, towels and bedlinen. The market is undergoing restoration and the traders have been moved temporarily to a vast marquee in the street outside. The smallest market on the route is **Concepció** in the Eixample, a charming steel-framed structure, with a 24-hour flower market on the upper side. The last stop on the tour is **Els Encants**, the furniture and flea market in Plaça de les Glòries, a lovely sprawl of gems and junk.

popcorn. Not much more than a *kiosko* itself, the friendly 'Dragon Café' serves breakfast all day, along with salads, nachos, guacamole and houmous, served tapas-style.

Euskal Etxea

Placeta Montcada 1-3 (93 310 21 85). Metro Barceloneta or Jaume I. **Open** *Bar* 10am-12.30am Mon-Fri, Sun; 10am-1.30am Sat. *Restaurant* 1-4pm, 8pm-midnight daily. **€. Tapas.** Map p73 B4 ⑳

A Basque cultural centre and the best of the city's many *pintxo* bars. Help yourself to dainty *jamón serrano* croissants, chicken tempura with saffron mayonnaise, melted provolone with mango and crispy ham, or a mini-brochette of pork, but hang on to the toothpicks spearing each one: they'll be counted up and charged for at the end.

Mosquito

C/Carders 46 (93 268 75 69, www. mosquito-tapas.com). Metro Arc de Triomf or Jaume I. **Open** 7pm-1am Mon-Wed; 1pm-1am Thur-Sun. **€. Asian.** Map p73 C3 ㉑

Mosquito's latest speciality in the world of Asian tapas is Chinese dumplings in myriad forms. Of the new dishes, the *xiaolong bao* (steamed pork dumplings) and crispy duck are more than toothsome, and the *amanida de col* (literally 'cabbage salad', but actually more like Korean *kimch'i*) is a zingy accompaniment. Mosquito is also excellent beers, some of which are brewed especially for the restaurant; try the *trigo* (wheat) beer, which is especially good.

Mudanzas

C/Vidrieria 15 (93 319 11 37). Metro Barceloneta or Jaume I. **Open** 10am-3am daily. **Bar.** Map p73 B5 ㉒

Eternally popular with all ages and nationalities, Mudanzas has a beguiling, old-fashioned look, with marble-topped tables, a black-and-white chequered floor and a rack of newspapers and

magazines, many of them in English. Its main drawback used to be that it got very smoky in the winter months, which of course is a thing of the past with the new legislation.

La Paradeta

C/Comercial 7 (93 268 19 39, www. laparadeta.com). Metro Arc de Triomf or Jaume I. **Open** 8-11.30pm Tue-Fri; 1-4pm, 8pm-midnight Sat; 1-4pm Sun. **€. Seafood.** Map p73 C4 ㉓

Superb seafood, served refectory-style. Choose from glistening mounds of clams, mussels, squid, spider crabs and other fresh treats, decide how you'd like it cooked (grilled, steamed or *a la marinera*), pick a sauce (Marie Rose, spicy local romesco, alioli or onion), buy a drink and wait for your number to be called. A great and cheap experience for anyone not too grand to clear their own plate.

Patxoca

C/Mercaders 28 (93 319 20 29). Metro Jaume I or Urquinaona. **Open** 9am-1am Mon-Thur; 9am-2am Fri; 11am-2am Sat; noon-8pm Sun. **€€. Catalan.** Map p73 A3 ㉔

Describing itself as '*agroecològic*', Patxoca endeavours to source produce locally (with the curious omission of most of its wines) and buys organic wherever feasible. The cornerstones of Catalan soul food are all present, from *cap i pota* (stew of calves' head and meat) to salt cod, while homesick Brits can take comfort in a local take on shepherd's pie (*pastis de vedella*) or cauliflower cheese.

En Petit Comité

NEW *C/Lluís el Piadós 2 (93 269 13 35, www.enpetitcomite.es). Metro Arc de Triomf.* **Open** 10am-midnight Tue-Thur; 10am-2.30am Fri, Sat; noon-midnight Sun **€€. French.** Map p73 C2 ㉕

The peaceful Plaça Sant Pere has never been well served with good places to eat or drink, so this relaxed, sunny and spacious new café has been joyfully received in the neighbourhood. French cheeses and charcuterie are the mainstays of the kitchen, served for the most part on toasted bread with a well-dressed salad.

Picnic

NEW *C/Comerç 1 (93 511 66 61, www.picnic-restaurant.com). Metro Arc de Triomf or Jaume I.* **Open** 12.30pm-5pm Mon, Sun; 12.30pm-5pm, 8.30pm-12.30am Tue-Sat, 12.30pm-5pm. **€€.**
Chilean/American. Map p73 C3 ㉖
Picnic took over this modest space in 2010 and gave it a rigorous makeover – while the exterior is still rather unlovely, inside it's a welcoming space, with country-kitchen bar stools, dramatic flower arrangements and lounge-y music. The food is influenced by the deep South and beyond, with corn chowder, fried green tomatoes and some tasty little crab cakes with fennel salad and crème fraîche, all served in half-portions. At weekends there's an excellent brunch: get there early for any chance of a table.

La Vinya del Senyor

Plaça Santa Maria 5 (93 310 33 79). Metro Barceloneta or Jaume I. **Open** noon-1am Mon-Thur; noon-2am Fri, Sat; noon-midnight Sun. **€€.**
Tapas/wine. Map p73 A5 ㉗
Though many pull up a chair simply to appreciate the splendours of Santa Maria del Mar's Gothic façade, it's a crime to take up the tables of the 'Wine of the Lord' without sampling a few of the excellent vintages on its list, along with some top-quality cheeses, hams and other tapas.

El Xampanyet

C/Montcada 22 (93 319 70 03). Metro Jaume I. **Open** noon-3.30pm, 7-11pm Tue-Sat; noon-3.30pm Sun. Closed 2wks Aug. **€. Tapas.** Map p73 B4 ㉘
The eponymous bubbly is actually a pretty low-grade cava, if truth be told, but a drinkable enough accompaniment

to the house tapa; a saucer of Cantabrian anchovies. Lined with coloured tiles, barrels and antique curios, the bar chiefly functions as a little slice of Barcelona history, and has been owned by the same family since the 1930s.

Shopping

Adolfo Domínguez

C/Ribera 16 (93 319 21 59, www.adolfodominguez.com). Metro Barceloneta. **Open** 10am-8.30pm Mon-Sat. **Map** p73 C5 ㉙
The women's department has finally caught up with the men's tailoring that for many years was Domínguez's forte. Expect to find sharp, flattering jackets, with surprisingly adventurous separates in luxurious materials, along with well-made shoes and bags.

Capricho de Muñeca

C/Brosoli 1 (93 319 58 91, www. caprichodemuneca.com). Metro Jaume I. **Open** 5-8.30pm Mon; noon-3pm, 5-8.30pm Tue-Sat. **Map** p73 A4 ㉚
Soft leather handbags in cherry reds, chocolate browns and violet made by hand just upstairs by designer Lisa Lempp. Sizes range from the cute and petit to the luxuriously large. Belts and wallets complement the handbags.

Como Agua de Mayo

C/Argenteria 43 (93 310 64 41, www.comoaguademayo.com). Metro Jaume I. **Open** 10am-8.30pm Mon-Fri; 10am-9pm Sat. **Map** p73 A4 ㉛
A temple for coquettish Carrie Bradshaw style on a mid-range budget. Think lots of mixing and matching of patterns with plenty of candy-bright shoes. Labels include Amaya Arzuaga, Antik Batik and Miriam Ocáriz; footwear comes courtesy of Otto et Moi, Pedro García and Chie Mihara. You might need to buzz to get in.

Custo Barcelona

Plaça de les Olles 7 (93 268 78 93, www.custo-barcelona.com). Metro

C/Montcada p71

Jaume I. **Open** 10am-9pm Mon-Sat; noon-8pm Sun. **Map** p73 B5 ❷

The Custo look is synonymous with Barcelona style, and the loud print T-shirts have spawned a thousand imitations. Custodio Dalmau's signature prints can now be found on everything from coats to jeans to swimwear for both men and women, but a T-shirt is still the most highly prized (and highly priced) souvenir for visiting fashionistas. There's also a Custo Vintage (Plaça del Pi 2, Barri Gòtic, 93 304 27 53), with clothes from past seasons.

Discos Juandó

C/Giralt el Pellisser 2B (93 319 16 74). Metro Jaume I. **Open** 10am-2pm, 4-8pm Mon-Sat. **Map** p73 B3 x

An old-school vinyl store specialising in soul and jazz but with a decent range of most other styles up to and including '80s new wave. Take a seat and flick through some copies of *Record Collector*, or peruse such oddities as the 'nude' section – albums with naked women on the front. Just don't come looking for techno or happy house.

Hatquarters

Plaça de la Llana 6 (93 310 18 02). Metro Jaume I. **Open** noon-9pm Mon-Sat. **Map** p73 A3 ❷

You won't find anything as vulgar as a tourist sombrero or the *titfer*. From raffia and tweed cadet caps, leather bucket hats to felt fedoras – by Goorin Bros, Cassel Goorin and Sant Cassel, among others – the simple application of any piece of headwear in this shop will get you past the toughest nightclub bouncer in town.

Ivo & Co

C/Rec 20 (93 268 33 31). Metro Arc de Triomf or Jaume I. **Open** 11am-3pm, 5-9pm Mon-Sat. **Map** p73 B4 ❸

If Cath Kidston were given free rein to create a fairytale Christmas in a Provençal farmhouse, the result would be something like Ivo & Co. This branch has wooden toys, knitted dolls, hand-stitched bunting and polka dots a go-go, while the branch opposite (Plaça Comercial 3, 93 268 86 31) focuses on homeware, with vintage-style crockery and wallpaper, table linen, hand-painted coat hangers and etched wine goblets.

Miriam Ponsa

C/Princesa 14, Born (93 295 55 62, www.miriamponsa.com). Metro Jaume I. **Open** 11am-8.30pm Mon-Sat. **Map** p73 B4 ❸

Miriam Ponsa's designs are aimed at affluent young urbanites with a taste for stripped-down, quasi-Japanese style. The clothes are generally loose fitting in style, and with a strong vertical silhouette, while materials can get pretty quirky; you might find yourself wondering how a T-shirt splattered in dripped latex or a hole-punched leather waistcoat could ever look so good.

MTX Barcelona

C/Rec 32 (93 319 43 44, www.mertxe-hernandez.com). Metro Barceloneta. **Open** 11am-9pm Mon-Sat. **Map** p73 B4 ❸

Right now, nobody in Barcelona is hipper than local designer Mertxe Hernández. Her clothes have the distinction of being utterly different and also immediately recognisable, with colourful, multilayered textiles slashed and restructured.

Mujer

C/Carders 28 (93 315 15 31). Metro Jaume I. **Open** 11am-3pm, 5-8pm Mon-Fri; 11am-8pm Sat. Closed last 2wks Aug. **Map** p73 B3 ❸

Run by the energetic Lulu, Mujer is the local nerve centre for expat parents. It stocks imported funky baby gear from the likes of Cath Kidston or Twisted Twee and is the perfect place to pick up a tiny Metallica T-Shirt.

There's also a range of maternity wear in stock, along with baby accessories, books, toys and a chill-out space for playing and breastfeeding.

On Land

C/Princesa 25 (93 310 02 11, www.on-land.com). Metro Jaume I. **Open** 5-8.30pm Mon; 11am-2pm, 5-8.30pm Tue-Fri; 11am-8.30pm Sat. Closed 1wk Aug. **Map** p73 B4 ❸⓿

This little oasis of urban cool has all you need to hold your head up high against the Barcelona hip squad: bags and wallets by Becksöndergaard and Can't Go Naked; cute dresses by Boba; elegant pencil skirts from Conni Kaminski; loose cotton trousers by IKKS and covetable T-shirts by Fresh from the Lab.

El Rei de la Màgia

C/Princesa 11 (93 319 39 20, www.elreidelamagia.com). Metro Jaume I. **Open** Sept-June 11am-2pm, 5-8pm Mon-Fri; 11am-2pm Sat. July, Aug 11am-2pm, 5-8pm Mon-Fri. **Map** p73 A4 ❹⓿

Cut someone in half, make a rabbit disappear or try out any number of other professional-quality stage illusions at the beautiful old 'King of Magic.' Less ambitious tricksters can practise their sleight of hand with the huge range of whoopee cushions and the like.

Vila Viniteca

C/Agullers 7 (902 32 77 77, www.vilaviniteca.es). Metro Jaume I. **Open** Sept-June 8.30am-8.30pm Mon-Sat. July, Aug 8.30am-8.30pm Mon-Fri; 8.30am-2pm Sat. **Map** p73 A5 ❹❶

This family-run business has built up a stock of more than 6,000 wines and spirits since 1932. Whether you want to blow €1,245 on a magnum of 2003 L'Ermita or just snag a €5 bottle of table wine, you'll find something to drink. The selection here is mostly Spanish and Catalan, but does cover international favourites. The new food shop next door at No.9 stocks fine cheeses, cured meats and oils.

Nightlife

Club Mix

C/Comerç 21 (93 319 46 96, www.clubmixbcn.com). Metro Jaume I. **Open** Apr-Sept 9pm-3am Tue-Thur; 9pm-4am Fri, Sat. Oct-Mar 9pm-3am Wed-Thur; 9pm-4am Fri, Sat. **Map** p73 C4 ❹❷

With an interior by local tastemaker Silvia Prada, a fashionable postcode and a menu of delicate finger foods, Mix attracts a professional, stylish crowd who enjoy both an after-work cocktail and an after-dinner piss-up. DJs play funk, soul, world beats and rare groove.

Diobar

C/Marquès de l'Argentera 27 (93 268 76 90). Metro Barceloneta. **Open** 11.30pm-3.30am Thur-Sat. **Map** p73 C5 ❹❸

The basement of a Greek restaurant is the unlikely setting for this cosy and wildly popular club. There's no plate throwing but instead, from Thursday to Saturday nights, it becomes a stone-walled temple of funk, soul and Latin beats as DJ Fred Spider hits the decks.

Arts & leisure

Aire de Barcelona

Passeig Picasso 22 (902 555 789, www.airedebarcelona.com). Metro Arc de Triomf or Jaume I. **Open** 10am-midnight daily. Baths (90 mins) €28; (incl 15-min massage) €39. **Map** p73 C4 ❹❹

These subterranean Arab-style baths are a superbly relaxing way to spend a couple of hours, and offer a range of extra massages in addition to the basic package of hot and cold pools, jacuzzi, saltwater pool, hammam and relaxation zone. Entrance is offered every two hours from 10am and reservations are advisable. If you've left your swimsuit at home, you can borrow or buy one.

MACBA p86

Raval

For at least a hundred years, the Raval has been the city's forbidden core, its dark 'other'. In the early 20th century, the area was notorious for its seedy theatres, brothels, anarchist groups and dosshouses. Gentrification has ensued in recent years, but, despite years of costly transformation, the old red-light district still retains a busy crew of prostitutes, transsexuals, drug addicts and poor labourers. Many of these unshiftable locals could have stepped straight from the pages of Jean Genet's *The Thief's Journal*, a chronicle of the time the writer spent here as a thieving, teenage rent boy during the 1920s. The Raval is now one of the most ethnically diverse places in Europe, with more than 70 different nationalities calling it home. Shop signs appear in a babel of languages, plugging everything from halal meat to Bollywood films and cheap calls to South America.

Dominating the Upper Raval is the Plaça dels Àngels, where the 16th-century Convent dels Àngels houses a gigantic almshouse, the Casa de la Caritat, converted into a cultural complex housing the MACBA and the CCCB.

Over the years, the square has become unofficial home to the city's skateboarders, and the surrounding streets have filled with restaurants and boutiques. Beneath C/Hospital in the Plaça Sant Agustí lies one of the Raval's more arresting pieces of architecture, the unfinished 18th-century Església de Sant Agustí (no.2, no phone, mass 11am, 1pm & 8pm Mon-Fri; 11am Sat; 11am, noon & 8pm Sun). The stone beams and jags protruding from its left flank (on C/Arc de Sant Agustí) and the undecorated sections of the Baroque façade show how work suddenly stopped when funding ran out.

Antic Hospital de la Santa Creu & La Capella

C/Carme 47-C/Hospital 56 (no phone).
Metro Liceu. **Open** 9am-11pm Mon-
Sat. La Capella (93 442 71 71) noon-
2pm, 4-8pm Tue-Sat; 11am-2pm Sun.
Admission free. **Map** p85 B3 **①**
There was a hospital on this site as
early as 1024, but in the 15th century it
expanded to centralise all the city's
hospitals and sanatoriums. By the
1920s, it was hopelessly overstretched,
and its medical facilities were moved
uptown to the Hospital Sant Pau. One
of the last patients was Gaudí, who
died here in 1926; it was also where
Picasso painted one of his first important pictures, Dead Woman (1903).

The buildings combine a 15th-
century Gothic core with Baroque and
classical additions. They're now given
over to cultural institutions, among
them the Catalan National Library, the
Institute of Catalan Studies and the
Royal Academy of Medicine, which
hosts occasional concerts. Highlights
include a neo-classical lecture theatre
complete with revolving marble dissec-
tion table (open 10am-2pm Mon-Fri),
and the entrance hall of the Casa de
Convalescència, tiled with Baroque
ceramic murals telling the story of St
Paul. La Capella, the hospital chapel,
has been converted into an exhibition
space for contemporary art. The courtyard is a popular spot for reading or
eating lunch.

CCCB (Centre de Cultura Contemporània de Barcelona)

C/Montalegre 5 (93 306 41 00,
www.cccb.org). Metro Catalunya.
Open 11am-8pm Tue, Wed, Fri-Sun;
11am-10pm Thur. **Admission**
1 exhibition €4.50; €3.40 reductions
& Wed. 2 exhibitions €6; €4.50
reductions & Wed. Free under-16s.
Free 1st Wed of mth & 8-10pm Thur;
3-8pm Sun. **Map** p85 B2 **②**

Spain's largest cultural centre was
opened in 1994 at the Casa de la Caritat,
a former almshouse, built in 1802 on
the site of a medieval monastery. The
massive façade and part of the courtyard remain from the original building;
the rest was rebuilt in dramatic contrast, all tilting glass and steel, by
architects Viaplana & Piñón, known
for the Maremàgnum shopping centre.
The CCCB's exhibitions can lean
towards heavy-handed didacticism,
but there are occasional gems.

MACBA (Museu d'Art Contemporani de Barcelona)

Plaça dels Àngels 1 (93 412 08 10/
www.macba.cat). Metro Catalunya.
Open late June-24 Sept 11am-8pm
Mon, Wed; 11am-midnight Thur, Fri;
10am-8pm Sat; 10am-3pm Sun. Late
Sept-23 June 11am-7.30pm Mon, Wed-
Fri; 10am-8pm Sat; 10am-3pm Sun.
Admission All exhibitions €7.50; €6
reductions. Annual pass €10. Permanent
collection €6; €4.50 reductions.
Temporary exhibitions €4; €3
reductions. Wed €3.50. **Map** p85 B2 **③**
The real show at the MACBA is the
building itself, Richard Meier's cool ice-
berg of a museum sitting imper-
turbably amid the ceaseless scrape and
clatter of skateboarders on the Plaça
dels Àngels. While the museum has
fattened up its holdings considerably
since opening in 1995, the shows are
often heavily political in concept and
occasionally radical to the point of inac-
cessibility, and queues to enter are
practically unheard of. Perhaps aware
of this, the MACBA's new director,
Bartomeu Marí, has expressed the
desire to put the thrill back into art.

The exhibits cover the last 50 years
or so; although there's no permanent
collection as such, some of the works
from the museum's holdings are usually on display. The earlier pieces are
strong on artists such as Antonio
Saura and Tàpies, who were members
of the Dau-al-Set, a group of radical
writers and painters much influenced

by Miró, who kick-started the Catalan art movement after the post-Civil War years of cultural apathy. Jean Dubuffet and Basque sculptors Jorge Oteiza and Eduardo Chillida also feature. Works from the last 40 years are more global, with the likes of Joseph Beuys, Jean-Michel Basquiat, AR Penck and photographer Jeff Wall.

Event highlights 'Volume. Collections of the MACBA and Fundació La Caixa.' (28 Oct 2011-1 Apr 2012).

Palau Güell

C/Nou de la Rambla 3 (93 317 39 74/www.palauguell.cat). Metro Drassanes or Liceu. Closed until April/May 2011. Map p85 C4 ④

A fortress-like edifice shoehorned into a narrow six-storey sliver, the Palau Güell was Gaudí's first major commission, begun in 1886 for textile baron Eusebi Güell. After major structural renovation, it is expected to fully reopen in spring 2011.

Once this happens, visitors can look around the subterranean stables, with an exotic canopy of stone palm fronds on the ceiling and the ground floor. Here the vestibule has ornate Mudéjar carved ceilings from which the Güells could snoop on their arriving guests through the jalousie trellis-work; at the heart of the house lies the spectacular six-storey hall complete with musicians' galleries and topped by a dome covered in cobalt honeycomb tiles.

Sant Pau del Camp

C/Sant Pau 101 (93 441 00 01). Metro Paral·lel. Open 10am-1.30pm, 4-7pm Mon-Sat. Mass 8pm Sat (Spanish); noon Sun (Catalan). Admission Visits €3; €2 reductions; free under-14s. Mass free. No credit cards. Map p85 A4 ⑤

The name, St Paul in the Field, reflects a time when the Raval was still countryside. In fact, this little Romanesque church is over 1,000 years old; the date carved on its most prestigious headstone – that of Count Guifré II Borrell, son of Wilfred 'the Hairy' and inheritor

of all Barcelona and Girona – is AD 912. The church's impressive façade includes sculptures of fantastical flora and fauna along with human grotesques. The tiny cloister is another highlight with its extraordinary Visigoth capitals, triple-lobed arches and central fountain.

Eating & drinking

Au Port de la Lune

Plaça Sant Galdric s/n (93 270 38 19). Metro Liceu. Open 1.30-4pm, 9pm-midnight Mon, Wed-Sat; 1.30-4pm Tue, Sun. €€€. No credit cards. French. Map p85 C3 ⑥

A tomato's toss from the Boqueria market is this sunny little French bistro, chipped and battered in parts but ultimately charming. The menu is a mix of the delightful (oysters, cassoulet, clafoutis) and the ever so slightly shabby, but it's difficult not to feel reassured by a blackboard that reads, 'there is no ketchup and no Coke, and there never will be'.

Bar Kasparo

Plaça Vicenç Martorell 4 (93 302 20 72). Metro Catalunya. Open 9am-10pm Tue-Sat. Closed mid Dec-mid Jan. No credit cards. Café. Map p85 C2 ⑦

Still the best of the various café terraces now sitting on the edges of quiet, traffic-free Plaça Vicenç Martorell, Kasparo serves tapas, bocadillos, salads and a varying selection of more substantial dishes, available all day. There is no indoor seating, so this is more of a warm weather proposition.

Bar Lobo

C/Pintor Fortuny 3 (93 481 53 46, www.grupotragaluz.com). Metro Catalunya. Open 9am-midnight daily. €€. Café. Map p85 C2 ⑧

The watchword is moody (not least among the waiting staff) in this stark, monochrome space with punky artwork from celebrated graffiti artists. It comes alive with DJs and studied lounging at night, however, and by day its terrace is a peaceful space for coffee or breakfast, given the proximity to La Rambla. Recent changes have brought about more of a focus on food, and lunchtimes can get packed.

Bar Marsella

C/Sant Pau 65 (93 442 72 63). Metro Liceu. **Open** 10pm-2.30am Mon-Thur; 10pm-3am Fri, Sat. No credit cards. **Bar**. Map p85 B4 ⑨
Opened in 1820 by a native of Marseilles, who may just have changed the course of Barcelona's artistic history by introducing absinthe, still a mainstay of the bar's delights. Untapped 100-year-old bottles of the stuff sit in glass cabinets alongside old mirrors and William Morris curtains, probably covered in the same dust kicked up by Picasso and Gaudí.

Bar Mendizábal

C/Junta de Comerç 2 (no phone). Metro Liceu. **Open** 8.30am-midnight daily. No credit cards. **Café**. Map p85 B3 ⑩
Considered something of a classic, Bar Mendizábal has been around for decades, its multicoloured tiles and serving-hatch a feature in thousands of holiday snaps. Really it's little more than a hole in the wall, from which juices, sandwiches and soup are ordered, and carried to tables on the other side of the road. Hours may vary according to the weather.

Bar Resolís

C/Riera Baixa 22 (93 441 29 48). Metro Liceu. **Open** 5pm-1am daily. **€**. **Tapas**. Map p85 B3 ⑪
A favourite with traders from the vintage clothing shops on the pedestrianised C/Riera Baixa, Resolís blends a trad look and run-of-the-mill tapas (tortilla, manchego cheese, prawns) with an immaculate selection of vinyl and some fanciful foodstuffs (like ceviche with oriental sauce). In the summer months, its serving-hatch ensures that the alley alongside it is rammed.

Biblioteca

C/Junta de Comerç 28 (93 412 62 21/www.bibliotecarestaurant.com). Metro Liceu. **Open** 8-11.30pm Mon-Sat. Closed 2wks Aug. **€€**. **Mediterranean**. Map p85 B3 ⑫
A tranquil and elegant space with beige, minimalist decor and a display of cookbooks – hence the name. And from Bocuse to Bourdain, they are all for sale, and their various influences collide in the menu. Increasingly, though, it draws from the Catalan culinary canon, with a good *esquixada* (salt cod salad) or a reasonable onion *coca* (flat, crispy bread) with anchovies to start, followed by gamier mains.

Boadas

C/Tallers 1 (93 318 95 92). Metro Liceu. **Open** noon-2am Mon-Thur; noon-3am Fri-Sat. No credit cards. **Cocktails**. Map p85 C2 ⑬
Set up in 1933 by Miguel Boadas, born to Catalan parents in Havana (where he became the first barman at the legendary La Floridita), this classic cocktail bar has changed little since Hemingway used to come here. In a move to deter the hordes of rubbernecking tourists, they have instituted a smart dress code.

Buenas Migas

Plaça Bonsuccés 6 (93 318 37 08). Metro Liceu. **Open** 8am-midnight daily. **€€**. **Vegetarian**. Map p85 C2 ⑭
A doggedly wholesome place, known for its red gingham and pine, and chewy spinach tart. The speciality, however, is tasty focaccia with various toppings, along with the usual high-fibre, low-fun cakes you expect to find in a vegetarian café. Its terrace sprawls across the wide pavement and street.

Cafè de les Delícies

Rambla del Raval 47 (93 441 57 14). Metro Liceu. **Open** 8am-11pm Mon-Wed; 8am-1am Thur; 11am-3am Fri,

The writing's on the wall

Graffiti turns legit.

Call it art, call it vandalism. Either way, the city council wasn't pleased when shopkeepers and artists got together to do something about the spraypaint tagging that plagues the city. Barcelona's taggers aren't fussed about where they spray – ancient doors, historic monuments and, above all, the steel shutters that cover shop fronts. The city's clean-up brigades wash the tags off walls, but can't touch the shutters, which are at least partly the responsibility of the shopkeepers.

Two groups, Persianas Lliures (Free Roller Blinds) and Enrotlla't, approached shopkeepers with the idea that they select an artist on their books to paint their blinds, with the degree of artistic licence to be agreed by the two parties. Some represent the shop's commercial activity, others are more abstract. In one weekend, Enrotlla't painted 47 blinds in the Gràcia district. To the taggers, who perhaps see themselves as artists too, the painted blinds are out of bounds and they remain tag-free.

Terrific. A civic solution to a civic problem, and one that brightens up the built environment. Terrific unless you are the council, which has started fining shopkeepers €600 a time for what it regards as vandalism. The city authorities claim the art is as much as an intrusion on the public space as 'washing hung from balconies'. Last year the city fined 165 businesses for altering their façades. 'The law regards graffiti as something that soils the public space, devalues our heritage and visually degrades the urban fabric,' a city spokesman said.

Jordi Llobell, Enrotlla't's founder, says its mission is to encourage the best art. 'The shopkeepers can visit our website, www.enrotllat.org, and see the work of the various artists and choose the one that is most to their taste,' he says. 'It's a huge contradiction that the city won't let us paint in public spaces, even with the owners' permission, when the same council mounts expensive exhibitions about graffiti in art galleries.'

Sat; 11am-1am Sun. Closed 2wks mid Aug. No credit cards. **Café**. **Map** p85 B3 ⓳

After an overhaul in the kitchen, the delightful Cafè de les Delicies is now serving breakfast, along with tapas and light dishes in its dining room at the back. Off the corridor there's a snug with armchairs, but otherwise the buzzing front bar is the place to be, with its theatre-set mezzanine, fabulous 1970s jukebox, shelves of books and reams of club flyers.

Dos Trece

C/Carme 40 (93 301 73 06, www. dostrece.net). Metro Liceu. **Open** 10am-2am Mon-Thur; 10am-3am Fri-Sun. **€€**. **Global**. **Map** p85 C2 ⓰

Thanks to a recent easing of the council's draconian measures to cut down live music in the city, Dos Trece's cosy basement space once again jumps to DJs and jam sessions. Earlier in the evening, however, it functions as another dining room – this one with cushions and candles for post-prandial lounging. Apart from a little fusion confusion (ceviche with nachos, and all manner of things with yucca chips) the food is not half bad for the price, and includes one of the few decent burgers to be had in Barcelona.

Elisabets

C/Elisabets 2-4 (93 317 58 26). Metro Catalunya. **Open** 7.30am-11pm Mon-Thur, Sat; 7.30am-2am Fri. Closed 3wks Aug. **€**. No credit cards. **Catalan**. **Map** p85 C2 ⓱

Also open in the mornings for breakfast, and late at night for drinking at the bar, Elisabets maintains a sociable local feel. Dinner, which is served only on Fridays, is actually a selection of tapas, and otherwise only the set lunch or myriad *bocadillos* are served. The lunch deal is terrific value, with *osso buco*, vegetable and chickpea stew, baked cod with garlic and parsley, and roast pork knuckle all making regular appearances on the menu.

Las Fernández

C/Carretes 11 (93 443 20 43). Metro Paral·lel. **Open** 9pm-1am Tue-Sun. Closed 2wks Aug. **€**. **Spanish**. **Map** p85 A3 ⓲

The inviting pillar-box red entrance is a beacon of cheer on one of Barcelona's less salubrious streets. Inside, the three Fernández sisters have created a bright and unpretentious bar/restaurant that specialises in wine and food from their native León. Alongside *cecina* (dried venison), gammon and sausages from the region, there are lighter Mediterranean dishes and generous salads: think smoked salmon with mustard and dill; pasta filled with wild mushrooms; and sardines with a citrus *escabeche*.

Granja M Viader

C/Xuclà 4-6 (93 318 34 86, www.granjaviader.cat). Metro Liceu. **Open** 5-8.30pm Mon; 9am-1.30pm, 5-8.30pm Tue-Sat. Closed 1wk Aug. **Café**. **Map** p85 C2 ⓳

The emblematic Catalan chocolate milk drink Cacaolat was invented in this old *granja* (milk bar) in 1931, and naturally it is still on offer, along with strawberry and banana milkshakes, *orxata* (tiger nut milk) and hot chocolate. It's an evocative, charming place with century-old fittings and enamel adverts, but be warned that the waiters refuse to be hurried.

Las Guindas

C/Sant Pau 126 (mobile 670 437 709). Metro Paral·lel. **Open** 7pm-2.30am Mon-Thur, Sun; 7pm-3am Fri, Sat. No credit cards. **Bar**. **Map** p85 A4 ⓴

Las Guindas is a long narrow bar with a crimson-hued retro look, an edgy mural and DJs fighting for turntable space to show off their acquisitions of vinyl from the 1950s to the '70s. Monday night is rockabilly night, but the rest of the week you're as likely to hear northern soul or boogaloo. For all this, Las Guindas is refreshingly attitude-free and all comers are made to feel welcome.

El Jardí

C/Hospital 56 (93 329 15 50,
www.eljardibarcelona.es). Metro Liceu.
Open 9am-11pm Mon-Sat. **€**. **Tapas**.
Map p85 B3 ㉑

The courtyard of the Gothic Antic
Hospital is a tranquil, tree-lined spot a
million miles from the hustle of
C/Hospital and nearby La Rambla.
Terrace café El Jardí actually has two
separate bars – go to the lesser-known
one, further from the entrance, for a
better chance of a table. Breakfast
pastries and all the usual tapas are present
and correct, along with pasta dishes,
quiches and salads.

Juicy Jones

C/Hospital 74 (93 443 90 82). Metro
Liceu. **Open** 1-5pm, 8pm-midnight
daily. **€**. **Vegetarian**. **Map** p85 B3 ㉒

Alongside its two menus, one
European and one Indian, this colourful vegan restaurant has an inventive
list of juices and smoothies, salads and
filled baguettes. While its heart is in the
right place, it's mostly aimed at back-
packers and staffed, it would seem, by
somewhat clueless language-exchange
students. Bring a book.

London Bar

C/Nou de la Rambla 34 (93 318 52 61).
Metro Liceu. **Open** 2pm-3am Mon-
Thur; 2pm-3.30am Fri, Sat. **Bar**. **Map**
p85 B4 ㉓

Since it had its live music licence
revoked, this beloved classic, smoky
old bar has had to rely on the pool table
or the occasional football match to
entertain its patrons. The TV screen is
hidden at the back, however, and easily
avoided; there are plenty of other
things to feast your eyes on, from the
period posters to the graceful swirls of
the turn-of-the-century woodwork.

Mam i Teca

C/Lluna 4 (93 441 33 35). Metro Sant
Antoni. **Open** 1-4pm; 8pm-midnight
Mon, Wed-Fri, Sun; 8.30pm-midnight
Sat. **€€**. **Catalan**. **Map** p85 B2 ㉔

A bright little tapas restaurant with
only three tables, so it pays to reserve.
All the usual tapas, from anchovies to
cured meats, are rigorously sourced,
and complemented by superb daily
specials such as organic *botifarra*, pork
confit and asparagus with shrimp.

Olivia

C/Pintor Fortuny 22 (93 318 63 80).
Metro Catalunya. **Open** Oct-May 9am-
9pm Mon-Sat; 10am-9pm Sun. June-
Sept 9am-9pm Mon-Sat. No credit
cards. **Map** p85 C2 ㉕

The love of a good homemade carrot
cake knows no international bound-
aries, and popular newcomer Olivia
sees a good mix of races (not to mention ages and sexualities). Its other uni-
versally admired facets include hot
ciabatta sandwiches (try avocado, brie
and sun-dried tomato); great breakfasts;
Illy coffee; fruit smoothies, and Miles
Davis playing on the stereo.

Organic

C/Junta de Comerç 11 (93 301 09
02/www.antoniaorganickitchen.com).
Metro Liceu. **Open** 1-5pm, 6pm-
midnight daily. **€€**. **Vegetarian**.
Map p85 B3 ㉖

The last word in refectory chic, Organic
is better designed and lighter in spirit
than the majority of the city's veggie
spots. Friendly staff usher you inside
and give you a rundown on options; an
all-you-can-eat salad bar, a combined
salad bar and main course, or the full
whammy – salad, soup, main course
and dessert. Beware the extras, drinks
and so on, which can hitch up the prices.

Pla dels Àngels

C/Ferlandina 23 (93 329 40 47, www.
semproniana.net). Metro Universitat.
Open 1.30-4pm, 9-11.30pm daily. **€**.
Mediterranean. **Map** p85 B2 ㉗

Appropriately, given its position opposite MACBA, Pla dels Àngels is a riot of
colour and chimera, something that
translates to its menu. The salads might
include mango, yoghurt and mint oil, or

El ACONTECIMIENTO
DISCOGRAFICO
... AÑO

La Concha p95

radicchio, serrano ham and roasted peppers, followed by a short list of pasta and gnocchi dishes and a couple of meat ones. The cheap set lunch includes two courses and a glass of wine.

Quiet Man

C/Marqués de Barberà 11 (93 412 12 19). Metro Liceu. **Open** 6pm-2am Mon-Thur; 6pm-3am Fri, Sat; 2pm-2am Sun. **Bar**. Map p85 B4 ㉘

One of the first and best of the city's many oirish pubs, the Quiet Man is a peaceful place with wooden floors and stalls that mostly eschews the beautiful game for occasional poetry readings and pool tournaments. There is Guinness (properly poured) and Murphy's, and you're just as likely to see Catalans as you are homesick expats or British tourists.

Ravalo

Plaça Emili Vendrell 1 (93 442 01 00). Metro Sant Antoni. **Open** 1-4pm, 8pm-midnight Tue-Thur; 1-4pm, 8pm-12.30am, Fri, Sat; 8pm-midnight Sun. **€**. **Pizza**. Map p85 B2 ㉙

Perfect for fans of the thin and crispy, Ravalo's table-dwarfing pizzas take some beating, thanks to flour (and a chef) imported from Naples. Most of the pizzas come with the cornerstone toppings you'd expect in any pizzeria; less familiar offerings include the pizza soufflé, filled with ham, mushrooms and an eggy mousse (better than it sounds). The restaurant's terrace overlooking a quiet square is open year-round.

Sésamo

C/Sant Antoni Abat 52 (93 441 64 11). Metro Sant Antoni. **Open** 8pm-midnight Tue-Sun. Closed Aug. **€€**. **Vegetarian**. Map p85 A2 ㉚

Sésamo's head cook recently took up the reins of management, and revamped the menu a little: for a while the front room was offering meaty Argentinian fare. However, it didn't really take off, and the place has gone back to concentrating on excellent vegetarian cooking, offering

an interesting bunch of dishes – crunchy polenta with baked pumpkin, gorgonzola and radicchio; spicy curry with wild rice; and a selection of Japanese tapas – in a buzzing space.

Silenus

C/Àngels 8 (93 302 26 80, www. silenus.es). Metro Liceu. **Open** 1.30-4pm, 8.30-11.30pm Mon-Thur; 1.30-4pm, 8.30pm-midnight Fri, Sat. **€€€**. **Mediterranean**. Map p85 B2 ㉛

Named after one of the drunken followers of the god Dionysus, Silenus is nonetheless all about restraint. Its quiet dining room has an air of scuffed elegance, with chipped and stained walls whereon the ghost of a clock is projected. The food, too, is artistically presented. It's not especially cheap, but the set lunch is generally a good bet, offering dishes ranging from Caesar salad to crunchy gnocchi with creamed spinach, or spicy *botifarra* with puréed potatoes.

Los Toreros

C/Xuclà 3-5 (93 318 23 25). Metro Catalunya. **Open** 6pm-midnight Mon-Wed, Sun; 6pm-1am Thur-Sat. **€€€**. No credit cards. **Spanish**. Map p85 C2 ㉜

For many this will be the Spanish experience they were after: a warren of yellowing dining rooms, the walls lined with bullfighting memorabilia, including a huge stuffed bull's head, a riotous atmosphere, delightfully friendly waiters, and carafes of cheap and decent house red. Most go for the set meals, which generally comprise old-school starters (melon with ham, *arroz cubano*) followed by grilled meats, but there's also a long list of tapas, paella and some generous salads.

Els Tres Tombs

Ronda Sant Antoni 2 (93 443 41 11). Metro Sant Antoni. **Open** 6am-2.30am Mon-Thur, Sun; 6am-3am Fri, Sat. **€**. **Tapas**. Map p85 A2 ㉝

Not, perhaps, the most inspired tapas bar in town, with its overcooked patatas bravas, sweaty manchego and loos that leave a lot to be desired, but Els Tres Tombs is still a long-time favourite because of its pavement terrace and proximity to the Sunday morning book market. The tres tombs in question are nothing more ghoulish than the 'three turns' of the area performed by a procession of men on horseback during the Festa dels Tres Tombs in January.

La Verònica

Rambla de Raval 2-4 (93 329 33 03). Metro Liceu. **Open** *Sept-July* noon-5pm, 7pm-midnight Mon-Wed; noon-5pm, 7pm-12.30am Thur; noon-5pm, 7pm-1am Fri; noon-1am Sat; noon-midnight Sun. *Aug* 7pm-12.30am Mon-Thur, Sun; 7pm-1am Fri, Sat. €€. **Pizza**. Map p85 B3 ㉞

La Verònica's shortcomings (its huge popularity with young foreigners and the minuscule spacing between tables foremost among them) are all but hidden by night, when candles add a cosy glow to the red, orange and yellow paintwork. Its pizzas are crisp, thin and healthy, and come with such toppings as smoked salmon, or apple, gorgonzola and mozzarella. Salads are plentiful and inventive, and there is a short, reliable wine list.

La Xina

C/Pintor Fortuny 3 (93 342 96 28, www.grupotragaluz.com). Metro Catalunya. **Open** 1-11.30pm Mon-Thur, Sun; 1pm-12.30am Fri, Sat. €€. **Chinese**. Map p85 C2 ㉟

La Xina's Shanghai chic owes much to Alan Yau's Hakkasan in London, with its lacquered teak screens, satin and velvet seating and club lighting – nothing less than you'd expect from the team behind the Tragaluz restaurants. Straightforward Chinese food can be difficult to find in Barcelona, and La Xina does little to buck the trend, with its carpaccios and Madras curry, but there is some decent dim sum, and plenty of wok dishes.

Shopping

The Raval is known for its great selection of shops selling vintage clothing, particularly those along the C/Riera Baixa.

Discos Castelló

C/Tallers 3 & 7 (93 302 59 46, http://castellodiscos.com). Metro Catalunya. **Open** 10am-8.30pm Mon-Sat. Map p85 C2 ㊱

Discos Castelló once dominated this street with a cluster of record shops catering to different tastes, but the economic crisis has sadly diminished this empire to two small shops, each with a different speciality in music: No.3 is devoted to classical; the largest shop, No.7 does hip hop, rock and alternative pop, and also stocks T-shirts and accessories.

Free

C/Ramelleres 5 (93 301 61 15, www.freeskate.com). Metro Catalunya. **Open** 11.30am-8.30pm Mon-Sat. Map p85 C2 ㊲

A skate emporium that has grown exponentially to cater for Barcelona's ever expanding population of enthusiasts, who mostly hang out around the nearby MACBA. For boys, there's casualwear from Stüssy, Carhartt et al; girls get plenty of Compobella and Loreak Mendian. The requisite chunky or retro footwear comes courtesy of Vans and Etnies.

Nightlife

Bar Pastis

C/Santa Mònica 4 (mobile 634 938 422, www.barpastis.com). Metro Drassanes. **Open** 7pm-2.30am Tue-Thur, Sun; 7pm-3.30am Fri, Sat. Map p85 B4 ㊳

This quintessentially Gallic bar once served pastis to visiting sailors and denizens of the Barrio Chino underworld. It's a Barcelona classic and still has a louche feel: floor-to-ceiling clippings and oil paintings, Edith Piaf on the stereo, and paper cranes swaying from the ceiling. There's live music every night (see website for details).

Big Bang

C/Botella 7 (no phone, www.bigbang bcn.net). Metro Liceu or Sant Antoni. **Open** *Bar* 9.30pm-2.30am Tue-Thur, Sun; 9.30pm-3am Fri, Sat. *Gigs* around 10pm-1am Fri, Sat. *Jam session* 10.30pm-1am Sun. No credit cards. **Map** p85 A2/3 ➌➒

Big Bang is decked out like a New York jazz club, circa 1930, with the low-lit smokiness and bar stool seating that that implies. The diner-style tiled floor leads from the bar to the tiny stage, where groups of talented musicians play swing, rock 'n' roll, bebop and every other vintage genre that should never have gone out of style. All you'll need is your Stetson and just a few euros for beer; shows are almost always free.

La Concha

C/Guàrdia 14 (93 302 41 18). Metro Drassanes. **Open** 5pm-2.30am Mon-Thur, Sun; 5pm-3am Fri, Sat. No credit cards. **Map** p85 B4 ➍➋

Papered with posters of vintage Spanish sexpot Sara Montiel and filled with hookah smoke, La Concha is a gem of dusty fabulousness that stands in direct contrast to all the slick and pretentious glamour of most of the newer late-night bars. It's under Moroccan ownership and there are plans to introduce tea and baklava in the afternoon.

Jazz Sí Club

C/Requesens 2 (93 329 00 20, www. tallerdemusics.com/jazzsi-club). Metro Sant Antoni. **Open** 7.45-10.30pm Tue; 8.30-11pm Mon, Wed-Fri; 7.45-11pm Sat; 6.30-10pm Sun. No credit cards. **Map** p85 A2 ➍➊

Tucked into a Raval sidestreet, with cheap shows every night and no-nonsense cheap bar grub, this truly authentic place is well worth seeking out. Since it functions as both a venue for known-in-the-scene locals and an auditorium for students of the music school across the street, it's packed to the brim with students, teachers, music lovers and players, and a lively time is guaranteed. Nights vary between jazz, flamenco and Cuban, and there are jam sessions on Tuesdays and Saturdays.

Moog

C/Arc del Teatre 3 (93 301 72 82, www.masimas.com). Metro Drassanes. **Open** midnight-5am Mon-Thur, Sun; midnight-6am Fri, Sat. **Map** p85 C4 ➍➋

Moog's been around for as long as Barcelona's been cool, and is something of an ambassador for the city's techno scene. It's admittedly a bit of an odd club, however: long, narrow and enclosed, with the air conditioning pumping away – it's a bit like partying on an aeroplane. The two floors are rather hilariously divided along gender lines: girls shake to pop and 1980s upstairs, while there's non-stop hard house and techno downstairs for the boys. It's packed seven days a week, and Angel Molina, Laurent Garnier and Jeff Mills have all played here.

La Paloma

C/Tigre 27 (93 301 68 97, www.la paloma-bcn.com). Metro Universitat. **Map** p85 B2 ➍➌

This extraordinary and much-loved dancehall is currently closed while it's fighting noise complaints, but the owners hope to be able to reopen the doors some time in the future. Arrive early and you'll see older *barcelonins* in full eveningwear elegantly circling the dancefloor. Take a seat in one of the plush balconies to admire the chandeliers and belle époque fittings. Once the foxtrot and tango have finished, DJs mix anything from funk and Latin to electro and acid. But phone first: no one knows when or how this battle will end.

Barceloneta
& the Ports

From industrial slum to leisure port, Barcelona's shoreline transformation is the result of two decades of development, which started in preparation for the 1992 Olympics and just kept on going. The seafront got a second blast of wind in its sails from the 2004 Fòrum event, which spawned a huge new swimming and watersports area, resculpted beaches and a park. Other leisure facilities in the area are the spa centre of Poliesportiu Marítim (Passeig Marítim 33-35) and the Club de Natació Atlètic Barceloneta (Plaça del Mar). The final grand project at the far end of Barcelona's waterfront is a state-of-the-art marine zoo with four different ecosystems. Despite protest from environmentalists, it's due to open in 2014.

Running between the *barrio* of Barceloneta and the palm-lined promenade alongside the Port Vell, Passeig Joan de Borbó leads to the Nova Bocana development, which is currently under construction. The complex will combine high-end leisure facilities and offices and is dominated by Ricardo Bofill's W Hotel (see p171). This marks the beginning of Barcelona's seven kilometres of beach.

At the far end of the Passeig Marítim, the gateway to the Port Olímpic is heralded by the twin skyscrapers of the Hotel Arts and the Torre Mapfre, and Frank Gehry's shimmering copper *Fish* sculpture. Behind it is the Vila Olímpica, the Olympic Village created for the games in 1992, with gardens, a cinema, four beaches, and a leisure marina. These days, the low population density and lack of cafés and shops leaves it devoid of Mediterranean charm. The wide empty boulevards do, however, lend themselves to sculpture, including a jagged pergola on Avda Icària by Enric Miralles and Carme Pinós.

Sights & museums

Monument a Colom

Plaça Portal de la Pau (93 302 52 24). Metro Drassanes. **Open** *May-Sept* 9am-8.30pm daily. *Oct-Apr* 9am-6.30pm daily. **Admission** €3; €2 reductions; free under-4s. **Map** p98 A3 ❶

Inspired by Nelson's Column, and complete with eight majestic lions, the Christopher Columbus monument was designed for the Universal Exhibition of 1888. Positioned at the sea end of La Rambla, it allegedly marks the spot where Columbus docked in 1493 after his discovery of the Americas, and the carvings illustrate the key moments in his voyages. Columbus's white hair comes courtesy of the city pigeons, so take appropriate cover if you decide to take the tiny lift up inside the column to the vertiginous viewing platform.

Museu d'Història de Catalunya

Plaça Pau Vila 3 (93 225 47 00, www. mhcat.cat). Metro Barceloneta. **Open** 10am-7pm Tue, Thur-Sat; 10am-8pm Wed; 10am-2.30pm Sun. **Admission** *All exhibitions* €5; €4 reductions; free under-7s & over-65s. *Temporary exhibitions* €3; €2 reductions; free under-7s; free to all 1st Sun of mth. **Map** p98 C3 ❷

The Catalan History Museum spans the Lower Paleolithic era right up to Jordi Pujol's proclamation as President of the Generalitat in 1980. It offers a virtual chronology of the region's past, through two floors of text, film, animated models and reproductions of everything from a medieval shoemaker's shop to a 1960s bar. Hands-on activities, such as trying to lift a knight's armour or irrigating lettuces with a Moorish water wheel, add a little pzazz to the rather dry early history; to exit the exhibition, visitors walk

over a huge 3D map of Catalonia. Every section has a decent introduction in English; the reception desk can offer in-depth English-language museum guides free of charge, and the English website is also very complete. Excellent temporary exhibitions typically examine recent aspects of regional politics and history, while the huge rooftop café terrace has unbeatable views over the city and marina.

Museu Marítim

Avda Drassanes (93 342 99 20, www.mmb.cat). Metro Drassanes. **Closed until 2013. Map** p98 A2 ❸

The soaring arches and vaults of these vast shipyards (*drassanes*) that contain the Maritime Museum represent one of the most perfectly preserved examples of civil Gothic architecture in Spain. In medieval times, the shipyards sat right on the water's edge and were used to dry-dock, repair and build vessels for the royal fleets.

The finest of these was Don Juan de Austria's galley, from which he commanded the fleet at Lepanto that defeated the Ottoman navy: a full-scale replica is the mainstay of the collection. With the aid of an audio guide, the maps, mastheads, nautical instruments, multimedia displays and models show you how shipbuilding and navigation techniques have developed over the years. The admission price also covers entrance to the beautiful 1917 *Santa Eulàlia* schooner docked nearby in the Moll de la Fusta. Note that the museum is closed for renovation until 2013.

Eating & drinking

1881

Plaça Pau Vila 3 (93 221 00 50, www. sagardi.es). Metro Barceloneta. **Open** 9.30am-midnight Mon-Thur, Sun; 9.30am-1am Fri, Sat. **Café. Map** p98 C3 ❹

There's no need to buy a ticket to the Museu d'Història de Catalunya to make the most of this little-known rooftop

BARCELONA BY AREA

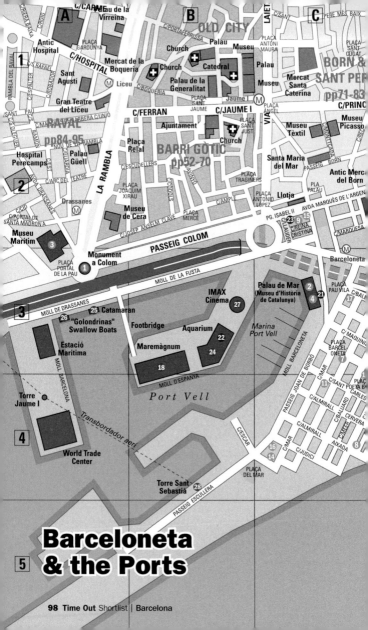

Barceloneta & the Ports

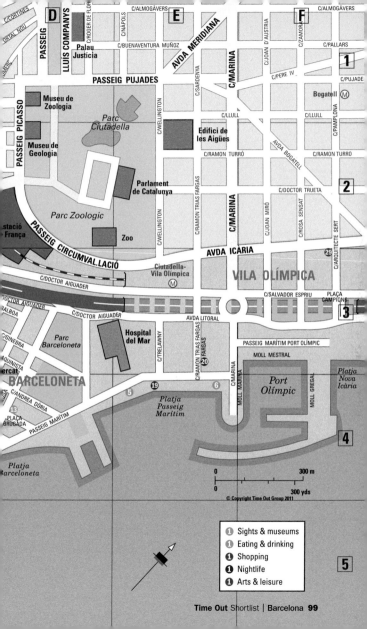

museum café with fabulous views. The set lunches don't break any ground gastronomically, but are reasonable enough, or you can take coffee and a croissant to its vast terrace and watch the boats bobbing in the harbour.

Agua

Passeig Marítim 30 (93 225 12 72, www.grupotragaluz.com). Metro Barceloneta/bus 45, 57, 59, 157. **Open** 1-3.45pm, 8-11.30pm Mon-Thur, Sun; 1-4.30pm, 8pm-12.30am Fri, Sat. **€€€**. **Mediterranean**. **Map** p99 E4 ❺

Agua's main draw is its large terrace overlooking the beach, but the relaxed dining room is usually buzzing. The menu rarely changes, but regulars never tire of the competently executed monkfish tail with *sofregit*, the risotto with partridge, and fresh pasta with juicy prawns. Scrummy puddings include marron glacé mousse and sour apple sorbet. Book ahead, especially for weekends and lunchtimes.

Bestial

C/Ramón Trias Fargas 2-4 (93 224 04 07). Metro Barceloneta. **Open** 1-3.45pm, 8-11.30pm Mon-Thur, Sun; 1-3.45pm, 8pm-12.30am Fri, Sat. **€€€**. **Italian**. **Map** p99 E4 ❻

A peerless spot for alfresco seaside dining, with tiered wooden decking and ancient olive trees. Bestial's dining room is also a stylish affair, with black-clad waiters sashaying along sleek runways, their trays held high. The food is modern Italian: mini-pizzas, rocket salad with parma ham and a lightly poached egg, tuna with black olive risotto and all the puddings you'd hope to find – panna cotta, tiramisu and limoncello sorbet. At weekends, a DJ takes to the decks, and drinks are served until 2am.

Can Ganassa

Plaça de la Barceloneta 6 (93 221 75 86. www.canganassa.com). Metro Barceloneta. **Open** 9am-mid Tue-Sun. Sat. **€€**. **Tapas**. **Map** p98 C3 ❼

It's chaotic, it's noisy, it's full of gruff old men competing to be heard above the fruit machines – it's great. And besides, there are tables outside. Good tapas are nearly all on display, so you don't need to worry about flexing your Catalan, just point. Try the '*bomba Ganassa*'; a huge potato and bacon croquette served with *all i oli* and a fiery chilli sauce.

Can Majó

C/Almirall Aixada 23 (93 221 54 55). Metro Barceloneta. **Open** 1-4pm, 8-11.30pm Tue-Sat; 1-4pm Sun. **€€€**. **Seafood**. **Map** p98 C4 ❽

Famous for its oysters, scallops, whelks, Galician clams, and just about any other mollusc you care to mention. While the menu reads much as you'd expect for a Barceloneta seafood restaurant, with plates of shellfish or (exemplary) fish soup to start, followed by rich paellas and exquisitely tasty *fideuà*, the quality is a cut above the norm. Sit inside the dapper green and yellow dining room, or within the periwinkle blue picket fence, overlooking the sea.

Can Paixano

C/Reina Cristina 7 (93 310 08 39, www.canpaixano.com). Metro Barceloneta. **Open** 9am-10.30pm Mon-Sat. Closed 3wks Aug-Sept. No credit cards. **Bar**. **Map** p98 C2 ❾

The 'Champagne Bar', as it's invariably known, has a huge following among young Catalans and legions of foreigners who think they discovered it first. It can be impossible to talk, get your order heard or move your elbows, and yet it's always mobbed for its age-old look and atmosphere, dirt-cheap bottles of house cava and (literally) obligatory sausage butties.

Can Ramonet

C/Maquinista 17 (93 319 30 64, www.canramonet.com). Metro Barceloneta. **Open** noon-midnight daily. Closed 2wks Jan, 1wk Xmas. **€€€**. **Seafood**. **Map** p99 D3 ❿

Tucked away in the *barrio* of Barceloneta, this quaint, rose-coloured space with two quiet terraces is mostly overlooked by tourists, and, consequently, it suffers none of the drop in standards of some of the paella joints on the seafront. Spectacular displays of fresh seafood show what's on offer that day, but it's also worth sampling the velvety fish soup and the generous paellas.

Can Solé

C/Sant Carles 4 (93 221 50 12, www.cansole.cat). Metro Barceloneta. **Open** 1.30-4pm, 8-11pm Tue-Sat; 1.30-4pm Sun. Closed 2wks Aug. €€€. **Seafood**. Map p98 C4 ⑪

Portly, jovial waiters have been charming monied regulars for over a hundred years at Can Solé. Over time, many of these diners have added to the framed photos, sketches and paintings that line the sky-blue walls. What continues to lure them is the freshest shellfish (share a plate of *chipirones* to start) and fillets of wild turbot, lobster stews and sticky paellas. Beware the steeply priced extras (coffee, cover).

La Cova Fumada

C/Baluard 56 (93 221 40 61). Metro Barceloneta. **Open** 9am-3.15pm Mon-Wed; 9am-3pm, 6-8.15pm Thur, Fri; 9am-1.15pm Sat. Closed Aug. No credit cards. €. **Tapas**. Map p98 C4 ⑫

An authentic family-run *bodega*, hugely popular with local workers, where you'll need to arrive early for a cramped and possibly shared table. Said to be the birthplace of the spicy potato *bomba*, La Cova Fumada also turns out a great tomato and onion salad, delicious chickpeas with *morcilla* (black pudding) and unbeatable marinated sardines. Note that it normally only opens at lunchtime.

Filferro

C/Sant Carles 29 (93 221 98 36). Metro Barceloneta. Open 10am-1am Tue-Thur, Sun; 10am-2am Fri, Sat. No credit cards. €. **Tapas**. Map p99 D4 ⑬

BCN Slow

A guide to the good life.

BCN Slow, a city council publication, is a collection of 23 itineraries intended to show another side of the city by way of plazas, patios, parks and cemeteries; a Barcelona that is quiet, crowd-free and abundant in fresh air and foliage.

Writer Isabel de Villalonga leaves no *barrio* untrodden and photographer Jordi Play gets up very early indeed to present Barcelona as it can occasionally be glimpsed: village-like, a place where amiable locals huddle in duffle coats at La Boqueria's Bar Pinotxo (see p59), take morning jogs around Montjuïc castle, or perform traditional cottage-industry tasks, such as making bread or musical instruments.

Some of the routes don't seem terribly relaxing: there's a 10km stroll along the beachfront to the industrial area of Besòs, a hike up the steep streets of Zona Alta, and a wander through the high-rises of business district 22@. There is also, if Play's photographs are meant to offer suggestions, an ill-advised tour of the backstreets of the Gòtic quarter in the dark.

Yet if used off-peak and selectively, *BCN Slow* does direct you to places easily missed: pretty Passatge Permanyer in Eixample, Parc Turó in Sant Gervasi, Plaça de la Concòrdia in Les Corts. It's also a worthy reminder that a short ride on public transport can take you to charming Horta, or up to the views and Modernista buildings of leafy Vallvidrera.

Simply but edgily decorated with red 1950s lampshades and rusted iron balustrades, this Italian-owned café is a restful, sunny spot for breakfast, lunch or tapas, with tables outside on a quiet square. As well as a good range of fresh fruit juices (try the Trifàsic, with carrot, pear and lemon), there are pastries, toasted sandwiches, pasta and salads.

Kaiku

Plaça del Mar 1 (93 221 90 82). Metro Barceloneta. **Open** 1-3.30pm Tue-Sun. Closed 3wks Aug & 1wk Dec. €€€.
Seafood. Map p98 C4 ⑭
With its simple look, missable façade and paper tablecloths, Kaiku looks a world apart from the upmarket seafood restaurants that pepper this *barrio*, but its dishes are in fact sophisticated takes on the seaside classics. A salad starter comes with shavings of foie gras or red fruit vinaigrette, and paella is given a rich and earthy spin with wild mushrooms. Book ahead for a terrace table.

Set Portes

Passeig Isabel II 14 (93 319 30 33, www.7portes.com). Metro Barceloneta. **Open** 1pm-1am daily. €€€.
Seafood. Map p98 C2 ⑮
The eponymous seven doors open on to as many dining salons, all kitted out in elegant 19th-century decor. Long-aproned waiters bring regional dishes, served in enormous portions, including a stewy fish *zarzuela* with half a lobster, a different paella daily (shellfish, for example, or rabbit and snails), and a wide array of fresh seafood or heavier dishes such as black-bean stew with pork sausage and herbs, and *orujo* sorbet to finish. Reservations are available only for certain tables; without one, get there early or expect a long wait outside.

El Suquet de l'Almirall

Passeig Joan de Borbó 65 (93 221 62 33, www.suquetdelalmirall.com). Metro Barceloneta. **Open** 1.15-4pm, 8.30-11pm Tue-Sat; 1.15-4pm Sun. Closed 2wks Aug. €€€. **Seafood.** Map p98 C4 ⑯

One of the famous beachfront *xiringuitos* that was moved and refurbished in time for the 1992 Olympics, El Suquet remains a friendly, family-run concern, despite the smart decor and mid-scale business lunchers. The fishy favourites range from *xató* salad to *arròs negre* and include a variety of set menus, such as the 'blind' selection of tapas, a gargantuan taster menu and, most popular, the *pica-pica*, which includes roast red peppers with anchovies, a bowl of steamed cockles and clams, and a heap of *fideuà* with lobster.

El Vaso de Oro

C/Balboa 6 (93 319 30 98). Metro Barceloneta. **Open** noon-11.45pm Mon-Fri; 12.30pm-11.45pm Sat, Sun. Closed Sept. No credit cards. €€.
Tapas. Map p98 C3 ⑰
The popularity of this long, narrow cruise ship-style bar tells you everything you need to know about the tapas, but it also means that he who hesitates is lost when it comes to ordering. Elbow out a space and demand, loudly, *choricitos*, *bravas*, *solomillo* (cubed steak) or *atún* (tuna, which here comes spicy). The beer (its handling and pouring) is also a point of great pride.

Shopping

Maremagnum

Moll d'Espanya (93 225 81 00, www.maremagnum.es). Metro Drassanes. **Open** 10am-10pm daily. Map p98 B3 ⑱
When Viaplana and Piñon's shopping and leisure centre opened in 1995, it was the place to hang out. After years of declining popularity, it's ditched most of the bars and taken a step upmarket: residents now include chocolate shop Xocoa, Calvin Klein and Parisian accessories shop Lollipops. All the high-street staples are present (Mango, H&M) and the ground floor focuses on the family market, with sweets, children's clothes and a Barça shop. There's also a handful of tapas restaurants.

Club de Natació Atlètic
Barceloneta p96

Nightlife

CDLC

Passeig Marítim 32 (93 224 04 70, www.cdlcbarcelona.com). Metro Ciutadella-Vila Olímpica. **Open** noon-3am Mon-Fri; noon-4am Fri, Sat. **Map** p99 E4 ⑲

Carpe Diem Lounge Club, to give the venue its full name, remains at the forefront of Barcelona's splash-the-cash, see-and-be-seen celeb circuit – the white beds flanking the dancefloor, guarded by a clipboard hostess, are perfect for showing everyone who's the daddy. Alternatively, for those not celebrating recently signed, six-figure record deals, funky house and a busy terrace provide an opportunity for mere mortals (and models) to mingle and discuss who's going to finance their next drink and, secondly, how to get chatting to whichever member of the Barça football team has just walked in.

Club Catwalk

C/Ramón Trias Fargas s/n (93 221 61 61, www.clubcatwalk.net). Metro Ciutadella-Vila Olímpica. **Open** midnight-6am Thur-Sun. **Map** p99 E3 ⑳

Maybe it's the name or maybe it's the location, but most of the Catwalk queue seems to think they're headed straight for the VIP room – that's crisp white collars and gold for the boys and short, short skirts for the girls. Inside it's suitably snazzy; upstairs there's R&B and hip hop, but the main house room is where most of the action is, with everything from electro-house to minimal beats.

Le Kasbah

Plaça Pau Vilà 1 (Palau del Mar) (mobile 667 166 783, www.otto zutz.com). Metro Barceloneta. **Open** *June-Sept* midnight-3.30am daily. *Oct-May* midnight-3.30am Wed-Sat. **Map** p98 C3 ㉑

A white awning over terrace tables heralds the entrance to this decidedly louche bar behind the Palau de Mar. Inside, a North African harem look seduces a young and up-for-it mix of tourists and students on to its plush cushions for a cocktail or two before they depart for other venues. But as the night progresses, so does the music, from chillout early in the night to full-on boogie after midnight, when it gets packed.

Mondo

Edifici IMAX, Moll d'Espanya (93 221 39 11, www.mondobcn.com). Metro Barceloneta or Drassanes. **Open** 11.30pm-3.30am Wed-Sat. **Map** p98 B3 ㉒

Arrive by yacht or Jaguar – anything less might not get you past the door. Upscale dining alongside amazing views of the port precedes late-night caviar and champagne house parties with DJs from Hed Kandi and Hôtel Costes. Multiple intimate VIP rooms provide privacy, pleasure and prestige.

Sala Monasterio

Passeig Isabel II 4 (93 319 19 88, www.salamonasterio.com). Metro Barceloneta. **Open** 9.30pm-2.30am Mon-Thur, Sun; 9.30pm-3am Fri, Sat. No credit cards. **Map** p98 C2 ㉓

Its entrance is easily missed; go in past the bar at street level and descend to this low-ceilinged, bare-brick cavern to hear all nature of jamming and live music on a great sound system. On Mondays there are singer-songwriters, rock jams on Tuesdays, Wednesday sees Brazilian music, and Thursday blues jams. The selection of music at weekends varies.

Arts & leisure

L'Aquàrium

Moll d'Espanya, Port Vell (93 221 74 74, www.aquariumbcn.com). Metro Barceloneta or Drassanes. **Open** *Oct-May* 9.30am-9pm Mon-Fri; 9.30am-9.30pm Sat, Sun. *June, Sept* 9.30am-9.30pm daily. *July, Aug* 9.30am-11pm daily. **Admission** €17.50; €12.50-€14.50 reductions; free under-4s. **Map** p98 B3 ㉔

The main draw here is the Oceanari, a giant shark-infested tank traversed via a glass tunnel on a slow-moving conveyor belt, but other aquaria house shoals of kaleidoscopic fish. The upstairs section is devoted to children: for pre-schoolers, Explora! has 50 knobs-and-whistles activities, such as turning a crank to see how ducks' feet move or climbing inside a mini-submarine, though much of the equipment is looking a bit the worse for wear. Older children should head to Planet Aqua – an extraordinary split-level circular space with Humboldt penguins.

Catamaran Orsom

Portal de la Pau, Port de Barcelona (93 221 82 83, www.barcelona-orsom. com, www.barcelonaspeedboat.com). Metro Drassanes. **Sailings** (approx 1hr 30mins) *Oct-Apr* call to confirm times. *May-Sept* noon, 3pm, 6pm daily. **Tickets** €12.50; €9.50 reductions; free under-4s. **Map** p98 A3 **㉕**
This 23m (75ft) sail catamaran is the largest in Barcelona. Departing from the jetty just by the Monument a Colom, it chugs up to 80 seafarers round the Nova Bocana harbour area, before unfurling its sails and peacefully gliding across the bay. There are 8pm jazz cruises from June to September.

Las Golondrinas

Moll de Drassanes (93 442 31 06, www. lasgolondrinas.com). Metro Drassanes. **Tickets** €5.50-€11.50; €9 reductions; free under-4s. **Map** p98 A3 **㉖**
Departing from the jetty just by the Monument a Colom, this 23m (75ft) sail catamaran is the largest in Barcelona – it chugs up to 80 seafarers round to the Nova Bocana harbour area before unfurling its sails and peacefully gliding across the bay. There are evening jazz/chill out cruises at 6pm and 8pm at weekends from July to August (€14.90, €12.90 reductions; free under-4s) and a new speedboat trip runs to the Fòrum and back (50mins, €10.95, €9.50 reductions, free under-4s).

IMAX Port Vell

Moll d'Espanya, Port Vell (93 225 11 11, www.imaxportvell.com). Metro Barceloneta or Drassanes. **Tickets** €8.70-€10. **Map** p98 B3 **㉗**
The predictable programming lets down the IMAX experience, and only if you're very lucky will you catch anything that's not about sharks, dinosaurs or adventure sports. If these rock your boat, however, you're in for a treat. Note that not all films are 3D; check the website to see which is which.

Teleférico del Port

Torre de Sant Sebastià, Barceloneta (93 441 48 20). Metro Barceloneta. **Open** Closed until 2013. **Map** p98 B4 **㉓**
These rather battered cable cars do not appear to have been touched – except for the installation of lifts – since they were built for the 1929 Expo, but that's about to change as they close for renovation. They provide sky-high views over Barcelona on their grinding, squeaking path from the Sant Sebastià tower at the very far end of Passeig Joan de Borbó to the Jaume I tower in front of the World Trade Center; the final leg ends at the Miramar lookout point on Montjuïc.

Yelmo Icària Cineplex

C/Salvador Espriú 61, Vila Olímpica (information 93 221 79 12, tickets 902 22 09 22, www.yelmocineplex.es). Metro Ciutadella-Vila Olímpica. **Tickets** Mon €6; Tue-Sun €7.50; €6 before 3pm & reductions. **Map** p99 F3 **㉙**
A vast multiplex, which has all the atmosphere of the near permanently empty shopping mall that surrounds it. But what it lacks in charm, it makes up for in choice, with 15 screens offering Hollywood blockbusters and mainstream foreign and Spanish releases. Weekends are seat-specific, so queues tend to be slow-moving; if you can, it's worth booking your seat online before you go.

BARCELONA BY AREA

Fundació Joan Miró p109

Montjuïc & Poble Sec

Maybe it was all those years of living within its walls, but the people of Barcelona seem to prefer to huddle and jostle amid the city's streets than high above the town on the hill gazing down over the city. The spectacular views came to the world's attention during the 1992 Olympic Games, but these days few bother to climb up for some fresh air on Tibidabo and Montjuïc, the city's remarkably underused hills.

In a city with as few parks as Barcelona, the hills of Montjuïc offer a precious green lung, along with some outstanding museums. Scattered over the landward side are buildings from the 1992 Olympic Games; facing the sea are a lighthouse and an enormous cemetery. At the top of the hill, all but invisible from below, is the heavily fortified Castell de Montjuïc, a dark and brooding symbol of the centuries Catalonia spent under Castilian rule.

Poble Sec, the name of the neighbourhood between Montjuïc and the Avda Paral·lel, actually means 'dry village'; it was 1894 before the thousands of poor workers who lived on the flanks of the hill celebrated the installation of the area's first fountain (still standing in C/Margarit). These days, Poble Sec is a friendly, working-class area of quiet, relaxed streets and leafy squares.

The name Paral·lel derives from the fact that the avenue coincides exactly with latitude 41° 44' N, one of Ildefons Cerdà's more eccentric conceits. This was the prime centre of Barcelona nightlife during the first half of the 20th century, and full of theatres and music halls. A statue on the corner adjoining C/Nou de la Rambla commemorates Raquel Meller, a star of the street who went on to celebrity around the world. She now stands outside notorious live-porn venue, the Bagdad.

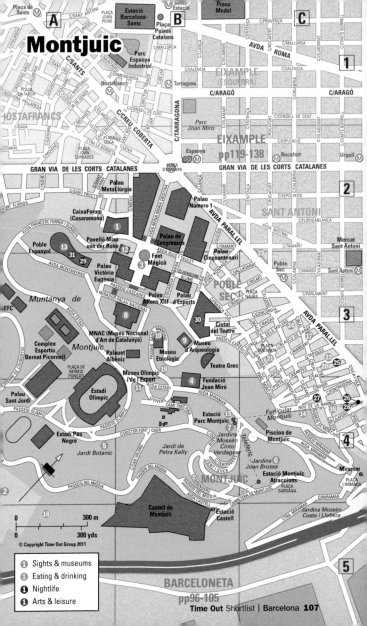

Montjuïc

Plaça de Sants

Estació Barcelona-Sants

Sants-Estació

Preso Model

Plaça Països Catalans

Parc Espanya Industrial

Hostafrancs

Tarragona

Espanya

HOSTAFRANCS

EIXAMPLE (ESQUERRA)

C/ARAGÓ

Parc Joan Miró

EIXAMPLE pp119-138

Rocafort

Urgell

GRAN VIA DE LES CORTS CATALANES

GRAN VIA DE LES CORTS CATALANES

PLAÇA D'ESPANYA

SANT ANTONI

Palau Metal·lúrgia

Palau Número 1

CaixaForum (Casaramona) **1**

Pavelló Mies van der Rohe **12**

Poble Espanyol **13** **31** **29**

Palau Victòria Eugènia

Font Màgica **3**

Palau de Congressos

Palau Cinquantenari

Mercat Sant Antoni

Sant Antoni

Poble Sec

POBLE SEC

Muntanya de

Palau Alfons XIII

Palau d'Esports

MIRADOR PALAU NACIONAL

8

30

Ciutat del Teatre

AVDA PARAL·LEL

Complex Esportiu Bernat Picornell

Montjuïc

MNAC (Museu Nacional d'Art de Catalunya) **10**

Palauet Albéniz

9 Museu d'Arqueologia

Museu Etnològic

Teatre Grec

Museu Olímpic i de l'Esport **11**

19

Fundació Joan Miró **4**

Palau Sant Jordi

Estadi Olímpic

15 Estació Parc Montjuïc

Funicular Montjuïc

Piscina de Montjuïc

Estadi Pau Negre

5

Jardí Botànic

Jardí de Petra Kelly

Jardins Mossèn Cinto Verdaguer

Jardins Joan Brossa

MONTJUÏC

6 Estació Montjuïc Atraccions

PLAÇA SARDANA

Miramar

PLAÇA D'ARMADA

Castell de Montjuïc

Estació Castell

Jardins Mossèn Costa i Llobera

18

0 — 300 m
0 — 300 yds

© Copyright Time Out Group 2011

BARCELONETA pp96-105

- ❶ Sights & museums
- ❶ Eating & drinking
- ❶ Nightlife
- ❶ Arts & leisure

CaixaForum

Sights & museums

CaixaForum

Casaramona, Avda Francesc Ferrer i Guàrdia 6-8 (93 476 86 00, www. fundacio.lacaixa.es). Metro Espanya. **Open** 10am-8pm Mon-Fri, Sun; 10am-10pm Sat. **Admission** free. **Map** p107 A/B2 ❶

One of the masterpieces of industrial Modernisme, this red-brick former textile factory was designed by Puig i Cadafalch in 1911. It spent most of the last century in a sorry state, acting briefly as a police barracks and then falling into dereliction. Fundació La Caixa, the charitable arm of Catalonia's largest savings bank, bought the building and set about the reconstruction. The original brick volume was supported, while the ground below was excavated to house a strikingly modern entrance plaza by Arata Isozaki, a Sol LeWitt mural, an auditorium, a bookshop and a library. In addition to the permanent contemporary art collection, there are three spaces for temporary exhibitions – often among the most interesting in the city.

Cementiri Sud-Oest

C/Mare de Déu de Port 54-58 (93 484 19 70). Bus 38. **Open** 8am-6pm daily. **Admission** free. **Map** p107 A4 ❷

Designed by Leandro Albareda in 1880, this enormous necropolis rests at the side of the motorway out of town, and is a daily reminder to commuters of their own mortality. The dead were originally placed in four sections: one for Catholics, one for Protestants, one for non-Christians and a fourth for aborted foetuses. It now stretches over the south-west corner of the mountain, with family tombs stacked five or six storeys high. Many, especially those belonging to the gypsy community, are a riot of colour and flowers. The Fossar de la Pedrera park memorialises those fallen from the International Brigades and the Catalan martyrs from the Civil War. There is

also a Holocaust memorial and a mausoleum to the former president of the Generalitat Lluís Companys.

Font Màgica de Montjuïc

Plaça Carles Buïgas 1 (93 316 10 00). Metro Espanya. **Shows** (every 30 mins) *May-Sept* 9.30-11pm Thur-Sun. *Dec-Apr* 7-9pm Fri, Sat. Closed Oct, Nov. **Map** p107 B3 ❸

Still using its original plumbing, the 'magic fountain' works its wonders with 3,600 pieces of tubing and more than 4,500 light bulbs. On summer evenings after nightfall, you can see a pastel-coloured array of founts swell and dance to music ranging from the 1812 *Overture* to Freddie Mercury and Montserrat Caballé's *Barcelona*. A new piece sees the fountain choreographed to soundtracks from films, including *Blade Runner*, *Gladiator* and *Lord of the Rings*.

Fundació Joan Miró

Parc de Montjuïc s/n (93 443 94 70, http://fundaciomiro-bcn.org). Metro Paral·lel then Funicular de Montjuïc. **Open** *July-Sept* 10am-8pm Tue, Wed, Fri, Sat; 10am-9.30pm Thur; 10am-2.30pm Sun. *Oct-June* 10am-7pm Tue, Wed, Fri, Sat; 10am-9.30pm Thur; 10am-2.30pm Sun. **Guided tours** *Temporary exhibitions* 11.30pm Sat. *Permanent exhibition* 11.30pm Sun. **Admission** *All exhibitions* €8.50; €6 reductions. *Temporary exhibitions* €4; €3 reductions; free under-15s. **Map** p107 B4 ❹

The building, designed by Josep Lluís Sert, is approachable, light and airy. Its white walls and arches house a collection of more than 225 paintings, 150 sculptures and all of Miró's graphic works, plus some 5,000 drawings. The collection, highlighting Miró's trademark use of primary colours and simplified organic forms symbolising stars, the moon, birds and women, occupies the second half of the space. On the way to the sculpture gallery is Alexander Calder's rebuilt Mercury

Fountain, originally on display at the Spanish Republic's pavilion at the 1937 Paris Fair. In other works, Miró is portrayed as a cubist (*Street in Pedralbes*, 1917), naive (*Portrait of a Young Girl*, 1919) and surrealist (*Man and Woman in Front of a Pile of Excrement*, 1935). In the upper galleries, large, black-outlined paintings from Miró's final period precede works with political themes. Outside is a small sculpture garden.

Jardí Botànic

C/Doctor Font i Quer (93 426 49 35, www.jardibotanic.bcn.cat). Metro Paral·lel then Funicular de Montjuïc or 50,55 bus. **Open** *Nov-Jan* 10am-5pm daily. *Feb-Mar, Oct* 10am-6pm daily. *Apr-May, Sept* 10am-7pm daily. *June-Aug* 10am-8pm daily. **Admission** €3.50; €2.60 reductions; free under-16s. Free after 3pm Sun & all day last Sun of month. No credit cards. **Map** p107 A4 ❺

After the original 1930s botanical garden was disturbed by the construction for the Olympics, the only solution was to build an entirely new replacement. This opened in 1999, housing plants from seven global regions with a climate similar to that of the Western Mediterranean. Everything about the futuristic design, from the angular concrete pathways to the raw sheet steel banking (and even the design of the bins), is the antithesis of the naturalistic, Gertrude Jekyll-inspired gardens of England. It is meticulously kept, with all plants being tagged in Latin, Catalan, Spanish and English along with their date of planting, and features wonderful views across the city.

Jardins de Joan Brossa

Plaça Dante (010, www.bcn.cat/parcsijardins). Metro Paral·lel, then Funicular de Montjuïc or 50,55 bus. **Open** 10am-sunset daily. **Admission** free. **Map** p107 C4 ❻

Set in five hectares of the former fairground, Montjuïc's latest park is part-forest, with 40 tree species, and part-urban playground. As well as a climbing frame, there are various wooden creations designed for children, allowing them to play tunes and pump water.

Jardins Mossèn Costa i Llobera

Ctra de Miramar 1 (010, www.bcn.cat/parcsijardins). Metro Paral·lel, then Funicular de Montjuïc or 50,55 bus. **Open** 10am-sunset daily. **Admission** free. **Map** p107 B4 ❼

The port side of Montjuïc is protected from the cold north wind, creating a microclimate that's two degrees centigrade warmer than the rest of the city, – ideal conditions for 800 species of the world's cacti. This extraordinary collection has been closed to the public for some time while funding for essential maintenance is sought.

MNAC (Museu Nacional d'Art de Catalunya)

Palau Nacional, Parc de Montjuïc (93 622 03 76, www.mnac.cat). Metro Espanya. **Open** 10am-7pm Tue-Sat; 10am-2.30pm Sun. **Admission** (valid 2 days) *Permanent exhibitions* €8.50; €6 reductions. *Temporary exhibitions* €5.50-€3.50. Combined ticket with Poble Espanyol €12. Free over-65s, under-16s and 1st Sun of mth. **Map** p107 B3 ❽

'One museum, a thousand years of art' is the slogan of the National Museum, and the collection provides a dizzying overview of Catalan art from the 12th to the 20th centuries. In recent years, the museum has added an extra floor to absorb the holdings of the section of the Thyssen-Bornemisza collection previously kept in the Pedralbes convent, along with the mainly Modernista holdings from the former Museum of Modern Art in Ciutadella park, a fine photography section, coins and the bequest of Francesc Cambó, founder of the autonomist Lliga Regionalista, a regionalist conservative party.

The highlight of the museum, however, is still the Romanesque collection.

MNAC (Museu Nacional d'Art
de Catalunya)

As art historians realised that scores of solitary tenth-century churches in the Pyrenees were falling into ruin – and with them were disintegrating extraordinary Romanesque mural paintings that had served to instruct villagers in the basics of the faith – the laborious task was begun of removing the murals from the church apses. The display here features 21 mural sections in loose chronological order.

A highlight is the tremendous *Crist de Taüll* from the 12th-century church of Sant Climent de Taüll. The Gothic collection is also excellent and starts with some late 13th-century frescoes, which were discovered in 1961 and 1997 when two palaces in the city were being renovated. There are carvings and paintings from local churches, including works by the indisputable Catalan masters of the Golden Age, Bernat Martorell and Jaume Huguet. The highlight of the Thyssen collection is Fra Angelico's *Madonna of Humility* (c1430), while the Cambó bequest contains some wonderful Old Masters. Also unmissable is the Modernista collection: it includes Ramon Casas' mural of himself and Pere Romeu on a tandem, which decorated the café frequented by Picasso, Els Quatre Gats (see p63). The rich collection of decorative arts includes original furniture from Modernista houses.

Museu d'Arqueologia de Catalunya

Passeig de Santa Madrona 39-41 (93 423 21 49, www.mac.cat). Metro Poble Sec. **Open** 9.30am-7pm Tue-Sat; 10am-2.30pm Sun. **Admission** €3; €2.10 reductions; free under-16s, over-65s. No credit cards. **Map** p107 B3 ⑨

The time frame for this archaeological collection starts with the Palaeolithic period, and there are relics of Greek, Punic, Roman and Visigothic colonisers, up to the early Middle Ages. A massive Roman sarcophagus is carved with scenes of the rape of Persephone,

and an immense statue of Aesculapius, the god of medicine, towers over one room. A few galleries are dedicated to the Mallorcan Talayotic cave culture, and there is an exemplary display on the Iberians – the pre-Hellenic, pre-Roman inhabitants of south-eastern Spain. An Iberian skull with a nail driven through it effectively demonstrates a typical method of execution from that time. The display ends with the marvellous, jewel-studded headpiece of a Visigoth king. One of the best-loved pieces, naturally, is an alarmingly erect Priapus, found during building work in Sants in 1848 and kept under wraps 'for moral reasons' until 1986.

Museu Etnològic

Passeig de Santa Madrona 16-22 (93 424 68 07, www.museuetnologic.bcn. cat). Metro Poble Sec. **Open** June-Sept 10am-6pm Tue-Sat; 11am-8pm Sun. *Oct-May* 10am-7pm Tue, Thur, Sat; 10am-2pm Wed, Fri; 10am-2pm, 3-8pm Sun. **Admission** €3.50; €1.70 reductions; free under-12s and 1st Sun of mth. No credit cards. **Map** p107 B3 ⑩

The Ethnology Museum houses a vast collection of items, from Australian Aboriginal boomerangs to rugs and jewellery from Afghanistan, although by far the most comprehensive collections are from Catalonia. Of the displays upstairs, most outstanding are the Moroccan, Japanese and Philippine exhibits, though there are also some interesting pre-Columbian finds. The attempts to arrange the pieces thematically, however, are not altogether successful: a potentially fascinating exhibition called 'Taboos', for instance, turned out to be a rather limp look at nudity in different cultures.

Museu Olímpic i de l'Esport

Avda Estadi 60 (93 292 53 79, www. fundaciobarcelonaolimpica.es). Metro Paral·lel then Funicular de Montjuïc or 50,55 bus. **Open** Apr-Sept 10am-8pm

Montjuïc & Poble Sec

Tue-Sat; 10am-2.30pm Sun. *Oct-Mar* 10am-6pm Tue-Sat; 10am-2.30pm Sun. **Admission** €4.50; €2.50 reductions; free under-14s & over-65s. **Map** p107 B4 ⓫

Opened in 2007 in a new building across from the stadium, the Olympic and Sports Museum gives an overview of the Games (and, indeed, all games) from ancient Greece onwards. As well as photos and film footage of great sporting moments and heroes, there is an array of memorabilia (Ronaldinho's boots, Mika Häkkinen's Mercedes), along with a collection of opening ceremony costumes and Olympic torches. Perhaps more entertaining are the interactive displays, such as one that compares your effort at the long jump with that of the pros.

Pavelló Mies van der Rohe

Avda Francesc Ferrer i Guàrdia (93 423 40 16, www.miesbcn.com). Metro Espanya. **Open** 10am-8pm daily. **Admission** €4.50; €2.30 reductions; free under-18s. **Map** p107 B2 ⓬

Mies van der Rohe built the Pavelló Alemany (German Pavilion) for the 1929 Universal Exhibition not as a gallery but as a simple reception space, sparsely furnished by his trademark 'Barcelona Chair'. The pavilion was a founding monument of modern, rationalist architecture, with its flowing floor plan and a revolutionary use of materials. Although the original pavilion was demolished after the exhibition, a fine replica was built on the same site in 1986, the simplicity of its design setting off the warm tones of the marble and expressive Georg Kolbe sculpture in the pond.

Poble Espanyol

Avda Francesc Ferrer i Guàrdia 13 (93 325 78 66, www.poble-espanyol. com). Metro Espanya. **Open** *Village & restaurants* 9am-8pm Mon; 9am-2am Tue-Thur; 9am-5am Fri, Sat; 9am-midnight Sun. *Shops* Dec-May 10am-6pm daily. June-Aug 10am-8pm daily.

Sept-Nov 10am-7pm daily. **Admission** €8.90; €5.60-€6.60 reductions; *family ticket* €20; free under-4s. *Night ticket* €5.50. *Combined ticket with MNAC* €12. **Map** p107 A2 ⓭

Built for the 1929 Universal Exhibition and designed by the Modernista architect Puig i Cadafalch, this composite Spanish village is charming and kitsch by turns, depending on your taste, and features reproductions of traditional buildings and squares from every region in Spain. The cylindrical towers at the entrance are copies from the walled city of Ávila, and lead on to a Castilian main square, a tiny whitewashed street from Arcos de la Frontera in Andalucia, the 16th-century House of Chains from Toledo, and so on. There are numerous bars and restaurants, a flamenco tablao and more than 60 shops selling Spanish crafts.

Refugi 307

C/Nou de la Rambla 169 (93 256 21 22, www.museuhistoria.bcn.cat). Metro Paral·lel. **Open** *Guided tour, by appointment only* 11am, noon, 2pm (Catalan), 1pm (Spanish) Sat, Sun. **Admission** €3. No credit cards. **Map** p107 C4 ⓮

About 1,500 Barcelona civilians were killed during the air bombings of the Civil War, a fact that the government has long silenced. As Poble Sec particularly suffered the effects of bombing, a large air-raid shelter was built partially into the mountain at the top of C/Nou de la Rambla – one of some 1,200 in the entire city. Now converted into a museum, it is worth a visit.

Telefèric de Montjuïc (cable car)

Estació Funicular, Avda Miramar (93 318 70 74, www.tmb.net). Metro Paral·lel then Funicular de Montjuïc or 50, 55 bus. **Open** *Nov-Feb* 10am-6pm daily. *Mar-May, Oct* 10am-7pm daily. *June-Sept* 10am-9pm daily. **Tickets** *one way* €6.30, €4.70 reductions; *return*

Time Out Shortlist | Barcelona **113**

€9, €6.30 reductions; free under-4s.
No credit cards. **Map** p107 B4 ⑮
The rebuilt system has eight-person
cable cars that soar from the funicular
all the way up to the castle.

Eating & drinking

Bar Seco

*Passeig Montjuïc 74 (93 329 63
74). Metro Paral·lel.* **Open** 9am-8pm
Mon-Wed; 9am-1am Thur; 10am-
1.30am Fri, Sat; 10am-midnight Sun.
Closed 2wks Aug. No credit cards.
Bar. **Map** p107 C4 ⑯
The 'Dry Bar' is, in fact, anything but,
and its ethical, friendly choices range
from local beers and organic wines to
fairtrade Brazilian cachaça. Despite a
quiet location, it has already gathered a
following for the quality of its Italian-
Spanish vegetarian dishes and tapas,
its fresh milkshakes and a heavenly
home-made chocolate and almond cake.

La Bella Napoli

*C/Margarit 12 (93 442 50 56).
Metro Paral·lel.* **Open** 1.30-4pm,
8.30pm-midnight Tue-Sun. **€€**.
Italian. **Map** p107 C3 ⑰
The welcoming Neapolitan waiters at
La Bella Napoli are happy to talk you
through the long list of antipasti and
pasta dishes, while you can't go
wrong with the crispy baked pizzas –
such as the Sofia Loren, complete with
provolone, basil, bresaola, cherry
tomatoes, rocket and parmesan. Beer
is Moretti, the wine list all-Italian; in
fact the only thing lacking authenticity is the catalogue of pre-made
ice-cream desserts, but there is own-
made tiramisu.

La Caseta del Migdia

*Mirador del Migdia, Passeig del
Migdia (mobile 617 956 572). Bus 55
or funicular, then 10min walk.* **Open**
June-Sept 8pm-1am Wed-Fri; noon-2am
Sat; noon-1am Sun. *Oct-May* noon-
sunset Sat, Sun. No credit cards.
Bar. **Map** p107 A5 ⑱

Completely alfresco, high up in a clear-
ing among the pine trees, this is a magical space, scattered with deckchairs,
hammocks and candlelit tables. DJs
spinning funk, rare groove and lounge
alternate surreally with a faltering
string quartet; food is pizza and other
munchies. To find it, cut through the
Brossa gardens from the funicular and
follow the Camí del Mar footpath south
around the castle. Be aware that it's
much cooler up here than in town.

La Font del Gat

*Passeig Santa Madrona 28 (93 289 04
04). Funicular Parc Montjuïc/bus 50,
55.* **Open** 1-4pm Tue-Sun. Closed 3wks
Aug, 2wks Christmas. **€€**. **Catalan**.
Map p107 B3 ⑲
A welcome watering hole perched high
on Montjuïc between the Miró paintings and ethnological museums. The
small, informal-looking restaurant has
a surprisingly sophisticated menu:
ravioli with truffles and wild mushrooms, for example, or foie gras with
Modena caramel. However, most come
for the set lunch: start with scrambled
egg served with Catalan sausage and
peppers or a salad, follow it with
baked cod or chicken with pine nuts
and basil, and finish with fruit or a
simple dessert. For tables outside, you
pay a surcharge.

Quimet i Quimet

*C/Poeta Cabanyes 25 (93 442 31 42).
Metro Paral·lel.* **Open** noon-4pm, 7-
10.30pm Mon-Fri; noon-4pm Sat. Closed
Aug. **€€**. **Tapas**. **Map** p107 C3 ⑳
Packed to the rafters with dusty bottles
of wine, this classic but minuscule bar
makes up for its lack of space with
great tapas. The specialities are *conser-
vas* (shellfish preserved in tins), which
aren't always to non-Spanish tastes,
but the *montaditos* (sculpted tapas
served on bread) are spectacular. Try
salmon sashimi with cream cheese,
honey and soy, or cod, passata and
black olive pâté. Get there early for any
chance of a table.

Quimet i Quimet

The Return of El Molino

Barcelona's answer to the Moulin Rouge is revived.

In its heyday, El Molino – a 110-year-old music hall fronted with a weather-beaten windmill – was one of a dozen on Paral·lel, an avenue that once boasted a backstreet Broadway appeal. In 1908 it was renamed Petit Moulin Rouge after the Parisian club, in 1929 gained its sails and in 1936 tossed the 'Petit'. El Molino once offered naughty spectacles, complete with vedettes, and attracted illustrious clientele including Italian filmmaker Federico Fellini. It managed to thwart the censorship of dictator General Franco, albeit with 'Rouge' dropped from its name as Barcelona's signs were purged of their communist associations, but it deteriorated, and closed in 1997.

Reopened in October 2010, it has retained its basic function as a musical theatre, lit up with neon and with red-rimmed sails that rotate during performances. A new silver building billows from the back; inside there is a bar with a view and space for one-off cultural events. Architects BOPBAA have maintained the original interior structure of the theatre itself, which, as if to compensate for El Molino's cream-washed façade, is redder than ever. The venue has a capacity of 250 and seats are at tables. Alcohol is served during performances, as is a set menu.

The inaugurating show, Made In Paral·lel (continuing to run in 2011), revived El Molino's cabaret past with a corsets-and-feathers extravaganza. While the owners evaluate whether cabaret can kick it like before, the programme is varied. Flamenco is set for Tuesday nights: Poco Ruido y Mucho Duende comes under the artistic direction of flamenco singer Mayte Martín and guests include acclaimed *cantaor* Enrique Morente. A burlesque festival in May and a tango festival in September also draw big names into the little windmill. On Saturday nights Los Unique Saturdays is run by veteran DJ Raúl Orellana, with select club DJs spinning from 1am to 4am. ■ C/Vila i Vilà 99 (93 205 91 11, www.elmolinobcn.com).

La Soleá

Plaça del Sortidor 14 (93 441 01 24).
Metro Poble Sec. **Open** noon-midnight
Tue-Sun. **€**. No credit cards. **Global**.
Map p107 C3 ㉑

An unassuming but jolly neighbourhood joint, with a sunny terrace on the Plaça del Sortidor. There's barely a continent that isn't represented on the menu, which holds houmous, tabouleh and goat's cheese salad plus juicy hamburgers served with roquefort or mushrooms, alongside smoky tandoori chicken, Mexican tacos, vegetable samosas and slabs of Argentine beef. Between 4pm and 8.30pm, the kitchen is officially closed, but simple platters of cold hams, cheeses and so on are served.

The Tatami Room

NEW *C/Poeta Cabanyes 22 (93 329 67 40, www.thetatamiroom.net). Metro Paral·lel.* **Open** 7pm-1am daily.
€€. **Japanese** Map p107 C3 ㉒

Opened in December 2010 by a trio of Japanophile Brits, the Tatami Room is based on the concept of *izakayas* – which very nearly equate to the local idea of tapas bars, only with more comfortable seating. Downstairs in a cosy basement-bar there are sunken tables and tatami mats to sit on (your footwear stays in a neat space underneath), at which you can chow down on shared plates of grilled yakitori brochettes, sashimi, tempura, noodle and rice dishes.

Tickets

NEW *Avda Paral·lel 164 (93 292 42 50, www.ticketsbar.es). Metro Poble Sec.* **Open** check website for details.
Map p107 C3 ㉓

Superchef Ferran Adrià's new tapas venture hadn't quite opened as this guide went to press, but is set to be the next big thing and thus worth inclusion here. A large space, it will house a dining room where avant-garde tapas will be served, and, alongside, a small bar (named 41º) for cocktails and fancy bar snacks.

Tinta Roja

C/Creu dels Molers 17 (93 443 32 43, www.tintaroja.net). Metro Poble Sec. **Open** 8.30pm-2am Thur; 8.30pm-3am Fri, Sat. Closed 2wks Aug. No credit cards. **Bar**. Map p107 C3 ㉔

This smooth, mysterious bar was once a dairy farm, but these days it's an atmospheric spot for a late-night drink. Push through the depths of the bar and you'll be transported to a Buenos Aires-style bordello/theatre/cabaret/circus with plush red velvet sofas, smoochy niches and an ancient ticket booth. Tango classes are held on Wednesday nights.

Nightlife

Barcelona Rouge

C/Poeta Cabanyes 21 (93 442 49 85). Metro Paral·lel. **Open** 7pm-2.30am Wed, Sun; 7pm-3am Thur-Sat. No credit cards. Map p107 C3 ㉕

Ah, cosy! This is a pretty little place done up with throw rugs, vintage lamps that don't do a whole lot (the lighting concept is the uncomplicated 'dark') and dusty sofas. Later in the night it gets packed with singing, decked-out thirtysomethings who don't mind getting tipsy in a place where it costs a fair bit of coin to do so. There are occasional live shows (normally Sundays).

La [2]

C/Nou de la Rambla 111-113 (93 441 40 01, www.sala-apolo.com). Metro Paral·lel. **Open** *Concerts* 8pm daily. *Club* midnight-6am Mon, Tue; 12.30-6am Wed-Sat. Map p107 C4 ㉖

La [2], downstairs from Sala Apolo, has excellent sounds, an intimate layout and the only hip flamenco night in the city (which runs on Mondays from May to September). The music is reliably good, with performances by more cultish artists than those that play next door. Punters can stay on for indie-rock club Nitsa upstairs.

BARCELONA BY AREA

Maumau

C/Fontrodona 33 (93 441 80 15, www.maumaunderground.com). Metro Paral·lel. **Open** 11pm-2.30am Thur-Sat. Closed Aug. No credit cards. **Map** p107 C4 **27**

Ring the bell by the anonymous grey door (and be warned that C/Fontrodona doglegs just when you thought the street had run out). Inside, a large warehouse space is humanised with colourful projections, Ikea-style sofas and scatter cushions, as well as a friendly, laid-back crowd. These days Maumau has taken a step upmarket and is more of a lounge bar, and its latest speciality is the G&T, with 25 different types of gin available.

Sala Apolo

C/Nou de la Rambla 113 (93 441 40 01, www.sala-apolo.com). Metro Paral·lel. **Open** *Concerts* 8.30pm daily. *Club* midnight-6am Mon-Sat. **Map** p107 C4 **28**

Sala Apolo, one of Barcelona's most popular clubs, is a 1940s dancehall, which means a great atmosphere but bad acoustics, though a new sound system has improved matters. Live acts range from Toots & the Maytals to Killing Joke, but note that buying tickets for the band doesn't provide admission to the club night: you'll need to re-enter for that, and pay an extra charge. On Wednesdays, the DJs offer African and Latin rhythms; on Thursdays, it's funk, Brazilian, hip hop and reggae; and Fridays and Saturdays are an extravaganza of bleeping electronica.

La Terrrazza

Poble Espanyol, Avda Francesc Ferrer i Guàrdia 13 (93 272 49 80, www.laterrrazza.com). Metro Espanya. **Open** May-mid Oct midnight-6am Thur-Sat. **Map** p107 A2 **29**

Gorgeous, glamorous and popular (mostly with the young, hair-gel-and-heels brigade), La Terrrazza is a nightclub that's the stuff of Hollywood dreams. Here, you can wander through the night-time silence of Poble Espanyol to the starry patio that's the dancefloor for one of the more surreal experiences you can have with a highly priced gin & tonic in your hand. Gazebos, lookouts and erotic paintings add to the magic of it all. So what if the music is mostly crowd-pleasing house tunes, with the occasional big-name DJ, but no one truly fabulous? That's not really what you came here for.

Arts & leisure

Mercat de les Flors

Plaça Margarida Xirgú, C/Lleida 59, Poble Sec (93 426 18 75, www.mercatflors.org). Metro Poble Sec. **Box office** 1hr before show. No credit cards. **Map** p107 B3 **30**

British theatre director Peter Brook is credited with transforming this former flower market into a venue for the performing arts in 1985, when he was looking for a place to stage his legendary production of the *Mahabharata*. After decades of diffuse programming, the Mercat has finally focused in on national and international contemporary dance, and offers a strong programme that experiments with unusual formats and mixes in new technologies and live music.

El Tablao de Carmen

Poble Espanyol, Avda Francesc Ferrer i Guàrdia 13 (93 325 68 95, www.tablaodecarmen.com). Metro Espanya. **Open** 8.30-11pm Tue-Sun. **Shows** 6.45pm, 10pm Tue-Sun. **Map** p107 A3 **31**

This rather sanitised version of the flamenco tablao sits in faux-Andalucian surroundings in the Poble Espanyol. You'll find both stars and new young talent, displaying the various styles of flamenco singing, dancing and music. It's advisable to book (up to a week ahead in summer). The admission charge includes entry to the Poble Espanyol after 7pm.

La Pedrera (Casa Milà) p127

Eixample

With its show-stopping Modernista architecture, elegant boutiques and cutting-edge restaurants, the Eixample forms the crucible for Barcelona's image as a city of design. Its extraordinary waffle-iron street layout was designed as an extendible matrix for future growth, gradually coming to connect Barcelona with outlying villages in Europe's first expansive work of urban planning. The period of construction coincided with Barcelona's golden age of architecture: the city's bourgeoisie employed Gaudí, Puig i Cadafalch, Domènech i Montaner and the like to build them ever more daring townhouses in an orgy of avant-garde one-upmanship.

Most of the sites of interest for visitors are within a few blocks of the grand central boulevard of Passeig de Gràcia, which ascends directly from the city's central square of Plaça Catalunya. Incorporating some of Barcelona's finest Modernista gems, it is the showpiece of the Quadrat D'Or (Golden District) – a square mile of open-air museum between C/Muntaner and C/Roger de Flor that contains 150 protected buildings.

A particularly striking Modernista masterpiece is Puig i Cadafalch's 1901 Palau Macaya at Passeig de Sant Joan 108. Other buildings of interest include the tiled Mercat de la Concepció on C/Aragó, designed by Rovira i Trias, and the turret-topped Casa de les Punxes, another by the prolific Puig i Cadafalch, which combines elements of Nordic Gothic with Spanish plateresque. Further down C/Roger de Llúria, the Casa Thomas and the Palau Montaner were both designed by Lluís Domènech i Montaner, while on C/Casp stands one of Gaudí's lesser-known works, the Casa Calvet. Look right to see the egg-topped

Plaça de Braus Monumental (C/Marina 749), but the city's last active bullring is now mainly frequented by tour buses from the Costa Brava; out of season, it hosts tatty travelling circuses.

Sights & museums

Casa Amatller

Passeig de Gràcia 41 (93 496 12 45, www.amatller.com). Metro Passeig de Gràcia. **Open** 10am-8.30pm daily. *Guided tour* noon Fri. **Admission** free; guided tour €10; free under-12s. **Map** p120 C3 ❶

Built for the chocolate baron Antoni Amatller, this playful building is one of Puig i Cadafalch's finest creations. Inspired by 17th-century Dutch townhouses, it has a distinctive stepped Flemish pediment with a ceramic façade incorporating lively sculptures by Eusebi Arnau. These include chocolatiers at work, almond trees and blossoms (after the family name) and Sant Jordi slaying the dragon.

Casa Àsia

Avda Diagonal 373 (93 238 73 37, www.casaasia.org). Metro Diagonal. **Open** 10am-8pm Tue-Sat; 10am-2pm Sun. **Admission** free. **Map** p121 D2 ❷

This cultural centre for Asia and the Asian Pacific is housed in the ornate Palau Baró de Quadras, designed by Puig i Cadafalch in 1904. If you can tear your eyes away from the building's array of lavish carvings and mosaics, there are a variety of excellent temporary exhibits covering anything from modern Chinese abstract art to Iranian graphics. The underlying function of this organisation, however, is the promotion of Asian culture in Barcelona, with language courses, international conferences and cinema seasons (often subtitled in English). It also features an excellent multimedia library on the fourth floor, which allows visitors to hire CDs, DVDs and books on presentation of a passport or ID card.

Casa Batlló

Passeig de Gràcia 43 (93 216 03 06, www.casabatllo.cat). Metro Passeig de Gràcia. **Open** 9am-8pm daily. **Admission** €17.80; €14.25 reductions; free under-11s. **Map** p120 C3 ❸

Gaudí and his long-time collaborator Josep Maria Jujol took an ordinary apartment block and remodelled it inside and out for textile tycoon Josep Batlló between 1902 and 1906. The result is one of the most impressive and admired of all Gaudí's creations, although opinions differ on what the building's remarkable façade actually represents – particularly its polychrome shimmering walls, sinister skeletal balconies and scaly humpbacked roof. Some say it's the spirit of carnival, others a Costa Brava cove. But the most popular theory takes into account Gaudí's deep patriotism, claiming that it is a representation of Sant Jordi and the dragon: the cross on top being the knight's lance, the roof the dragon's back, and the balconies below the skulls and bones of its hapless victims.

Fundació Antoni Tàpies

C/Aragó 255 (93 487 03 15, www.fundaciotapies.org). Metro Passeig de Gràcia. **Open** 10am-7pm Tue-Sun. **Admission** €7; €5.60 reductions; free under-16s. **Map** p120 C3 ❹

Antoni Tàpies exploded on to the art scene in the 1950s, when he began to incorporate wastepaper, mud and rags into his paintings, eventually moving on to whole pieces of furniture, running water and girders. As Barcelona's most celebrated living artist, his trademark abstract expressionism graces everything from wine bottle labels to theatre posters. The artist set up the Tàpies Foundation in 1984, and crowned the building with a glorious tangle of aluminium piping and ragged metal netting (*Núvol i Cadira*, or *Cloud and Chair*). The building, extensively renovated in 2010, is one of the

Sagrada Família p127

earliest examples of Modernisme to combine exposed brick and iron and is now a cultural centre and museum dedicated to the man himself.

Fundació Joan Brossa

C/Provença 318 (93 467 69 52, www.fundacio-joan-brossa.cat). Metro Diagonal or Verdaguer. **Open** 10am-2pm, 3-7pm Mon-Fri. Closed Aug. **Admission** free. **Map** p121 D3 **⑤**

Joan Brossa, polymathic artist (1919-98), left his fingerprints all over his home city, not only in physical sculptures such as the letters spelling 'Barcino' by the cathedral or the Illusory Clock outside the Teatre Poliorama on La Rambla, but also in his vast legacy of poems, theatre plays, tireless campaigning for the Catalan language and the Espai Brossa theatrical space in the Born. The foundation's permanent collection fills three white rooms with some 35 of Brossa's visual and object poems along with posters, manuscripts, books and photographs, plus screenings of some of his short films.

Fundació Suñol

Passeig de Gràcia 98 (93 496 10 32, www.fundaciosunol.org). Metro Diagonal. **Open** 4-8pm Mon-Sat. **Admission** €5; €2.50 reductions. No credit cards. **Map** p121 D2 **⑥**

The foundation's two floors house the contemporary art collection of businessman Josep Suñol. At any one time, 100 works of painting, sculpture or photography are on show, shuffled every six months from an archive of 1,200 pieces amassed over 35 years. Catalan and Spanish artists (Picasso, Miró and Pablo Gargallo) predominate, augmented by international big names like Warhol, Giacometti and Man Ray.

Fundación Alorda Derksen

C/Aragó 314 (93 272 62 50, www.fundacionad.com). Metro Girona or Passeig de Gràcia. **Open** 10am-1pm,

4-7pm Wed, Fri; 10am-2pm, 4-8pm Sat. Closed Aug. **Admission** €5; €3 reductions; free under-13s. No credit cards. **Map** p121 D3 **⑦**

Manuel Alorda and his wife Hanneke Derksen opened this impressive contemporary art gallery in 2008. Some pieces in the inaugural exhibition came from their private collection but, as a patron of Tate Modern and the MACBA, Alorda's connections have allowed him to borrow high-profile works of art that have never before been seen in Barcelona. These include works from Damien Hirst's *Butterfly* series and photorealist paintings based on the birth of Hirst's son. Catalan conceptual artist Jaume Plensa's body sculpture of metal letter 'cells' also impresses.

Fundación Francisco Godia

C/Diputació 250 (93 272 31 80, www.fundacionfgodia.org). Metro Passeig de Gràcia. **Open** 10am-8pm Mon, Wed-Sun. **Admission** €6.50; €3.25 reductions; free under-5s. **Map** p120 C4 **⑧**

Transplanted in late 2008 from a first-floor flat to this building, the Casa Garriga Nogués – a Modernista masterpiece in its own right – this vast private art collection now has enough room to breathe, with two floors of exhibition space. Godia was a Formula 1 driver for Maserati in the 1950s who funnelled his considerable fortune into an impressive array of medieval religious art, historic Spanish ceramics, sculpture and modern painting. The permanent collection largely consists of medieval sculptures and paintings, including Alejo de Vahia's *Pietà*, and a Baroque masterpiece by Luca Giordano, along with some outstanding Romanesque sculptures. The inaugural temporary exhibition on the ground floor showcases Godia's contemporary collection, with pieces by Eduardo Chillida, Picasso, Antoni Tàpies and Joan Miró.

Hospital de la Santa Creu i Sant Pau

C/Sant Antoni Maria Claret 167 (93 291 90 00, www.santpau.cat). Metro Sant Pau Dos de Maig. **Open** Call for details. **Map** p121 F2 ⑨

When part of the roof of the gynaecology department collapsed, it was clear that the restoration of Domènech i Montaner's century-old Modernista 'garden city' hospital was unavoidable. In 2009, the last of the departments were transferred to the modern building and the old complex ceased to function as a hospital, although there are tentative plans to turn part of it into a museum of Modernisme. Renovations will take another decade or so, but the complex remains open to visitors. A World Heritage Site, the hospital consists of 20 pavilions abundantly adorned with the Byzantine, Gothic and Moorish flourishes that characterise the architect's style, all set in peaceful gardens. The public enjoy free access to the grounds, and guided tours (€10; €5 reductions) in English are held daily at 10am, 11am, noon and 1pm.

Museu de Carrosses Fúnebres

C/Sancho de Avila 2 (93 484 17 10). Metro Marina. **Open** 10am-1pm, 4-6pm Mon-Fri; 10am-1pm Sat, Sun. **Admission** free. **Map** p121 F5 ⑩

This obscure and macabre museum is hard to find – ask at the reception desk of the Ajuntament's funeral service and, eventually, a security guard will take you down to a silent and shuddersome basement housing the world's largest collection of funeral carriages and hearses dating from the 18th century through to the 1950s.

Museu de la Música

L'Auditori, C/Padilla 155 (93 256 36 50, www.museumusica.bcn.cat). Metro Glòries. **Open** 10am-6pm Mon, Wed-Fri, Sat; 10am-8pm Sun. **Admission** €4; €3 reductions; free under-16s. **Map** p121 F5 ⑪

The Music Museum comprises over 1,600 instruments, presented like precious jewels on red velvet in glass cases, along with multimedia displays, interactive exhibits and musical paraphernalia. Spanning ancient civilisations to the modern day, instruments from all corners of the globe are represented; the museum's world-class collection of guitars from the 17th century is a high note.

Museu del Modernisme Català

C/Balmes 48 (93 272 28 96, www.mmcat.cat). Metro Passeig de Gràcia. **Open** 10am-8pm Mon-Sat; 10am-2pm Sun. **Admission** €10; €7-€5 reductions; free under-5s. No credit cards. **Map** p120 C4 ⑫

Inaugurated in 2010, this private collection includes work by all the heavyweights of the Modernisme movement. There is a Gaudí-designed kissing chair, some extravagant ecclesiastical pieces by Puig i Cadafalch, tiled bedheads by Gaspar Homar, marble sculptures by Josep Llimona and paintings by Santiago Rusiñol, Joaquim Mir and Ramon Casas. The furniture created by lesser-known craftsmen also includes some stunning pieces, with a collection of marquetry escritoires.

Museu del Perfum

Passeig de Gràcia 39 (93 216 01 21, www.museudelperfum.com). Metro Passeig de Gràcia. **Open** 10.30am-1.30pm; 4.30-8pm Mon-Fri; 11am-2pm Sat. **Admission** €5; €3 reductions; free under-5s. No credit cards. **Map** p120 C4 ⑬

In the back room of the Regia perfumery sits this collection of nearly 5,000 scent bottles, cosmetic flasks and related objects. You'll find all manner of unguent containers, from a pre-dynastic Egyptian tube of black eye make-up to Edwardian atomisers and a prized double-flask pouch that belonged to Marie Antoinette. Rare bottles, among them a garish Dalí creation for Schiaparelli, are displayed in the second chamber.

Museu Egipci de Barcelona

*C/València 284 (93 488 01 88,
www.museuegipci.com). Metro
Passeig de Gràcia.* **Open** 10am-8pm
Mon-Sat; 10am-2pm Sun. **Admission**
€11; €8 reductions; free under-5s.
Map p121 D3 ⑭

One of the finest collections of Ancient
Egyptian artefacts in Europe, it's owned
by prominent Egyptologist Jordi Clos
and spans 3,000 years of Nile-drenched
culture. The exhibits include religious
statuary – such as the massive baboon
heads used to decorate temples – everyday copper mirrors and alabaster head-
rests, and some really rather moving
infant sarcophagi. Outstanding pieces
include some painstakingly matched
fragments from the Sixth Dynasty
Tomb of Iny, mummified cats, baby
crocodiles and falcons, and a 5,000-
year-old bed.

Parc de l'Estació del Nord

*C/Almogàvers 27-61 (no phone).
Metro Arc de Triomf.* **Open** 10am-
sunset daily. **Admission** free.
Map p121 F5 ⑮

Otherwise known as Parc Sol i Ombra
(meaning 'Sun and Shadow'), this small
park is home to three pieces of landscape art in blue and white ceramic by
New York sculptor Beverly Pepper.
Along with a pair of incongruous white
stone entrance walls, *Espiral Arbrat*
(*Tree Spiral*) is a spiral bench set under
the cool shade of lime-flower trees,
while *Cel Caigut* (*Fallen Sky*) is a 7m-
high (23ft) ridge rising from the grass.
The colourful tile work recalls Gaudí's
trencadís smashed-tile technique.

Parc Joan Miró (Parc de l'Escorxador)

*C/Tarragona (no phone). Metro
Espanya.* **Open** 10am-sunset daily.
Map p120 A3 ⑯

Covering an area the size of four
city blocks, the old slaughterhouse
(*escorxador*), demolished in 1979, provided a much-needed park, although
there's little greenery. Palms and pines
are dwarfed by Miró's sculpture *Dona
i Ocell* (*Woman and Bird*) getting its
feet wet in a rather grim cement lake;
there's also a playground.

La Pedrera (Casa Milà)

*C/Provença 261-265 (93 484 59 00,
www.caixacatalunya.cat/obrasocial).
Metro Diagonal.* **Open** Jan-Feb, Nov-
Dec 9am-6pm daily. Mar-Oct 9am-8pm
daily. **Admission** €11; €6 reductions;
free under-13s. **Map** p121 D3 ⑰

Gaudí's Casa Milà apartment block
(known as La Pedrera, or 'the stone
quarry') has no straight lines and is a
stupendous feat of architecture, the
culmination of Gaudí's experimental
attempts to recreate natural forms
with bricks and mortar (not to mention ceramics and even smashed-up
cava bottles). Now a UNESCO World
Heritage Site, its marine feel is completed by Jujol's tangled balconies,
doors of twisted kelp ribbon, sea-
foamy ceilings and interior patios as
blue as a mermaid's cave. It is supported entirely by pillars, without a
single master wall, allowing great
swathes of natural light to come in
through the vast asymmetrical windows of the façade.

La Pedrera houses an art gallery showing international artists, while the
upstairs focuses on Gaudí the architect.
Visit a reconstructed Modernista flat on
the fourth floor, with a sumptuous bed-
room suite by Gaspar Homar, while an
exhibition offering an overview of
Gaudí's career is located in the attic,
framed by parabolic arches worthy of a
Gothic cathedral. Best of all is the roof of
the building with its trencadís-covered
ventilation shafts: their heads are shaped
like the helmets of medieval knights,
which led the poet Pere Gimferrer to dub
the spot 'the garden of warriors'.

Sagrada Família

*C/Mallorca 401 (93 207 30 31,
www.sagradafamilia.org). Metro
Sagrada Família.* **Open** Apr-Sept 9am-
8pm daily. Oct-Mar 9am-6pm daily.

Admission €12; €10 reductions; free under-11s. *Guided tour* €4. *Lift to spires* €2.50. **Map** p121 F3 ⑱

The Temple Expiatori de la Sagrada Família manages to be both Europe's most fascinating building site and Barcelona's most emblematic creation. In the 1930s, anarchists managed to destroy Gaudí's intricate plans and models for the building by setting fire to them, which means that the ongoing work is a matter of conjecture and considerable controversy; the putative completion date of 2020 is looking increasingly optimistic.

Gaudí, buried beneath the nave of the Sagrada Família, dedicated more than 40 years of his life to the project, the last 14 exclusively, and the crypt, the apse and the nativity façade, all of which were completed in his lifetime, are the most beautiful elements of the church. The latter, facing C/Marina, looks at first glance as though some careless giant has poured candlewax over a Gothic cathedral, but closer inspection reveals that every protuberance is an intricate sculpture of flora, fauna or a human figure, combining to form an astonishingly moving stone tapestry depicting scenes from Christ's life. The other completed façade, the Passion, which faces C/Sardenya, is more austere, with vast diagonal columns in the shape of bones and haunting sculptures by Josep Maria Subirachs. Japanese sculptor Etsuro Sotoo has chosen to adhere more faithfully to Gaudí's intentions, and has fashioned six more modest musicians at the rear of the temple, as well as the exuberantly coloured bowls of fruit to the left of the nativity façade.

Eating & drinking

Alkimia

C/Indústria 79 (93 207 61 15). *Metro Joanic or Sagrada Família.* **Open** 1.30-3.30pm, 8.30-11pm Mon-Fri. Closed 3wks Aug. €€€€. **Catalan**. **Map** p121 F2 ⑲

Chef Jordi Vilà is hugely respected, and turns out complex dishes that play with Spanish classics – for instance, liquid *pa amb tomàquet* with fuet sausage, or wild rice with crayfish and strips of tuna on a bed of foamed mustard. There is also an enviably stocked wine cellar. What is lacking, however, is a great deal of warmth in either the minimalist dining room or from the occasionally tight-lipped waiting staff.

Bar Mut

C/Pau Claris 192 (93 217 43 38). *Metro Diagonal.* **Open** noon-11pm Tue, Wed; noon-midnight Thur-Sat; noon-4pm Sun. €. **Tapas**. **Map** p121 D2 ⑳

Bar Mut has an ineffably Gallic feel, with its etched glass, bronze fittings, chanteuses on the sound system, and Paris prices. The tapas are undeniably superior, however: try everything from a carpaccio of scallops and sea urchin to fried eggs with foie gras. Breakfast dishes include haricot beans with *morcilla* and wild mushrooms. *Formidable*.

La Bodegueta

Rambla de Catalunya 100 (93 215 48 94). *Metro Diagonal.* **Open** 7am-1.30am Mon-Sat; 6pm-1am Sun. €€. **Tapas**. **Map** p120 C3 ㉑

This delightful old bodega, with a pretty tiled floor, is unreconstructed, dusty and welcoming, supplying students, businessmen and anyone else in between with an endless supply of reasonably priced wine, vermouth on tap and prime-quality tapas. The emphasis is on locally sourced products (try Montserrat tomatoes with tuna), and old favourites such as *patatas bravas*.

Café del Centre

C/Girona 69 (93 488 11 01). *Metro Girona.* **Open** 8am-11pm Mon-Fri; 5pm-midnight Sat. Closed 2wks Aug. **Café**. **Map** p121 D4 ㉒

Possibly the only café of its type left in the Eixample, with a delightfully dusty air, Modernista wooden banquettes, walls stained with the nicotine of ages and marble tables sitting on a chipped chequered floor that almost certainly dates back to the bar's opening in 1873. It's still in the hands of the same family, whose youngest members' attempts to instigate change haven't progressed much beyond a list of fruit teas.

Casa Calvet

C/Casp 48 (93 412 40 12). Metro Urquinaona. **Open** 1-3.30pm, 8.30-11pm Mon-Sat. Closed 2wks Aug. **€€€€**. **Catalan**. Map p121 D4 ㉓

One of Gaudí's more understated buildings from the outside, Casa Calvet has an interior full of glorious detail in the carpentry, stained glass and tiles. The food is up to par, with surprising combinations almost always hitting the mark: sole with pistachio sauce and sautéed aubergine; scallops with black olive tapenade and wild mushroom croquettes, and roast beef with apple sauce and truffled potatoes. Puddings are superb – try goat's cheese cream with pistachio and beetroot ice-cream.

Cinc Sentits

C/Aribau 58 (93 323 94 90, www. cincsentits.com). Metro Passeig de Gràcia or Universitat. **Open** 1.30-3pm, 8.30-10.30pm Tue-Sat. Closed - 2wks Aug. **€€€€**. **Catalan**. Map p120 B3 ㉔

Talented chef Jordi Artal shows respect for the classics (flat *coca* bread with foie gras and crispy leeks, duck magret with apple) while adding a personal touch to dishes such as Palamós prawn in *ajoblanco* (garlic soup) with cherries and an ice-cream made from their stones. Save room for the artisanal Catalan cheeses. After a long wait, Cinc Sentits has finally received a well-deserved Michelin star, so be prepared to book.

Dry Martini

C/Aribau 162-166 (93 217 50 72). FGC Provença. **Open** noon-12.30am Mon-Thur; 1pm-3am Fri; 6.30pm-3am Sat; 6.30pm-12.30am Sun. **Cocktails**. **Map** p120 B2 ㉕

A shrine to the eponymous cocktail, which is honoured in Martini-related artwork and served in a hundred forms. All the trappings of a trad cocktail bar are here (bow-tied staff, leather banquettes, drinking antiques and wooden cabinets displaying a century's worth of bottles) but there's a notable lack of stuffiness: the barmen welcome all comers and the music is more trip hop than rat pack.

Federal

NEW *C/Parlament 39 (93 187 36 07, www.federalcafe.es). Metro Sant Antoni.* **Open** 8am-10pm Tue-Thur; 8am-1am Fri, Sat; 9am-5.30pm Sun. **Map** p120 A5 ㉖

Australian-run Federal exudes a breezy oceanside chic not often seen in Sant Antoni – a barrio of old-timers and market-goers. Spacious, open to the street and crowned with a pretty little roof garden, it offers own-made cupcakes, excellent brunch (try the skillet of eggs, pancetta, caramelised onion and crème fraîche) and copies of the *New Yorker* to leaf through.

Fonda Gaig

C/Còrsega 200 (93 453 20 20, www.fondagaig.com). Metro Hospital-Clínic. **Open** 1.30-3.30pm, 9-11pm Tue-Sat; 1.30-3.30pm Sun. **€€€€**. **Catalan**. Map p120 B2 ㉗

It's currently all the rage for Barcelona's top chefs to set up affordable offshoots and this one is under the guiding hand of Carles Gaig. The Fonda Gaig shtick is a return to Catalan basics, and the favourite dish here is the *canelons* – hearty, steaming tubes of pasta filled with shredded beef and topped with a fragrant béchamel. The dining rooms are smart, modern and wonderfully comfortable.

BARCELONA BY AREA

Bar Mut p128

Manairó

C/Diputació 424 (93 231 00 57, www. manairo.com). Metro Monumental. **Open** 1.30-4pm, 8.30-11pm Mon-Sat. €€€€. **Catalan**. **Map** p121 F4 ㉘

If you're curious to try postmodern haute cuisine (we're talking offal rather than the latest fancies from the Blumenthal school), Manairó is the place to start. Its divine tasting menu takes in small portions of Catalan specialities such as *cap i pota* (a stew of calves' head and feet) and langoustine with *botifarra* sausage and cod tripe, rendering them so delicately that the most squeamish diner will be seduced.

Moo

C/Rosselló 265 (93 445 40 00, www. hotelomm.es). Metro Diagonal. **Open** 1.30-3.45pm, 8.30-10.45pm Mon-Sat. Closed Aug. €€€€. **Catalan**. **Map** p121 D2 ㉙

The tables at Moo are as desirable as the rooms in its parent, Hotel Omm. Inventive cooking, overseen by the celebrated Roca brothers, is designed as half portions, the better to experience the full range, from sea bass with lemongrass to suckling pig with a sharp Granny Smith purée. Particular wines (from a list of 500) are suggested to go with every course, with many dishes even built around them: finish, for example, with 'Sauternes', the wine's bouquet perfectly rendered in mango ice-cream, saffron custard and grapefruit jelly.

Noti

C/Roger de Llúria 35 (93 342 66 73, www.noti-universal.com). Metro Passeig de Gràcia or Urquinaona. **Open** 1.30-3.30pm, 8.30-11.30pm Mon-Fri; 8.30pm-midnight Sat. €€€. **Mediterranean**. **Map** p121 D4 ㉚

Housed in the former offices of *El Noticiero* newspaper, which won awards for its design, Noti pulls in a glamorous selection of the great and the good for its globetrotting range of dishes. Centrally positioned tables surrounded by reflective glass and gold

panelling make celebrity-spotting unavoidable, but other reasons for coming here include steak tartare, squid stuffed with pigs' trotters and a good selection of French cheeses.

Routa

C/Enric Granados 10 (93 451 19 97, www.restaurant-routa.com). Metro Passeig de Gràcia or Plaça Universitat. **Open** 7.30-11pm Tue-Sat. €€€€. **Scandinavian**. **Map** p120 C4 ㉛

The young, talented Finnish chefs at Barcelona's first high-level Scando restaurant employ traditional techniques of smoking, salting and pickling to create delicacies such as smoked herring ravioli with ice-cream, or sweetbreads with horseradish jelly and beetroot risotto. Everything about the decor (or lack of it) yells Scandinavia, from the whitewashed walls and floor to the curtain of cut-out snowflakes dividing the dining room from the bar. For most this will be a tasty journey through the unknown, finishing with some elaborate petits fours.

Tapaç24

C/Diputació 269 (93 488 09 77, www.carlesabellan.com). Metro Passeig de Gràcia. **Open** 9am-midnight Mon-Sat. €€. **Tapas**. **Map** p121 D4 ㉜

A venture from chef Carles Abellan of Comerç 24 fame, this is an ostensibly old-school tapas bar; but among the lentils with chorizo or ham croquettes you'll find playful snacks more familiar to his many fans. The McFoie Burger is an exercise in fast-food heaven, as is the Bikini – a small version of his signature take on the ham and cheese toasty, this one with truffle.

La Taverna del Clínic

C/Rosselló 155 (93 410 42 21, http://latavernadelclinic.com). Metro Hospital Clínic or Diagonal. **Open** 7.30am-1.30am Mon-Sat; 1-11.30pm Sat. €. **Spanish**. **Map** p120 B2 ㉝

La Taverna del Clínic sums up much that is good about the Spanish sense of priorities. The lighting is hideous, the decor is cheap and crappy, the TV is permanently on, the walls and floor are tiled in the ugliest terrazzo imaginable, and yet the care that goes into the food is the match of many a luxury dining room. The menu concept is somewhere between tapas and restaurant, so you'll probably order a stack of dishes to share. Try the creamy morels with foie; a sticky oxtail stew made with Priorat wine; or a tiny skillet of chips, fried egg and crispy *jamón*. The octopus 'igloo' is also superb.

Tintoreria Dontell

NEW *C/Aribau 55, Eixample (93 452 07 20, www.tintoreriadontell. com). Metro Universitat.* **Open** 1-4pm, 8.30pm-2am daily. €€€. **Mediterranean. Map** p120 B3 ③④
See box right.

Tragaluz

Ptge de la Concepció 5 (93 487 01 96, www.grupotragaluz.com). Metro Diagonal. **Open** *Sept-July* 1.30-4pm, 8.30pm-midnight daily. *Aug* 1.30-4pm, 8.30pm-midnight Mon-Fri; 8.30pm-midnight Sat. €€€. **Mediterranean. Map** p120 C3 ③⑤
The stylish flagship for this extraordinarily successful restaurant group has weathered the city's culinary revolution well and is still covering new ground in Mediterranean creativity. It doesn't come cheap – the wine mark-up is particularly hard to swallow – but there's no faulting the likes of monkfish tail in a sweet tomato *sofrito* with black olive oil or cherry *consommé* for dessert.

Ty-Bihan

Ptge Lluís Pellicer 13 (93 410 90 02, www.tybihan.com). Metro Hospital Clínic. **Open** 1.30-3.30pm Mon; 1.30-3.30pm, 8.30-11.30pm Tue-Fri; 8.30-11.30pm Sat. Closed 3 wks Aug. €€. **Crêperie. Map** p120 B2 ③⑥
A small restaurant and centre for all things Breton, with live music on Wednesday nights. There's a blend of specialities of the region with Spanish produce in starters such as *andouille* sausage and *membrillo* (quince jelly), but from there on in it's French all the way. Try *galettes*, or scrumptious little blinis (with jam and cream). The Petite menu will take care of *les enfants*, while the Breton cider is a hit with the grown-ups.

Windsor

C/Còrsega 286 (93 415 84 83, www.restaurantwindsor.com). Metro Diagonal. **Open** 1.30-4pm, 8.30pm-midnight Mon-Fri; 8.30pm-midnight Sat. Closed Aug. €€€€. **Catalan. Map** p120 C2 ③⑦
Despite a smart but drab dining room, which attracts a preponderance of business-trippers, Windsor nevertheless serves some of the most creative and uplifting food around. Most dishes are based on Catalan cuisine – pigs' trotters stuffed with *cap i pota*, squab risotto – while others have a lighter, Mediterranean feel.

Xix Bar

C/Rocafort 19 (93 423 43 14, www. xixbar.com). Metro Poble Sec. **Open** 5pm-2.30am Mon-Thur; 5pm-3am Fri- 5pm-3am Sat. **Cocktails. Map** p120 A5 ③⑧
Xix (pronounced 'chicks', and a play on the street number, among other things) is an unconventional cocktail bar in the candlelit surroundings of a prettily tiled former *granja* (milk bar). It's dead cosy and just a little bit scruffy, which makes the list of 20 brands of gin all the more unexpected.

Shopping

Altaïr

Gran Via de les Corts Catalanes 616 (93 342 71 71, www.altair.es). Metro Universitat. **Open** 10am-8.30pm Mon-Sat. **Map** p120 C4 ③⑨
This is the largest travel bookshop in Europe; expect everything from guides

Kitchen confidential

Dining on the QT.

Tintoreria Dontell

Anyone who's ever been to Cuba, for example, knows that in some places the best dining experiences happen behind closed doors. The vogueish breed of restaurants that seems to be having a fashion moment in Barcelona right now doesn't always see a door as good enough cover, however, and you might find one behind a shop, a bar or even, say, a drycleaner's.

This last is the case of **Tintoreria Dontell** (geddit?, see left), a startlingly glitzy eaterie entered by keying in a code to open a door behind racks of freshly laundered dresses and jackets. From here a long corridor lined with white leather sofas and adorned with chandeliers leads to an unexpectedly cavernous and dimly lit dining room with an open kitchen down one side.

It drips with sugar-daddy glamour and therefore the quality of the food, quite honestly, comes as something of a surprise. Original and creative combinations, such as monkfish and courgette ravioli, or lamb sweetbreads with langoustines, come in half or full portions, beautifully presented and cooked with aplomb. Including a bottle from a very decently priced wine list, the bill comes to around €40 to €50 per head.

Other clandestine dining rooms around town currently include **Speakeasy**, which is entered through the kitchen at cocktail bar Dry Martini (see p129), and works hard to replicate the elegant jazz vibe of the era of Prohibition, and the recently opened **Mutis**. This last sits above Bar Mut (see p128), and provides live music and cabaret to complement some creative cooking.

After some success in London and New York, the concept of the 'pop-up restaurant', whereby flats, artists' studios and any space that looks cool enough becomes an ad hoc restaurant for the night, is also hitting Barcelona. These don't generally advertise, so you'll need to be fairly dogged in your pursuit, pestering any foodies you might meet for the latest intel.

to free eating in Barcelona and academic tomes on geolinguistics, to handbooks on successful outdoor sex and CDs of tribal music. It also stocks the usual hiking maps, travel guidebooks, multilingual dictionaries, travel diaries and equipment such as mosquito nets.

Camper

C/Pelai 13-37 (93 302 41 24, www.camper.com). Metro Catalunya. **Open** 10am-10pm Mon-Sat. **Map** p120 C5 ⓴
Mallorca-based Camper has sexed up its ladies' lines in recent years with high heels (albeit rubbery ones) and girly straps. Of course, it still has its round-toed and clod-heeled classics, and the guys still have their iconic bowling shoes.

Casa del Llibre

C/Passeig de Gràcia 62 (93 272 34 80, www.casadellibro.com). Metro Passeig de Gràcia. **Open** 9.30am-9.30pm Mon-Sat. **Map** p121 D3 ⓵
Part of a well-established Spanish chain, this bookstore offers a diverse assortment of titles that includes some English-language fiction. Glossy, Barcelona-themed coffee-table tomes with good gift potential sit by the front right-hand entrance.

Colmado Quilez

Rambla Catalunya 63 (93 215 23 56). Metro Passeig de Gràcia. **Open** *Jan-mid Oct* 9am-2pm, 4.30-8.30pm Mon-Fri; 9am-2pm Sat. *Mid Oct-Dec* 9am-2pm, 4.30-8.30pm Mon-Sat. **Map** p120 C3 ⓶
Colmados – old-school grocery stores – are relics of the time before the invasion of the supermarkets. This is one of the few surviving examples in the Modernista Eixample, with floor-to-ceiling shelves stacked full of gourmet treats: local preserved *funghi* in cute mushroom-shaped bottles (Delicias del Bosque), along with the store's own-label caviar, cava, saffron and anchovies.

El Corte Inglés

Plaça Catalunya 14 (93 306 38 00, www.elcorteingles.es). Metro Catalunya. **Open** 10am-10pm Mon-Sat. **Map** p121 D5 ⓸
The mothership of Spanish retail. This department store is the place for toiletries and cosmetics, fashion and homewares. It also houses a supermarket and a gourmet food hall in the basement, plus services from key cutting to currency exchange; on the top floor, there's a restaurant with great views (but service station-style food). The Portal de l'Àngel branch stocks CDs, DVDs, books, electronic equipment, stationery and sports gear.

Du Pareil au Même

Rambla Catalunya 95 (93 487 14 49, www.dpam.com). Metro Diagonal/FGC Provença. **Open** 10am-8.30pm Mon-Sat. **Map** p120 C3 ⓺
This French chain stocks everything a pint-sized fashionista might need, though the girls do a bit better than the boys. Newborns to 14-year-olds are served with a covetable range of funky and well-designed clothes at great prices.

Els Encants

C/Dos de Maig 177-187, Plaça de les Glòries (93 246 30 30, www.encants bcn.com). Metro Glòries. **Open** 9am-6pm Mon, Wed, Fri, Sat. *Auctions* 7-9am Mon, Wed, Fri. No credit cards. **Map** p121 F4 ⓹
The new location of this open-air flea market has been up in the air for years, but the Ajuntament has finally decided on the central plaza of the remodelled Sant Antoni market. It should open in 2012; until then, the market remains a crazy and chaotic antidote to the Glòries shopping mall next door, with teetering piles of everything from old horseshoes and Barça memorabilia to electrical gadgets, religious relics and ancient schoolbooks.

For furniture at a decent price, join the commercial buyers at the auctions from 7am, or arrive at noon, when unsold stuff drops in price. Don't forget to check out the vast warehouses on the market's outskirts, where you may find a bargain among the junk. Avoid Saturdays, when the crowds and the prices increase, and watch out for pickpockets.

Escribà

Gran Via de les Corts Catalanes 546 (93 454 75 35, www.escriba.es). Metro Urgell. **Open** 8am-3pm, 5-9pm Mon-Fri; 8am-9pm Sat, Sun. **Map** p120 B4 ④

Antoni Escribà, the 'Mozart of Chocolate', died back in 2004, but his legacy lives on. His team produces jaw-dropping creations for Easter, from a chocolate Grand Canyon to a life-size model of Michelangelo's *David*. Smaller miracles include cherry liqueur encased in red chocolate lips. The Rambla branch (La Rambla 83, 93 301 60 27) is situated in a pretty Modernista building.

FNAC

El Triangle, Plaça Catalunya 4 (93 344 18 00, www.fnac.es). Metro Catalunya. **Open** 10am-10pm Mon-Sat. **Map** p120 C5 ④

This French multimedia superstore supplies info and entertainment in all possible formats. The ground floor stocks magazines, along with a small café, ticket desk and a travel agent. Above are two floors of CDs, DVDs, computers, stereos, cameras and books in various languages.

Imaginarium

Passeig de Gràcia 103 (93 272 57 10, www.imaginarium.es). Metro Diagonal. **Open** 10am-8pm Mon-Thur; 10am-9pm Fri, Sat. **Map** p120 D2 ④

As well as the racks of excellent toys that made Imaginarium famous, the three-floor flagship of Spain's biggest toy chain has a hairdresser's, shoe department, computer zone, a multilingual book department, a play area

and reading corner. Expect craft activities, balloon-bending and puppet shows, while the top floor Saborea restaurant has organic food.

Josep Font

C/Provença 304 (93 487 21 10, www.josepfont.com). Metro Diagonal. **Open** *Sept-July* 3.30-8.30pm Mon; 10am-8.30pm Tue-Sat. Closed Aug. **Map** p121 D3 ④

Font's romantic and feminine designs are dripping with ribbons and ruffles yet somehow never stray into Barbara Cartland territory. Look for cute 1950s-inspired shorts suits, floral maxi dresses and sumptuous materials, from shimmery silks to mille-feuille chiffon.

Mango

Passeig de Gràcia 65 (93 215 75 30, www.mango.es). Metro Passeig de Gràcia. **Open** 10am-9pm Mon-Sat. **Map** p120 C3 ⑤

A small step up from Zara in quality and price, Mango's womenswear includes tailored trouser suits and skirts, knitwear and stretchy tops. Unsold items end up at the Mango Outlet (C/Girona 37, 93 412 29 35). **Other locations** Passeig de Gràcia 8-10 (93 412 15 99).

Muxart

Rambla de Catalunya 47, Eixample (93 467 74 23, www.muxart.com). Metro Passeig de Gràcia. **Open** 10am-8.30pm Mon-Sat. **Map** p120 C4 ⑤

Muxart sells shoes around which to build an outfit. The materials are refined, and the styles are sharp, avant-garde and blatantly designed to be seen – and heard. Lines for men and women are complemented by equally creative bags and accessories.

Santa Eulalia

Passeig de Gràcia 93 (93 215 06 74, www.santaeulalia.com). Metro Diagonal. **Open** 10am-8.30pm Mon-Sat. **Map** p120 C3 ⑤

Discount your blessings

Frugality is back in fashion.

Etxart & Panno

Bargain-hunters will find rich pickings along C/Girona, home to some of the city's best discount outlets: top addresses include the Mango outlet at no.37 (93 412 29 35, www.mangooutlet.es); gorgeous eveningwear and accessories from **Etxart & Panno** at No.40 (93 232 80 45, www.etxartpanno.com); and slinky designs from Catalan label **Javier Samorra** at No.38 (93 231 49 21, www.javiersamorra.com). Just off C/Girona, the **Desigual Outlet** (C/Diputació 323, 93 2720 66, www.desigual.com) offers the signature bright prints at bargain prices. A few blocks west are colourful, funky fashion and accessories from **Skunkfunk** (Ronda Sant Pere 31, 93 412 02 23, www.skunkfunk.com).

For pile-it-high, sell-it-cheap fashion, make for **Lefties** (Plaça Universitat 11, 93 317 50 70, www.lefties.com), the Zara outlet store, which stocks slightly faulty or end-of-line clothes and accessories for men, women and children (new stock arrives on Mondays and Thursdays). There's another branch in the **Maremagnum** shopping mall (93 225 81 00, www.mare magnum.com), which, as every barcelonin shopaholic knows, is open every day of the year.

Committed fashionistas should check out the 3-day biannual sales (usually held in August and November, check websites for details) organised by some stores. **Santa Eulalia** (see p135), has Balenciaga, Lanvin and all the top couture labels for less than half price. The original but wearable footwear designed by **Vialis** (C/Botànica 131, L'Hospitalet, 93 264 00 58, www.vialis.es) attracts lengthy queues of discerning women looking for discounts of up to 70 per cent on their colourful shoes, sandals and boots.

The **Heron City** mall (Passeig Andreu Nin 31, Nou Barris, 902 401 144, www.heroncity barcelona.com) has outlets from high-street fashion labels like Desigual, Mango and Lefties, as well as kids' shoes from Querolet.

Barcelona's oldest design house and a pioneer in the local catwalk scene, Santa Eulalia was founded in 1843 and remains a seriously upmarket proposition. The prêt-à-porter collection carries labels such as Balenciaga, Jimmy Choo and Stella McCartney. Services include bespoke tailoring and wedding wear for grooms. The C/Pau Casals branch is for men only.

Sephora

El Triangle, C/Pelai 13-37 (93 306 39 00, www.sephora.es). Metro Catalunya. **Open** 10am-10pm Mon-Sat. **Map** p120 C5 ❸
Sephora is your best bet for unfettered playing around with scents and make-up. Cosmetics and toiletries range from basic to high-end brands; there are also handy beauty tools, such as eyebrow tweezers and pencil sharpeners.

Vinçon

Passeig de Gràcia 96 (93 215 60 50, www.vincon.com). Metro Diagonal. **Open** 10am-8.30pm Mon-Sat. **Map** p121 D2 ❺
Keeping Barcelona's reputation as a city of cutting-edge design alive, the Vinçon building itself is a monument to the history of local design: the upstairs furniture showroom is surrounded by Modernista glory (you get a peek at Gaudí's La Pedrera); downstairs in the kitchen, bathroom, garden and other departments, everything is black, minimalist and hip. Although its not cheap, almost everything you buy here is, or will be, a design classic, be it a Bonet armchair or a Perfect Corkscrew.

Nightlife

Arena

Classic & Madre *C/Diputació 233* **VIP & Dandy** *Gran Via de les Corts Catalanes 593 (93 487 83 42, www.arenadisco.com). Metro Universitat.* **Open** *Winter* 12.30am-6am Fri, Sat. *Summer* 12.30am-6am Mon-Sat; 7.30pm-5am Sun. No credit cards. **Map** p120 C4 ❺

The four Arena clubs are still packing them in every week with a huge variety of gay punters. The USP is that you pay once, get your hand stamped and can then switch between all four clubs. Madre is the biggest and most full-on; VIP doesn't take itself too seriously and is popular with just about everyone; Classic is similarly mixed, if even cheesier; and, finally, Dandy bangs away with vintage chart hits.

Astoria

C/París 193-197 (93 414 63 62, www.opiumcinema.com). Metro Diagonal. **Open** 11.30pm-2.30am Tue-Thur, Sun; 11.30pm-3.30am Fri, Sat. Closed Aug. **Map** p120 C2 ❺
Astoria offers a break from the norm. For a start, the club is housed in a converted 1950s cinema, so the projections are actually watchable. There are three bars, plenty of comfortable seating and a small dancefloor; the very special get to sit on a heart-shaped cushion in the tiny VIP area. Somewhat inevitably, Astoria has become the domain of Barcelona's monied classes.

City Hall

Rambla Catalunya 2-4 (93 317 21 77, www.grupo-ottozutz.com). Metro Catalunya. **Open** 10.30pm-6am daily. **Map** p120 C4 ❺
City Hall ain't big, but it is popular. The music is mixed, from deep house to electro rock, and there's an older post-(pre-?) work crowd joining the young, tanned and skinny to show the dancefloors some love. Outside, the terrace is a melting pot of tourists and locals, who rub shoulders under the watchful (and anti-pot-smoking) eye of the bouncer.

D-Boy

Ronda Sant Pere 19-21 (93 318 06 86, www.matineegroup.com). Metro Urquinaona. **Open** midnight-6am Fri-Sat; 11.30pm-5.30am Sun. No credit cards. **Map** p121 D5 ❺

The much-loved Salvation recently reopened, after a €2m makeover and much fanfare, as D-Boy. With two spaces, one for house and another for deep house, and a huge darkroom, it's kept its megatron and go-gos, although its attitude and pricing policy could be said to exceed its actual charms.

Arts & leisure

L'Auditori

C/Lepant 150 (93 247 93 00, www. auditori.cat). Metro Marina. **Open** *Information* 8am-10pm daily. *Box office* 3-9pm Mon-Sat; 1hr before performance Sun. Closed Aug. **Map** p121 F5 ⑤⑨
Designed by Rafael Moneo and directed by Joan Oller, L'Auditori offers something for everyone. The 2,400-seat Pau Casals hall, dedicated to the Catalan cellist, provides a stable home for city orchestra OBC, now under the baton of conductor Eiji Oue. Look out for the revered Jordi Savall in a superb series of early music concerts called El So Original, running from October to April. An intimate 600-seat chamber space incorporates contemporary and world music, while experimental and children's work is staged in a 400-seat space named after jazz pianist Tete Montoliu.

Casablanca-Kaplan

Passeig de Gràcia 115 (93 218 43 45). Metro Diagonal. **Tickets** *Mon* €5. *Tue-Sun* €6.80. No credit cards. **Map** p121 D2 ⑥⓪
This comfortable four-screen cinema has recently made the move from dubbed films and now shows crowd-pleasers in their original languages.

Cinemes Méliès

C/Villarroel 102 (93 451 00 51, www.cinesmelies.net). Metro Urgell. **Tickets** *Mon* €4. *Tue-Sun* €6. No credit cards. **Map** p120 B4 ⑥①
The small, two-screen Cinemes Méliès is the closest that Barcelona comes to an arthouse theatre; idiosyncratic classics nestle alongside more recent films that aren't quite commercial enough for general release.

La Filmoteca de la Generalitat

Avda Sarrià 31-33 (93 410 75 90, http://cultura.gencat.net/filmo). Metro Hospital Clínic. **Tickets** €2.70; €2 reductions; €18 for 10 films. **Map** p120 A2 ⑥②
Funded by the Catalan government, the Filmoteca's programming can be a little dry, offering seasons of cinema's more recondite auteurs, alongside better-known classics. Books of 10 tickets bring down the price per film to a negligible amount. The 'Filmo' also runs an excellent library of film-related books, DVDs and magazines at Portal Santa Madrona 6-8 (93 316 27 80), just off La Rambla. Note that the Filmo is due to move to new premises in the Raval in late 2011.

Renoir-Floridablanca

C/Floridablanca 135 (93 228 93 93, www.cinesrenoir.com). Metro Sant Antoni. **Tickets** *Mon* €5.70. *Tue-Fri* €7. *Sat, Sun* €7.50. **Map** p120 B5 ⑥③
This, the more central of the Renoir cinemas, screens up to eight independent, offbeat American, British and Spanish films per day, though programming tends towards the worthy.
Other locations Renoir-Les Corts, C/Eugeni d'Ors 12, Les Corts (93 490 43 05).

Teatre Nacional de Catalunya (TNC)

Plaça de les Arts 1 (93 306 57 00, www.tnc.cat). Metro Glòries. Closed Aug. **Map** p121 F4 ⑥④
The Generalitat-funded theatre designed by Ricardo Bofill boasts three performance spaces. Director Sergi Belbel has opted for a good mix of contemporary and classical pieces and incorporated a fine dance programme. Works by new writers are normally performed in the more experimental Sala Tallers.

Park Güell p142

Gràcia

Dissent has been a recurring feature in Gràcia's history: streets boast names such as Llibertat, Revolució and Fraternitat; and for the 64 years preceding the Civil War, there was a satirical political magazine called *La Campana de Gràcia*, named after the famous bell in Plaça Vila de Gràcia. However, few vestiges of radicalism remain. Sure, the *okupa* squatter movement inhabits a relatively high number of buildings in the area, but the middle-class population has been waging an increasingly successful campaign to dislodge them.

Gràcia is both alternative and upmarket, and anything bigger than a shoebox costs a fortune to rent or buy, but for many, it's the only place to be in Barcelona. As a consequence, it radiates a sort of global chic of sleek bars, yoga centres, shiatsu, acupuncture and every form of holistic medicine, as well as piercing and tattoo parlours, dotted among the antique shops and *jamonerías*. It has more street life than other districts, but really comes into its own for a few days in mid August, when its *festa major* grips the entire city.

The district's Modernista gem is one of Gaudi's earliest and most fascinating works, the Casa Vicens, hidden away in C/Carolines. The building is a private residence and not open to visitors, but the castellated red brickwork and colourful tiled exterior with Indian and Mudéjar influences should not be missed; notice too the spiky wrought-iron leaves on the gates.

Sights & museums

Fundació Foto Colectània
C/Julián Romea 6, D2 (93 217 16 26, www.colectania.es). FGC Gràcia.
Open 11am-2pm, 5-8.30pm Mon-Sat.
Admission €3; €2 reductions. Free to all 1st Sat of mth. **Map** p140 B4 **❶**

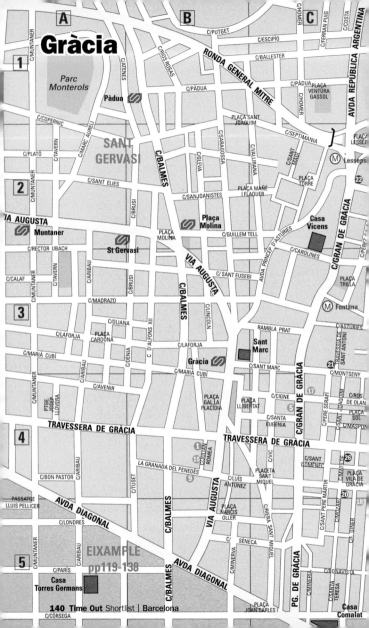

Gràcia

A **B** **C**

1

Parc Monterols

Pàdua

C/MUNTANER
C/ATENES
C/ROS ROSAS
C/PUTGET
C/PADUA
RONDA GENERAL MITRE
C/ESCIPIO
C/BALLESTER
C/FERRAN PUIG
C/COSTA
AVDA REPÚBLICA ARGENTINA
CHOMER
C/PÀDUA PLAÇA VENTURA GASSOL
CHOMER
C/SEPTIMANIA
PLAÇA LESSEPS

SANT GERVASI

C/COPERNIC
C/MARC AURELI
C/PLATÓ
C/TAVERN
C/SANT ELIES
C/BALMES
C/GLEVA
C/SARAGOSSA
C/VALLIRANA
C/SANT MARTI
PLAÇA SANT JOAQUIM

2

C/MUNTANER
C/BRUSI
C/SANJOANISTES
PLAÇA MARÈ I FLAQUER
PLAÇA TORRE
M Lesseps
22

VIA AUGUSTA
Muntaner

St Gervasi

Plaça Molina

Casa Vicens

C/RECTOR UBACH
C/TAVERN
C/ARIBAU
C/BRUSI
PLAÇA MOLINA
VIA AUGUSTA
C/GUILLEM TELL
C/CAROLINES
C/GRAN DE GRACIA
PLAÇA TRILLA

C/CALAF
C/MUNTANER
C/TAVERN
C/MADRAZO
VIA AUGUSTA
C/BALMES
C/SANT EUSEBI
AVDA PRINCEP D'ASTURIES

M Fontana

3

C/OLIANA
C/ALFONS XII
C/LINCOLN
RAMBLA PRAT
C/ASTURIES
TRAVESSIA DE SANT ANTONI

C/LAFORJA
PLAÇA CARDONA
C/DENIA
C/LAFORJA
Sant Marc
21
C/MONTSENY

C/MARIÀ CUBÍ
C/ARIBAU
Gràcia
C/MARIA CUBÍ
C/SANT MARC
C/GRAN DE GRACIA

C/AVENIR
PLAÇA GALLA PLACÍDIA
PLAÇA LLIBERTAT
C/CIGNE
17
C/PERE SERAFI
C/ROS D'OLAN
PLAÇA SOL
C/MASPON

C/MUNTANER
C/SANTA EUGENIA
C/SANTA

4

TRAVESSERA DE GRÀCIA

PTGE JOSEP LLOVERA
C/ARIBAU
TRAVESSERA DE GRÀCIA
CIVIC
PLAÇETA SANT MIQUEL
C/SANT DOMÈNEC
PLAÇA VILA DE GRACIA
26

C/BON PASTOR
1 C/LLUIS ROMEA
LA GRANADA DEL PENEDÉS
15
C/LLUIS ANTÚNEZ
20
18

9

PASSATGE LLUIS PELLICER
AVDA DIAGONAL
C/TUSET
C/BALMES
VIA AUGUSTA
PLAÇA NARCIS OLLER
C/RIERA SANT MIQUEL
C/SANT PERE MARTIR
C/MOZART
C/GINER

5

C/LONDRES
C/MUNTANER
C/CARIBAU
EIXAMPLE pp119-138
C/PARÍS
AVDA DIAGONAL
C/BALMES
C/SENECA
C/MINERVA
PG. DE GRÀCIA
C/BONAVISTA
C/SANTA TERESA

Casa Torres Germans

PLAÇA JOAN CARLES
Casa Comalat

C/CÓRSEGA

D

C/VERDI
BAIXADA
GLORIA
C/SOSTRES

E

C/OLOT Casa
Museu Gaudí

**Park
Güell** ❷

F

LTRA CARMEL
C/RAMIRO DE MAEZTU

AVDA HOSPITAL
MILITAR
CAMARE DE
C/DIEU DEL COLL
C/ALBIGESOS
AVDA COLL DEL PORTELL
C/MERCEDES
C/MARIANAO

1

C/VALLDOREIX
C/SANT
CUGAT
RAMBLA MERCEDES
C/LARRARD
C/ANTE QUERA

C/MAIGNON
AVDA SANT JOSEP DE LA MUNTANYA
Hospital
C/MOLIST
RAMBLA CAN TODA
RAMBLA PONPEU FABRIA

C/VERDI
C/MARE DE DÉU DE LA SALUT

C/SANTA
PERPETUA
TRAVESSERA DE DALT
RONDA DE GUINARDO

2

C/TORRENT DE L'OLLA
C/LA GRANJA
C/CARDENER
C/CAMELIES
C/ESCORIAL
CALEGRE DE DALT
C/CAMELIES

C/VERDI
C/SANT SALVADOR
TORRENT DE LES FLORS
C/BALCELLS

C/MARTI
PASSEIG AMUNT
C/SECRETARI COLOMA

PLAÇA
NORD
C/MARTI

C/TORRENT DE L'OLLA
⑭
GRÀCIA
C/PROVIDÈNCIA
PLAÇA ROVIRA
I TRIAS ④
❷⑤ C/PROVIDÈNCIA

3

PLAÇA
DIAMANT
⑫ ❸
PLAÇA
VIRREINA
⑯ C/LEGALITAT
C/REIG I BONET
CALEGRE DE DALT

C/L'OR
C/VERDI ㉗
⑥
C/L'ENCARNACIÓ
C/ESCORIAL
C/L'ENCARNACIÓ

C/QUEVILLERIES
C/PERLA ⑦
C/TORRENT D'EN VIDALET
MONTMANY
C/SANT LLUIS
C/SANT LLUIS
C/TAXDIRT

C/TORRENT DE L'OLLA
PLAÇA
REVOLUCIÓ
SETEMBRE
1868 ⑲ ⑩
C/TEROL
C/TORRIJOS
C/BRUNIQUER
TORRENT DE LES FLORS
PLAÇA
JOANIC
C/P/ I MARGALL
C/ROMANS

⑬
C/RAMON Y CAJAL ㉔
㉓
Ⓜ Joanic
C/SECRETARI COLOMA
C/P. LÀINEZ

TRAVESSERA DE GRÀCIA

4

C/PUIGMARTI
PLAÇA
JOHN
LENNON

C/SIRACUSA
⑪
PLAÇA
RASPALL
C/TORDERA
PASSEIG SANT JOAN
EIXAMPLE
pp119-138

C/TORRES
C/BANYOLES
C/BAILÉN
C/ROGER DE FLOR

C/FRATERNITAT
C/MILA I FONTANALS
C/MONISTROL
C/LLIBERTAT
C/SANTA
EULALIA
C/PERILL
C/CAMPRODON

❶ Sights & museums
❶ Eating & drinking
❶ Shopping
❶ Nightlife
❶ Arts & leisure

5

C/CÒRSEGA
C/CÒRSEGA

0 _____ 200 m
0 _____ 200 yds
© Copyright Time Out Group 2011

This private foundation is dedicated to the promotion of the work of major Spanish and Portuguese photographers from the 1950s to the present day. It also has an extensive library of Spanish and Portuguese photography books and monographs.

Park Güell

C/Olot (Casa-Museu Gaudí 93 219 38 11). Metro Lesseps or Vallcarca (for top entrance)/bus 24, 92. **Open** *Park* 10am-sunset daily. *Museum* Apr-Sept 10am-7.45pm daily. Oct-Mar 10am-5.45pm daily. **Admission** *Park* free. *Museum* €5.50; €4.50 reductions; free under-11s. **Map** p141 F1 ❷

Gaudí's brief for this spectacular project was to emulate the English garden cities so admired by his patron Eusebi Güell (hence the unusual spelling of 'park'): to lay out a self-contained suburb for the wealthy, but also to design the public areas. The idea never took off and the Güell family donated the park to the city in 1922.

It is a real fairy-tale place; the fantastical exuberance of Gaudí's imagination is breathtaking. The visitor was previously welcomed by two life-sized mechanical gazelles, although these were destroyed in the Civil War. The two gatehouses that do still remain were based on designs the architect made earlier for the opera *Hansel and Gretel*, one of them featuring a red and white mushroom for a roof. From here, walk up a splendid staircase flanked by multicoloured battlements, past the iconic mosaic lizard sculpture, to what would have been the main marketplace. Here, 100 palm-shaped pillars hold up a roof, reminiscent of the hypostyle hall at Luxor. On top of this structure you'll find the esplanade, a circular concourse surrounded by undulating benches in the form of a sea-serpent decorated with shattered tiles – a technique known as trencadís, which was actually perfected by Gaudí's overshadowed but talented assistant Josep Maria Jujol.

The park itself, now a UNESCO World Heritage Site, is magical, with twisted stone columns supporting curving colonnades or merging with the natural structure of the hillside. The park's peak is marked by a large cross and offers an amazing panorama of Barcelona and the sea beyond. Gaudí lived for a time in one of the two houses built on the site. It has since become the Casa-Museu Gaudí; guided tours, some of which are in English, are available. The best way to get to the park is on the 24 bus; if you go via Lesseps metro, be prepared for a steep uphill walk.

Eating & drinking

A Casa Portuguesa

C/Verdi 58 (93 368 35 28). Metro Fontana. **Open** 5pm-midnight Tue-Fri; 11am-3pm, 5pm-midnight Sat, Sun. €. **Café**. **Map** p141 D3 ❸

Fado provides the soundtrack at this mellow, tile-floored café-cum-deli, which is dedicated to all things nice from Portugal. Sit down with a coffee and a freshly made pastéis de Belém (little custard tarts with a dusting of cinnamon), or linger over a glass of wine and some nibbles. In the deli section, you can choose from a great selection of wines, preserves, pâtés, jams and cheeses.

Bodega Manolo

C/Torrent de les Flors 101 (93 284 43 77). Metro Joanic. **Open** 10am-5pm Tue, Wed; 10am-5pm, 9-midnight Thur, Fri; 12.30-5.30pm, 9-11pm Sat; noon-3pm Sun. Closed Aug. €. No credit cards. **Tapas**. **Map** p141 E3 ❹

A smoky but likeable old family *bodega* with a faded, peeling charm, barrels on the wall and rows of dusty bottles. Bodega Manolo specialises not only in reasonably priced wine, but in classy food: try the foie gras with port and apple, or a fresh anchovy salad with Greek yoghurt and tomato confit. Push through the bar to the dining room at the back.

Botafumeiro

*C/Gran de Gràcia 81 (93 218 42 30,
www.botafumeiro.es). Metro Fontana.*
Open 1pm-1am daily. €€€. **Seafood**.
Map p140 C4 ⑤
The speciality at this vast Galician
restaurant is seafood in every shape and
form, served with military precision by
a fleet of nautically clad waiters. The
sole cooked in cava with prawns is
superb, as are more humble dishes such
as a cabbage and pork broth typical of
the region. The platter of seafood (for
two) is an excellent introduction to the
various molluscs of the Spanish coast-
line. It can be hard to get a table at peak
times, but the kitchen is open all day.

Cantina Machito

*C/Torrijos 47 (93 217 34 14). Metro
Joanic.* **Open** 1-4pm, 7pm-1.30am daily.
€€. **Mexican**. **Map** p141 D3 ⑥
Every day is Day of the Dead in this
cheerily decked out little Mexican joint,
with its tissue paper bunting and
chaotic hubbub. The minuscule writing
on the menu and low lighting make for
some guesswork when placing your
order, but the choices are standard
enough – quesadillas, tacos, ceviche and
enchiladas – with a couple of surprises,
such as the tasting platter of insects.
Service can be slow and the kitchen a
little heavy-handed with the sauces, but
portions are huge and prices reasonable.

Châtelet

*C/Torrijos 54 (93 284 95 90). Metro
Fontana.* **Open** 6pm-2.30am Mon-Thur,
Sun, 6pm-3am Fri, Sat. **Bar**. No credit
cards. **Map** p141 D4 ⑦
Crammed with funkily mismatched flea
market finds, old movie posters, and
chandeliers, the Châtelet is part of a
small *gracienc* chain of bars with a
Parisian flavour. It has the edge over the
others thanks to its corner location near
the Verdi art cinema, with huge windows that open up completely in summer. Comfy sofas and armchairs plus
occasional film screenings make this a
favourite with an artsy, studenty crowd.

Envalira

*Plaça del Sol 13 (93 218 58 13).
Metro Fontana.* **Open** 1.30-4pm,
9pm-midnight Tue-Sat; 1.30-5pm
Sun. Closed Aug, 1wk Christmas, 1wk
Easter. €€. **Spanish**. **Map** p140 C4 ⑧
Most regions of Spain are represented
on the menu at this profoundly traditional restaurant, with a particular
emphasis on Galicia (*caldeirada
gallega* is a hearty fish stew, *lacón
con grelos* is gammon with turnip
tops and *tarta de Santiago* is an
almond cake). The Basque oxtail stew
is also very tasty. The dining room
could do with a lick of paint and some
subtlety in its lighting; arrive early
for the more comfy leather banquettes
at the front, and be sure to book ahead
at weekends.

Flash Flash

*C/Granada del Penedès 25 (93 237 09
90). FGC Gràcia.* **Open** 11am-1.30am
daily. **Bar**. **Map** p140 B4 ⑨
Opened back in 1970, this bar was a
design sensation in its day, with its
white leatherette banquettes and walls
imprinted with silhouettes of a life-size
frolicking, Twiggy-like model. They
describe it as a *tortilleria*, with 60 or so
tortilla variations available, alongside
a list of child-friendly dishes and adult-
friendly cocktails.

Gelateria Caffetteria Italiana

*Plaça Revolució 2 (93 210 23 39).
Metro Fontana or Joanic.* **Open**
4-8.45pm Mon-Thur; 4pm-midnight
Fri-Sun. Closed mid Dec-mid Jan.
€. No credit cards. **Ice-cream**.
Map p141 D4 ⑩
Run by an Italian mother and daughter, Caffetteria Italiana is famous for
its own-recipe dark chocolate ice-
cream – of which it runs out every
night. Other freshly made, additive-
free flavours include fig, strawberry,
peach: basically, whatever fruit happens to be in season. Prepare to queue
on summer evenings.

Cantina Machito p143

Himali

*C/Milà i Fontanals 68 (93 285 15
68). Metro Joanic.* **Open** 1-4.30pm,
8pm-midnight Tue-Sun. **€. Nepalese**.
Map p141 D4 ⑪
A comic metaphor for modern-day
Barcelona, Himali moved into what was
a local boozer, but has retained the silhouettes of famous Catalans – Dali and
Montserrat Caballé among them – on
the windows, while inside there are
Nepalese prayer flags and tourist
posters of the Himalayas. The alien and
impenetrable menu looks a bit daunt-
ing, but the waiters are useful with rec-
ommendations; or you could start with
momo dumplings or Nepalese soup, followed by *mugliaco kukhura* (barbecued
butter chicken in tomato sauce) or *khasi
masala tarkari* (baked spicy lamb). All
dishes include rice and nan bread.

Mesopotamia

*C/Verdi 65 (93 237 15 63). Metro
Fontana.* **Open** 8.30pm-10.45pm
Tue-Thur; 8.30-11.30pm Fri-Sat.
Closed 2wks Sept, 2wks Dec. **€€**.
No credit cards. **Iraqi. Map** p141 D3 ⑫
The policy at Barcelona's only Iraqi
restaurant is to have everything on the
menu at the same price, so that the cost
won't hold anybody back from ordering
what they want. The menu is based on
Arab 'staff of life' foods, such as yoghurt
and rice. Best value is the huge taster
menu, which includes great Lebanese
wines, a variety of dips for your *riqaq*
bread, bulgur wheat with aromatic roast
meats and vegetables, sticky baklava
and Arabic teas. Also good are the
potato croquettes stuffed with minced
meat, almonds and dried fruit.

La Nena

*C/Ramón y Cajal 36 (93 285 14 76).
Metro Fontana or Joanic.* **Open** 9am-
2pm, 4-10pm Mon-Wed; 10am-10.30pm
Thur-Sun. Closed Aug. No credit cards.
Café. Map p141 D4 ⑬
With whitewashed stone walls, piles of
books and games, and a gaily painted
table-and-chair set for children, La

Nena is wonderfully cosy, or would be
if the staff would only lighten up. The
speciality is sugar and spice and all
things nice; waffles, crêpes, hot chocolate, fresh juices and ice-cream.
Savoury delights include sandwiches
and toasted bread with various toppings. Note there is no alcohol.

Noise i Art

*C/Topazi 26 (93 368 48 21).
Metro Fontana.* **Open** 6pm-2am
Tue-Thur, Sun; 6.30pm-3am Fri,
Sat. **Map** p141 D3 ⑭
Colourful, pop art decor coupled with a
chilled and convivial atmosphere makes
this the perfect bar to sit and shoot the
breeze. It's occasionally livened up with
a flamenco session, and all the usual
Gràcia food staples, such as houmous
and tabbouleh, are served. We could live
without the Madonna and Depeche
Mode videos looping on a giant screen,
but the large spirit measures do help.

Octubre

*C/Julián Romea 18 (93 218 25 18).
Metro Diagonal/FGC Gràcia.* **Open**
1.30-3.30pm, 9-11pm Mon-Fri; 9-11pm
Sat. Closed Aug, 1wk Easter. **€€**.
Catalan. Map p140 B4 ⑮
Time stands still in this quiet little spot,
with its quaint old-fashioned decor,
swathes of lace and brown table linen.
Time often stands still, in fact, between
placing an order and receiving any
food, but this is all part of Octubre's
sleepy charm. Also contributing to its
appeal is a roll-call of reasonably
priced, mainly Catalan dishes, like
squid stuffed with meatballs on a bed
of *samfaina*, and pig's trotters with
fried cabbage and potato.

San Kil

*C/Legalitat 22 (93 284 41 79). Metro
Joanic.* **Open** 1-3pm, 8.30pm-midnight
Mon-Sat. Closed 2wks Aug. **€€**.
Korean. Map p141 E3 ⑯
If you've never eaten Korean food
before, it pays to gen up a bit before
you head to this bright and spartan

restaurant. *Panch'an* is the ideal starter for the beginner in this cuisine: four little dishes containing vegetable appetisers, one of which will be tangy *kimch'i* (fermented cabbage with chilli). Then try mouth-watering *pulgogi* – beef served sizzling at the table and eaten rolled into lettuce leaves – and maybe *bibimbap* – rice with vegetables (and occasionally meat) topped with a fried egg. Finish up with a shot of soju rice wine.

Shojiro

C/Ros de Olano 11 (93 415 65 48).
Metro Fontana. **Open** 1.30-3.15pm, 9-11.30pm Tue-Sat. Closed Aug. **€€**.
Japanese. Map p140 C4 ⑰
A curious but surprisingly successful mix of Catalan and Japanese applies to the decor as much as the food at Shojiro, with original mosaic flooring and dark-green paintwork setting off a clean feng-shuied look. There are only set meals on offer (drinks are all included in lunch). Dishes might include mackerel cooked with miso and white aubergine, followed by venison with wild mushrooms and black basil. Two puddings are also included in the price.

La Singular

C/Francisco Giner 50 (93 237 50 98).
Metro Diagonal or Fontana. **Open** 1.30-4pm, 9pm-midnight Mon-Thur; 1.30-4pm, 9pm-1am Fri; 9pm-1am Sat. Closed last wk Aug & 1st wk Sept. **€€**.
Mediterranean. Map p140 C5 ⑱
While this is often described as a lesbian-friendly restaurant, in fact that's the least noteworthy thing about it, and all are made welcome. Most come here for the good-value set lunch (salads and light pasta dishes to start, followed by dishes such as roast beef carpaccio with red cabbage and onion) in snug surroundings of red walls with pale green woodwork and a tiny, leafy patio. It can get noisy when full; it's best to come early and beat the rush. Reservations are necessary for Friday and Saturday nights.

Sureny

Plaça de la Revolució 17 (93 213 75 56).
Metro Fontana or Joanic. **Open** *Sept-June* 1-3.30pm Mon; 1-3.30pm, 8pm-midnight Tue-Thur; 1-4pm,8.30pm-1am Fri; 8.30pm-1am Sat; 8pm-midnight Sun. *July, Aug* 8pm-midnight Tue-Thur; 8.30pm-1am Fri, Sat; 8pm-midnight Sun. Closed 2wks Christmas. **€€**.
Tapas. Map p141 D4 ⑲
A well-kept gastronomic secret, Sureny boasts superb gourmet tapas and waiters who know what they're about. In addition to the usual run-of-the-mill tortilla 'n' calamares fare, look out for dishes such as tuna marinated in ginger and soy sauce, partridge, venison and other game when in season, and a sublime duck foie with redcurrant sauce.

Shopping

BCN Computers

C/Mozart 26 (93 217 61 66, www.bcn-computers.es). **Open** 10am-2pm, 4-8pm Mon-Fri, open Sat with appt. No credit cards.
Map p140 C5 ⑳
Everything for Macs and PCs: software in English, hardware and software installations, repairs for personal computers and laptops and ADSL support. There's English-speaking customer service and, unlike many local shops, staff offer a free evaluation of your computer's problems when you take it for repair.

Hibernian Books

C/Montseny 17 (93 217 47 96, www.hibernian-books.com). Metro Fontana. **Open** 4-8.30pm Mon; 10.30am-8.30pm Tue-Sat. No credit cards. **Map** p140 C4 ㉑
With its air of pleasantly dusty intellectualism, Hibernian feels like a proper British secondhand bookshop. There are books for all tastes, from bound early editions to classic Penguin paperbacks, biographies, cookbooks, poetry and plays – in all more than 30,000 titles. Part-exchange is possible here.

Feeling the crunch

A few suggestions for making your cèntims go further.

The global crisis has hit almost everybody, and tourists travelling with weak currencies such as the pound are feeling it. Here we provide a few budgeting tips that may help:

■ Municipal museums are free every Sunday, between 3 and 6pm.

■ Sales come between 7 January and early March, while summer sales are in July.

■ Free-entry contemporary art museums include: **Fundació Joan Brossa** (see p124); **CaixaForum** (p109); **Arts Santa Mònica** (see p54).

■ There is free museum entry across the board on 18 May for the Dia Internacional dels Museus. Many are also free on the night of the 17th for the Nit dels Museus.

■ Particularly good-value set lunches are served at **La Soleá** (see p117), **Himali** (see p145), **Kaiku** (see p102) and **Organic** (see p91).

■ Longer-term visitors with a library card get discounts at cinemas, theatres and bookshops.

■ Unsold theatre tickets are on sale at a 30 to 50 per cent discount from the Tiquet 3 box office in the main tourist office underneath Plaça Catalunya up to three hours before the start of the show.

■ Sample cheap but top quality seafood by serving yourself at **La Paradeta** (see p79).

■ Monday is discount day at most of the city's cinemas, though they occasionally drop their prices on Wednesdays.

■ If you intend to use a lot of public transport, it can be cheaper to buy a travelcard than the standard single ticket or T-10 carnet. TMB offers travelcards for 1-5 days that give unlimited access to all forms of public transport.

■ **Museu Frederic Marès** (see p57), the **CCCB** (see p86) and **Parc del Laberint** (see p159) are free or discounted on Wednesdays.

■ Carrer Girona in the Eixample is packed with remainder stores and factory outlets, such as Mango Outlet at No.37.

■ Save your paella experience for Thursday lunchtime when it is a standard feature on set menus.

Kwatra

C/Gran de Gràcia 262 (93 237 66 37).
Metro Lesseps. **Open** 11am-2.30pm,
4-8.30pm Mon-Sat. **Map** p140 C2 ㉒
This is urban trainer heaven, with the
latest models and limited-editions from
Nike, 555DSL, Vans, Adidas, Diesel,
Converse, Onitsuka Tiger, Quicksilver,
Puma and Roxy. There's also a small
but very covetable selection of bags
and T-shirts from the same labels.

Nightlife

Elèctric Bar

Travessera de Gràcia 233 (no phone,
www.myspace.com/electricbarcelona).
Metro Joanic. **Open** 7pm-2am Tue-
Thur, Sun; 7pm-3am Fri, Sat. Closed
last wk July, 1st wk Aug. No credit
cards. **Map** p141 E4 ㉓
Elèctric was the first bar in Gràcia to be
connected to the mains, yet this former
bastion of modernity seems not to have
changed since. An innocuous entry
opens into a sprawling bohemian den
that has an agenda as colourful as its
clientele: theatre, puppetry and storytelling on weekdays, live music at night.

Heliogabal

C/Ramón y Cajal 80 (no phone,
www.heliogabal.com). Metro Joanic.
Open 9pm-2.30am Mon-Wed, Sun;
9pm-3am Thur-Sat. *Concerts* 10pm.
No credit cards. **Map** p141 D4 ㉔
Loved by habitués of the Gràcia arts
scene, this low-key bar and performance venue is filled to bursting with
cutie pies in cool T-shirts who just
really adore live poetry. Events change
nightly, running from live music to
film screenings, art openings and readings, and programming focuses on
local talents. On concert nights, arrive
early for an 'at-least-I'm-not-standing'
folding chair.

KGB

C/Alegre de Dalt 55 (93 210 59 06,
www.salakgb.net). Metro Joanic.
Open 1-6am Thur-Sat. **Map** p141 F3 ㉕

KGB is a cavern-like space that was,
in its heyday, the rock 'n' roll disco
barn capital of the city and *'un after'*
where Sidecar heads would bolt at
6am on the weekend. It still remains
loud, whether featuring concerts or DJ
sessions. Thursday's concerts tend
towards pop rock, which then continues for the DJ sessions, while the occasional weekend gigs vary but are
followed by tech-house.

Vinilo

C/Matilde 2 (mobile 626 464 759,
http://vinilus.blogspot.com). Metro
Fontana. **Open** 7pm-2am Mon-Thur;
7pm-3am Fri, Sat; 7pm-12.30am Sun.
No credit cards. **Map** p140 C4 ㉖
Run by an affably hip family, Vinilo
seems like an artist's den masquerad-
ing as a neighbourhood bar. The walls
are papered with original prints and
concert posters; a silent television
plays 1980s cartoons on loop; the
sandwiches are big and delicious and
the beer selection certainly nothing to
scoff at. But it's really the music
that makes it: Sufjan Stevens, Coco
Rosie, Leonard Cohen… You'll wish
you lived here.

Arts & leisure

Verdi

C/Verdi 32 (93 238 79 90, www.
cines-verdi.com). Metro Fontana.
Tickets 1st screening Tue-Fri
€5.50. Mon €5. Tue-Fri €7.50. Sat,
Sun €8. **Map** p141 D3 ㉗
The five-screen Verdi and its four-
screen annexe Verdi Park on the next
street have transformed this corner of
Gràcia, bringing with them vibrant bars
and cheap eats for the crowds that flock
to their diverse programme of independent, mainly European and Asian cinema. At peak times, chaos reigns; arrive
early and don't mistake the line to enter
for the ticket queue, which can stretch
to Madrid on rainy Sundays.
Other locations Verdi Park,
C/Torrijos 49 (93 238 79 90).

Fòrum p158

Other Districts

Sants & Les Corts

Sants, or at least the immediate environs of Estació de Sants, which is all that most visitors see of the area, stands as a monument to the worst of 1970s urban design. Just outside the station is the forbidding Plaça dels Països Catalans, a snarl of traffic around a roundabout whose centrepiece looks like a post-Miró bus shelter. However, Sants merits a few hours' investigation for historic, if not aesthetic, reasons. Most routes of interest start and end at the hub of the barri, Plaça de Sants, halfway up C/Sants high street, where Jorge Castillo's *Ciclista* statue is also to be found. Also worth checking out are the showy Modernista buildings at nos.12, 130, 145 and 151, designed by local architect Modest Feu.

Another village engulfed by the expanding city in the 19th century, Les Corts ('cowsheds' or 'pigsties'), remains one of the most Catalan of the city's *barris*, but the rows of unlovely apartment blocks have stamped out any trace of its bucolic past. Something has been retained, however, in the Plaça de la Concòrdia, a quiet square with a tall bell tower. This anachronistic oasis houses the civic centre Can Deu, formerly a farmhouse and now home to a great bar. The area is much better known, though, for what happens every other weekend, when tens of thousands pour in to watch FC Barcelona, whose **Nou Camp** takes up much of the west of the barri.

Sights & museums

Parc de l'Espanya Industrial

C/Muntadas 1-37 (no phone). Metro *Sants-Estació.* **Open** 10am-sunset daily. **Admission** free.
In the 1970s, the owners of the old textile factory announced their intention to use

Parc Central del
Poblenou p158

the land to build blocks of apartments. The neighbourhood's residents, though, put their collective foot down and insisted on a park, which was eventually laid out in 1985. The result is a puzzling space, with ten watchtowers overlooking a boating lake with a statue of Neptune in the middle, flanked by a stretch of mud used by dog walkers, but little greenery. By the entrance children can climb over Andrés Nagel's *Drac*, a massive black dragon sculpture.

Eating & drinking

Fragments Café

Plaça de la Concòrdia 12, Les Corts (93 419 96 13, www.fragmentscafe.com). Metro Les Corts or Maria Cristina. **Open** 1.15pm-1am Tue, Wed; 1.15pm-2am Thur, Fri; 11.30am-2am Sat; 11.30am-1am Sun. Closed 2wks Christmas, 2wks Aug. **€€€. Tapas.**
A tapas bar with a classy look in the one remaining pocket of charm left in the neighbourhood of Les Corts. Sit on the tables out in the square or in the bar's own garden at the back (candlelit at night), and order some vermut (on tap here) and *gildas* (anchovies with chilli) before you so much as begin to peruse the menu. Later there are scrambled eggs with foie, juicy steaks, and homemade pasta.

La Parra

C/Joanot Martorell 3, Sants (93 332 51 34). Metro Hostafrancs. **Open** 8.30pm-12.30am Tue-Fri; 1.30-4.30pm, 8.30pm-12.30am Sat; 1.30-4.30pm Sun. Closed Aug. **€€€. Catalan.**
A charming converted 19th-century coaching inn with a shady vine-covered terrace. The open wood grill sizzles with various parts of goat, pig, rabbit and cow, as well as a few more off-piste items such as deer and even foal. Huge, oozing steaks are slapped on to wooden boards and accompanied by baked potatoes, calçots, grilled vegetables and *all i oli*, with jugs of local wines from the giant barrels.

Nightlife

Bikini

Avda Diagonal 547, Les Corts (93 322 08 00, www.bikinibcn.com). Metro Les Corts or Maria Cristina. **Open** midnight-5am Wed-Sat.
Bikini lost some muscle in recent years, with the big-name stars it once booked replaced by little-knowns and ageing rockers. However, it has shown a few signs of new life lately, offering shows from the likes of Martha Wainwright and the Ting Tings. Divide your time between the rooms playing hip hop, pop, lounge or Latin sounds.

Arts & leisure

Camp Nou – FC Barcelona

Avda Arístides Maillol, access 9, Les Corts (93 496 36 00/08, www.fcbarcelona.com). Metro Collblanc, Les Corts or Maria Cristina. **Open** *Museum* Apr-Sept 10am-8pm Mon-Sat; 10am-2.30pm Sun. Oct-Mar 10am-6.30pm Mon-Sat; 10am-2.30pm Sun. **Admission** *Guided tour* €17; €14 reductions; free under-5s.
Nou Camp, where FC Barcelona has played since 1957, is one of football's great stadiums. If you can't get there on match day but love the team, it's worth visiting the club museum. The excellent guided tour of the stadium takes you through the players' tunnel to the dugouts and then, via the away team's changing room, on to the President's box, where there is a replica of the European Cup, which the team won at Wembley in 1992 and again in Paris in 2006. The club museum commemorates those glory years. Last tour begins an hour before closing time.

Tibidabo & Collserola

Tibidabo is the dominant peak of the Collserola massif, with sweeping views of the whole of the Barcelona conurbation stretching out to the sea. The

Feelin' blue

The Natural History Museum gets a striking new home.

The Universal Forum of Cultures in 2004 was a vastly ambitious, wildly expensive attempt to put Barcelona back on the world map after the years basking in the afterglow of the 1992 Olympic Games. It was pretty much an unmitigated flop, but it did leave one legacy in the form of some architecturally striking buildings.

One such was Herzog and de Meuron's Edifici Fòrum, a glittering triangular creation, painted deep blue and criss-crossed with mirrored strips that give it a marine effect. Since the 2004 Forum, the building has mostly lain empty, apart from some slightly dreary municipal exhibitions on urbanism, and has only now been put to good use as the new home of the Museum of Natural History, now also known as the Museu Blau (Blue Museum).

This comprises the two collections of the former zoology and geology museums in the Parc de la Ciutadella, whose buildings will now be given over to archiving and studying the materials.

The new museum is said to be structured around James Lovelock's Gaia hypothesis, which views the earth as a self-regulating organism, though – so far, at least – this isn't obvious from the collection. Despite the breathlessly modern architecture that surrounds it, this is a strictly old-school affair of glass cases and formaldehyde jars, enlivened by some dramatic lighting and the odd touch screen.

It begins with the geology section, which includes meteorites, gems, crystals, radioactive minerals and rocks from the earth's lithosphere. There's an extensive collection of fossils and funghi, and then the zoology section begins, with dozens of stuffed animals, preserved insects and molluscs, though little attempt is made to contextualise them. Several animals from the collection have enjoyed a moment of fame being lent out for TV and theatre shows and the horned Mouflon skull was the direct inspiration for the Oscar-winning faun make-up in the film Pan's Labyrinth.

■ Museu Blau (see p158).

neo-Gothic Sagrat Cor church crowning the peak has become one of the city's most recognisable landmarks; it's clearly visible for miles around. At weekends, thousands of people head to the top of the hill in order to whoop and scream at the **funfair**.

Getting there on the **Tramvia Blau** (Blue Tram) and then the funicular railway is part of the fun; between the two is Plaça Doctor Andreu, a great place for an alfresco drink. For the best view of the city, either take a lift up Norman Foster's tower, the **Torre de Collserola**, or up to the mirador at the feet of Christ atop the Sagrat Cor.

The vast Parc de Collserola is more a series of forested hills than a park, its shady paths through holm oak and pine opening out to spectacular views. It's most easily reached by FGC train on the Terrassa-Sabadell line from Plaça Catalunya or Passeig de Gràcia, getting off at Baixador de Vallvidrera station.

Sights & museums

Tibidabo Funfair
Plaça del Tibidabo 3-4 (93 211 79 42, www.tibidabo.net). FGC Avda Tibidabo, then funicular. **Open** varies (see website). **Admission** *Cami del Cel* Mar-Dec €11.10 adults; €7 under 120cm; free under 90cm. *Parc d'Atraccions* (unlimited rides) €25.20, €9 under 120cm, free under 90cm. This hilltop fairground, dating from 1889, is investing millions in getting itself bang up to date, with the terrifying freefall Pendulum, a new rollercoaster and a hot-air balloon style ride for smaller children. The many other attractions include a house of horrors, bumper cars and the emblematic Avió, the world's first popular flight simulator when it was built in 1928. Don't miss the antique mechanical puppets and contraptions at the Museu d'Autòmats,

and there are hourly puppet shows at the Marionetàrium (from 1pm). At the weekends, there are circus parades at the end of the day and, in summer, street theatre.

Torre de Collserola
Ctra de Vallvidrera al Tibidabo (93 211 79 42, www.torredecollserola.com). FGC Peu Funicular then funicular. **Open** varies (see website). **Admission** €5; reductions €2.80-€3; free under-90cm. Barcelona's most visible landmark, Norman Foster's communications tower, was built in 1992 to transmit images of the Olympics around the world. Those who don't suffer from vertigo attest to the wonderful views of Barcelona and the Mediterranean from the top.

Eating & drinking

La Venta
Plaça Doctor Andreu, Tibidabo (93 212 64 55, www.restaurantelaventa.com). FGC Avda Tibidabo, then Tramvia Blau or bus 179. **Open** 1.30-3.15pm, 9-11.30pm daily. **€€€. Mediterranean**. La Venta's pretty Moorish-influenced interior plays second fiddle to the terrace: shaded by day and uncovered by night in summer, sealed and warmed with a wood-burning stove in winter. Of the food, complex starters include lentil and spider crab salad, and sea urchins au gratin (a must). Simpler but high-quality mains run from rack of lamb to delicate monkfish in filo pastry with pesto.

Nightlife

Mirablau
Plaça Doctor Andreu s/n, Tibidabo (93 418 58 79). FGC Avda Tibidabo then Tramvia Blau. **Open** 11am-4.30am Mon-Wed, Sun; 11am-6am Thur-Sat. **Admission** free. It doesn't get any more uptown than this, geographically and socially. Located at the top of Tibidabo, this little bar gets packed with the high rollers of

BARCELONA BY AREA

Barcelona, from local footballers living on the hill to international businessmen on the company card. Watch out for the view and the artificial wind that sweeps through the tropical shrubbery outside.

Zona Alta

Zona Alta (the 'upper zone', or 'uptown') is the name given collectively to a series of smart neighbourhoods including Sant Gervasi, Sarrià and Pedralbes that stretch out across the lower reaches of the Collserola hills. The centre of Sarrià and the streets of old Pedralbes around the monastery retain a flavour of the sleepy country towns these once were.

Gaudí fans are rewarded by a trip up to the **Pavellons de la Finca Güell** at Avda Pedralbes 15; its extraordinary and rather frightening wrought-iron gate features a dragon into whose gaping mouth the foolhardy can fit their heads. Once inside the gardens, via the main gate on Avda Diagonal, look out for a delightful fountain designed by the master himself. Across near Putxet is Gaudí's relatively sober **Col·legi de les Teresianes** (C/Ganduxer 85-105), while up towards Tibidabo, just off Plaça Bonanova, rises his Gothic-influenced **Torre Figueres** or Bellesguard.

Sights & museums

CosmoCaixa

C/Isaac Newton 26 (93 212 60 50, www.fundacio.lacaixa.es). Bus 60/FGC Avda Tibidabo. **Open** 10am-8pm Tue-Sun. **Admission** €3; €2 reductions; free under-7s. *Planetarium* €2; €1.50 reductions; free under-7s.

Said to be the biggest science museum in Europe, CosmoCaixa doesn't, perhaps, make the best use of its space. A glass-enclosed spiral ramp runs down an impressive six floors, but actually represents quite a long walk to reach the main collection five floors down. Here you'll find the Flooded Forest, a reproduction of a corner of Amazonia complete with flora and fauna, and the Geological Wall, along with temporary exhibitions. The Matter Room covers 'inert', 'living', 'intelligent' and 'civilised' matter, but, for all the fanfare made by the museum about taking exhibits out of glass cases and making scientific theories accessible, many of the displays still look dated.

On the plus side, the installations for children are excellent: the Planetarium pleases those aged five to eight, and the wonderful Clik (ages three to six) and Flash (seven to nine) introduce kids to science through games.

DHUB Barcelona/ Museu de Ceràmica

Palau Reial de Pedralbes, Avda Diagonal 686 (93 280 16 21, www.museuceramica.bcn.cat, www.dhub-bcn.cat). Metro Palau Reial. **Open** 10am-6pm Tue-Sun. **Admission** €4.20; €2.40 reductions. Free under-16s & 3-6pm Sun & all day 1st Sun of mth. No credit cards.

In 2008, the Museu Tèxtil, previously located in the Born, joined the ceramic and decorative arts museums in the Palau Reial de Pedralbes, built in the 1920s and briefly used as a royal palace. The textile, decorative arts and, in the future, a graphic arts collection form the new design mega-museum, the Disseny Hub Barcelona, which will be relocated to a new building in the Plaça de les Glòries in the future.

The Textile Museum provides a chronological tour of clothing and fashion, from its oldest piece, a man's Coptic tunic from a seventh-century tomb, through to Karl Lagerfeld. The Museum of Decorative Arts is informative and fun, and looks at the different styles informing the design of artefacts in Europe since the Middle Ages, from Romanesque to art deco and beyond. A second section is devoted to post-war Catalan design of objects as diverse as urinals and man-sized inflatable pens.

The Ceramics Museum is equally fascinating, showing how Moorish ceramic techniques from the 13th century were developed after the Reconquista with the addition of colours (especially blue and yellow) in centres such as Manises (in Valencia) and Barcelona. Upstairs is a display of 20th-century ceramics, with a room devoted to Miró and Picasso.

Monestir de Pedralbes

Baixada del Monestir 9 (93 256 21 22). FGC Reina Elisenda. **Open** *Apr-Sept* 10am-5pm Tue-Sat; 10am-8pm Sun. *Oct-Mar* 10am-2pm Mon-Sat; 10am-8pm Sun. **Admission** €7; €5 reductions; free under-16s. Free 1st Sun of mth & Sun 3pm-8pm.

In 1326, the widowed Queen Elisenda of Montcada used her inheritance to buy this land and build a convent for the Poor Clare order of nuns, which she soon joined. The result is a jewel of Gothic architecture with an understated single-nave church with fine stained-glass windows and a beautiful three-storey 14th-century cloister. The place was out of bounds to the general public until 1983, when the nuns, a closed order, opened it up as a museum in the mornings (when they escape to a nearby annexe). A fascinating insight into life in a medieval convent.

Parc de la Creueta del Coll

C/Mare de Déu del Coll 77 (no phone). Metro Penitents. **Open** 10am-sunset daily. **Admission** free.

Created from a quarry in 1987 by Josep Martorell and David Mackay, the team that went on to design the Vila Olímpica, this park boasts a sizeable swimming pool complete with a 'desert island' and a sculpture by Eduardo Chillida: a 50-ton lump of curly granite suspended on cables, called *In Praise of Water*.

Pavellons de la Finca Güell

Avda Pedralbes 7 (info 93 317 76 52, www.rutadelmodernisme.com). Metro Palau Reial. **Open** *Tours in English* 10.15am, 12.15pm Sat, Sun. **Admission** €6; €3 reductions. Free under-11s. No credit cards.

Businessman Eusebi Güell bought what is now Palau Reial in 1882 as a summer home, contracting Gaudí to remodel the entrance lodges and gardens for the estate. In 1883, they began to build what would be one of Gaudí's first projects for the Güell family.

The Porta del Drac (Dragon's Gate) used to be the private entrance for the Güell family, and was connected to the Güell home in Barcelona by a private, walled road. The Pavellons must be visited with a guide, and tours are offered in Spanish and English. Really though, it isn't much of a tour, lasting for about 25 minutes with a look at nothing more than the gate and the stables.

Tramvia Blau

Avda Tibidabo (Plaça Kennedy) to Plaça Doctor Andreu (93 318 70 74, www.tmb.cat). FGC Avda Tibidabo. **Open** *Nov-Mar* 10am-6pm Sat, Sun. *Apr-June* 10am-8pm daily. *July, Aug* 10am-8pm Mon-Fri. *Sept, Oct* 10am-8pm Sat, Sun. **Frequency** 20mins. **Tickets** €2.80 single; €4.30 return. No credit cards.

Barcelonins and tourists have been clanking 1,225m (4,000ft) up Avda Tibidabo in the 'blue trams' since 1902. In the winter months, when the tram only operates on weekends, a rather more prosaic bus (no.195) takes you up (or you can walk it in 15 minutes).

Eating & drinking

Hisop

Passatge Marimon 9, Sant Gervasi (93 241 32 33, www.hisop.com). Metro Hospital Clínic or Diagonal. **Open** 1.30-3.30pm, 8.30-11pm Mon-Fri; 9-11pm Sat. Closed 3wks Aug. **€€€€**. **Mediterranean**.

Run by two young, enthusiastic and talented chefs, Hisop aims to bring serious dining to the non-expense-account masses by keeping its prices on the low side and its service approachable. The €52 tasting menu is the most popular choice among diners, with dishes that vary according to the season but often include its rich 'monkfish royale' (served with its liver, a cocoa-based sauce and tiny pearls of saffron) and a pistachio soufflé with Kaffir lime ice-cream and rocket 'soup'.

El Petit Bangkok

C/Saragossa 87, Sant Gervasi (mobile 616 185 196). Metro Lesseps/FGC Plaça Molina. **Open** 7.30pm-midnight Tue-Thur; 1-3.30pm, 8pm-12.30am Fri-Sat. **€€. Thai**.

Unlike most Thai restaurants in Barcelona, with their trickling fountains, garlanded Buddhas and leafy settings, Petit Bangkok is cramped, bright, bare and a pain to get to. Unlike most Thai restaurants in Barcelona, however, Petit Bangkok serves really excellent food – authentic, hot and fantastically cheap, from an aromatic tom yam soup to spicy duck rolls. Reservations are essential.

Shopping

Pedralbes Centre

Avda Diagonal 609-615, Pedralbes (93 410 68 21, www.pedralbescentre. com). Metro Maria Cristina. **Open** 10am-9pm Mon-Sat.

The focus of this shopping centre is on upmarket clothes, accessories and homewares, with plenty of local names such as Elena Miró, Majoral jewellers and Luis Guirau in among the likes of Hello Kitty and Timberland. The cafés and restaurants appeal to ladies who lunch, with salad buffets and gourmet tapas. In winter, the mall's plaza is transformed into an ice-rink.

Nightlife

Elephant

Passeig dels Til·lers 1, Pedralbes (93 334 02 58). Metro Palau Reial. **Open** 11.30pm-4.30am Thur-Sat.

If you have a Porsche and a model girlfriend, this is where you meet your peers. Housed in an old mansion, Elephant is as elegant and hi-design as its customers. The big attraction is the outdoor bar and terrace dancefloor – though the low-key, low-volume house music doesn't inspire much hands-in-the-air action.

Luz de Gas

C/Muntaner 246 (93 209 77 11, www.luzdegas.com). FGC Muntaner. **Open** *Club* 1-5.30am daily. *Gigs* vary.

This lovingly renovated old music hall, garnished with chandeliers and classical friezes, is a mainstay on the live music scene and sure is one classy joint. In between visits from international artists and various benefits for local causes, you'll find nightly residencies: blues on Mondays, Dixieland jazz on Tuesdays, disco on Wednesdays, pop-rock on Thursdays, soul on Fridays and vintage and Spanish rock on weekends.

Sala BeCool

Plaça Joan Llongueras 5 (93 362 04 13, www.salabecool.com). Metro Hospital Clínic. **Open** *Gigs* 10pm Thur-Sat. *Club* midnight-5am Thur; 1am-6am Fri, Sat.

The latest from Berlin's minimal electro scene reaches Barcelona via this multifaceted concert space and club. After the live shows by local rock stars or international indie success stories, a packed and music-loving crowd throbs to sophisticated electronica and its bizarre attendant visuals. Upstairs, in the Red Room, DJs playing indie pop-rock provide an alternative to the pounding beats of the main room.

Poblenou

In its industrial heyday, Poblenou was known as 'little Manchester' due to the concentration of cotton mills. The old mills and other

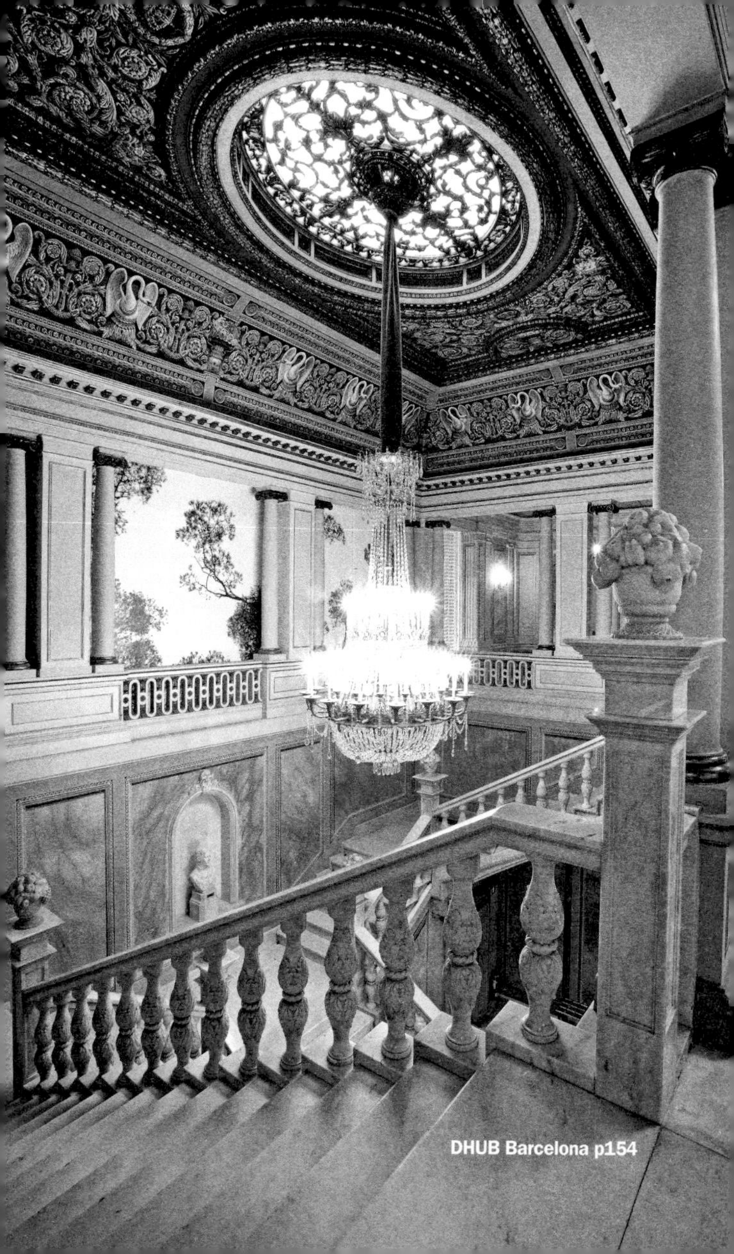
DHUB Barcelona p154

factories are now being bulldozed or remodelled as the district is rebranded as a technology and business district, snappily tagged 22@, which will exist side by side with the garages, exhaust fitters, wheel balancers and car washes that are a feature of the *barrio*.

Work is about to begin on remodelling the ghastly, traffic-choked Plaça de les Glòries, partly to open up the land around the hugely phallic **Torre Agbar**, and to form a gateway to the Diagonal Mar area and the new commercial and leisure area on the shoreline, known as the **Fòrum**, after the event in 2004 for which it was created. The tower, designed by French architect Jean Nouvel and owned by the Catalan water board, has been a bold and controversial project; it's not unlike London's famed Gherkin. Nouvel has also created the new, walled Parc Central del Poblenou, one of a number of highly designed gardens in Barcelona, which features giant plants, an island, a cratered lunar landscape and a perfumed garden.

Sights & museums

Museu Blau
Plaça Leonardo da Vinci 4-5, Parc del Fòrum, Poblenou (93 256 22 00, www.museuciencies.bcn.cat). Metro El Maresme-Forum. **Open** *Oct-May* 10am-7pm Tue-Fri; 10am-8pm Sat, Sun. *June-Sept* 10am-9pm Tue-Sun. **Admission** €7; free under-17s. See box p152.

Eating & drinking

Els Pescadors
Plaça Prim 1, Poblenou (93 225 20 18, www.elspescadors.com). Metro Poblenou. **Open** 1-3.45pm, 8-11.30pm daily. **€€€€. Seafood.**
In a forgotten, almost rustic square of Poblenou lies this first-rate fish restaurant, with tables under a canopy formed by two huge and ancient ombú trees. Suspend your disbelief with the crunchy sardine skeletons that arrive as an aperitif (trust us, they're delicious), and move on to tasty fried chipirones, followed by cod and pepper paella or creamy rice with prawns and smoked cheese. Desserts include the likes of strawberry gelatine 'spaghetti' in a citric soup.

Shopping

Barcelona Glòries
Avda Diagonal 208 (93 486 04 04, www.lesglories.com). Metro Glòries. **Open** *Shops* 10am-10pm Mon-Sat.
This mall, office and leisure centre has become a focus of local life. There are more than 220 shops, including a Carrefour supermarket, an H&M, a Mango and a Disney Store, facing on to a large, café-filled square decorated with jets of coloured water.

Diagonal Mar
Avda Diagonal 3, Poblenou (93 567 76 37, www.diagonalmar.com). Metro El Maresme-Forum. **Open** 10am-10pm Mon-Sat.
This three-level mall at the sea end of Avda Diagonal has a sea-facing roof terrace filled with cafés and restaurants. As well as major anchors, such as an Alcampo supermarket, Zara and FNAC, there's a particular emphasis on children's clothes and toy shops, plus plenty of smaller global brands (like Miss Sixty).

Nightlife

Razzmatazz
C/Almogàvers 122 (93 320 82 00, www.salarazzmatazz.com). Metro Bogatell or Marina. **Open** *Concerts* vary. *Club* 1-6am Fri, Sat.
This monstrous club's five distinct spaces form the night-time playground of seemingly all young Barcelona. There's indie rock in Razz Club, tech-house in the Loft, techno pop in Lolita,

electro pop in the Pop Bar and electro rock in the Rex Room. Live music runs from Arctic Monkeys to Bananarama.

Horta

Horta was once a picturesque little village that still remains aloof from the city that swallowed it in 1904. Originally a collection of farms (its name means 'market garden'), the *barrio* is still peppered with old farmhouses, such as Can Mariner on C/Horta, dating back to 1050, and the medieval Can Cortada at the end of C/Campoamor, which is now a huge restaurant located in beautiful grounds. An abundant water supply also made Horta the place where much of the city's laundry was done: a community of *bugaderes* (washer-women) lived and worked in lovely C/Aiguafreda, where you can still see their wells and open-air stone washtubs.

The Vall d'Hebron is a leafy area located just above Horta in the Collserola foothills. Here, formerly private estates have been put to public use; among them are the chateau-like Palauet de les Heures, now a university building. The area was one of the city's four major venues for the Olympics and is rich in sporting facilities, including public football pitches, tennis courts, and cycling and archery facilities at the Velòdrom. It's also home to one of Barcelona's major concert venues. Around these environs there are several striking examples of street sculpture, including Claes Oldenburg's *Matches* and Joan Brossa's *Visual Poem* (in the shape of the letter 'A').

Sights & museums

Parc del Laberint
Passeig dels Castanyers 1 (93 413 24 00, www.bcn.cat/parcsijardins). Metro Mundet. **Open** 10am-sunset daily.

Admission €2.17; €1.38 reductions; free under-6s, over-65s. Free Wed, Sun. No credit cards.

In 1791, the Desvalls family, owners of this marvellously leafy estate, hired Italian architect Domenico Bagutti to design gardens set around a cypress maze, with a romantic stream and a waterfall. The mansion may be gone (replaced with a 19th-century building), but the gardens are remarkably intact, shaded in the summer by oaks, laurels and an ancient sequoia. Best of all, the maze, an ingenious puzzle that intrigues those brave enough to try it, is still in use.

Eating & drinking

Can Travi Nou
C/Jorge Manrique s/n, Horta (93 428 03 01, www.gruptravi.com). Metro Horta or Montbau. **Open** 1.30-4pm, 8.30-11pm Mon-Sat; 1.30-4pm Sun. **€€€. Catalan**.
An ancient rambling farmhouse clad in bougainvillea and perched high above the city, Can Travi Nou offers wonderfully rustic dining rooms with roaring log fires in winter, while in summer the action moves out to a covered terrace in a bosky, candlelit garden. The food is hearty, traditional Catalan cuisine, though it's a little expensive for what it is; Can Travi Nou is really all about location, location, location.

L'Esquinica
Passeig Fabra i Puig 296, Horta (93 358 25 19). Metro Virrei Amat. **Open** 8am-midnight Tue-Fri; 8am-4pm, 6.30pm-midnight Sat; 8am-4pm Sun. Closed last 2wks Aug. **Tapas**.
Think of it not as a trek, but as a quest; queues outside are testament to the great value tapas. On especially busy nights you'll be asked to take a number, supermarket-style. Waiters will advise first-timers to start with *chocos* (creamy squid rings), *patatas bravas* with *all i oli*, *llonganissa* sausage and *tigres* (stuffed mussels). After which the world is your oyster, cockle or clam.

Essentials

Barceló Raval p169

Hotels

The economic downturn, or '*la crisis*' as the Spanish have it, has its flipside. The city's popularity during the last decade and a half has seen hotel prices reach excruciating levels. But thanks to the slowdown, hoteliers have had to rethink drastically, and while there are still plenty of luxury options for those who can afford it, creativity in the mid-range is starting to boom, with rooms ranging between €80 and €150 a night.

High season runs year-round and finding somewhere to lay your head at short notice can be tough. Hotels generally require you to guarantee your booking with credit-card details or a deposit; it's worth calling a few days before arrival to reconfirm the booking (get it in writing if you can; many readers have reported problems) and check the cancellation policy. Often you will lose the first night.

Hostales are more laid-back and don't always ask for a deposit.

To be sure of a room with natural light or a view, ask for an outside room (*habitació/habitación exterior*), which will usually face the street. Many of Barcelona's buildings are built around a central airshaft, and the inside rooms (*habitació/ habitación interior*) around them can be quite gloomy, albeit quieter. However, in some cases (especially in the Eixample), these inward-facing rooms look on to large, open-air patios or gardens, which benefit from being quiet and having a view.

Apartment rentals

Short-term apartment rental is a rapidly expanding market. Some firms rent out their own flats, while others act as intermediaries between apartment owners and visitors, taking a cut of the rents.

When renting, it pays to use a little common sense. Check the small print (payment methods, deposits, cancellation fees) and exactly what is included (cleaning, towels and so on) before booking. Note that apartments offered for rental tend to be very small.

Some of the many websites offering flats include: www.rentthesun.com, www.inside-bcn.com, www.oh-barcelona.com, www.barcelona-home.com, www.destinationbcn.com, www.rentaflatinbarcelona.com, and www.friendlyrentals.com.

Barri Gòtic & La Rambla

Bonic Guesthouse

C/Josep Anselm Clavé 9, 1º-4ª (mobile 626 05 34 34, www.bonic-barcelona.com). Metro Drassanes. €€.
Bonic is painted in daisy-fresh colours and has sunlight streaming through the windows and meticulously restored original features. The gregarious Fernando does all he can to make you feel at home. Free newspapers, tea, coffee and water, and flowers in the three immaculate, communal bathrooms all add up to an experience that raises the budget bar considerably.

Duc de la Victòria

C/Duc 15 (93 270 34 10, www.nh-hotels.com). Metro Catalunya. €€€.
The trusty NH chain has high standards, and this good-value downtown branch is no exception to the rule. The rooms, with a blue-and-beige colour scheme, may not be very exciting, but the superior quality beds ensure a sound night's sleep. Note the street has changed name from Duc de la Victòria.

H1898

La Rambla 109 (93 552 95 52, www.hotel1898.com). Metro Catalunya or Liceu. €€€.

A dapper luxury hotel in a 19th-century building, the former Philippine Tobacco Company headquarters. Rooms are candy-striped; one floor is all perky green and white, another is red and white, and so on. The more expensive rooms have wooden-decked terraces, while some of the suites have private plunge pools. There's also a rooftop deck with navy-tiled pool and luxurious four-poster day beds.

Hostal Fontanella

Via Laietana 71, 2º (93 317 59 43, www.hostalfontanella.com). Metro Urquinaona. €.
The splendid Modernista lift lends a somewhat unjustified aura of grandeur to this simply furnished 11-room *hostal*. The downside of the Fontanella's central location on a busy thoroughfare is that outward-facing rooms are abuzz with the sound of traffic. But it's clean and comfy, and double-glazing helps.

Hotel Bagués

NEW *La Rambla 105 (93 343 50 00, www.derbyhotels.com). Metro Liceu.* €€€.
The Bagués is built on to the lovely listed exterior of an 1850s mansion, previously the showroom for venerable Catalan jewellery brand Bagués. Rooms draw from a palette restrained in colour to blacks and neutrals but with a sensuous mix of woods, plaster, leather, gold leaf, glass and slate. The bar/restaurant is a little overblown for some tastes, but the rooftop bar and pool are everything you need; a fitness centre/spa is planned.

Hotel Barcelona Catedral

C/Capellans 4 (93 304 22 55, www.barcelonacatedral.com). Metro Jaume I. €€€.
This newcomer to the city's heart is modern and relaxed, with a lobby that doubles as a funky lounge and cocktail bar. Rooms, while not particularly exciting, are bright and comfortable, with vast bathrooms and king-size beds. A garden terrace and a rooftop deck with pool are further pluses.

ESSENTIALS

Hotel Duquesa de Cardona

Passeig Colom 12 (93 268 90 90, www.hduquesadecardona.com). Metro Drassanes or Jaume I. €€€.

This elegantly restored 16th-century palace retains many original features and is furnished with natural materials – wood, leather, silk and stone – complemented by a soft colour scheme. Deluxe rooms and junior suites on the higher floors have views out across the harbour. Guests can sunbathe on the roof terrace and then cool off in the mosaic-tiled plunge pool.

Hotel Medinaceli

Plaça del Duc de Medinaceli 8 (93 481 77 25, www.gargallo-hotels.com). Metro Drassanes. €€€.

Rooms in this restored palace are done out in soothing rusty shades. Some of the bathrooms have jacuzzi baths, while others come with massage showers. Repro versions of the sofa Dali created, inspired by Mae West's lips, decorate the lobby, to match the crimson velvet thrones in the courtyard. Rooms overlooking the street can be noisy.

Hotel Le Méridien Barcelona

La Rambla 111 (93 318 62 00, www.barcelona.lemeridien.com). Metro Liceu. €€€€.

After a €23-million refurb, Le Meridien has maintained its conservative look, opting for classy hardwood floors, polished marble and leather furnishings, along with Egyptian cotton bedlinen, rain showers and plasma-screen TVs. However, at this price you'd expect more facilities: a rooftop pool, perhaps, or at least a decked terrace. Under-12s stay free.

Hotel Neri

C/Sant Sever 5 (93 304 06 55, www. hotelneri.com). Metro Jaume I. €€€€.

Arguably the sexiest boutique in town, in a former 18th-century palace. The lobby-cum-library teams flagstone floors with red velvet chaises longues and lashings of gold leaf, though rooms are more

---

SHORTLIST

Best new luxury hotels
- Hotel Bagués (see p164)
- Hotel Espanya (see p171)
- Mandarin Oriental (see p175)
- W Hotel (see p171)

Best chain hotels
- Barceló Raval (see p169)
- Room-mate Emma (see p176)

Best budget hotels
- Barcelona Urbany (see p176)
- Bonic Guesthouse (see p164)
- Hotel Curious (see p171)

Old-style class
- Casa Fuster (see p176)
- Hotel Claris (see p174)
- Hotel Majestic (see p174)

Designer glitz
- Hotel Murmuri (see p174)
- Hotel Soho (see p175)
- Neri Hotel (see left)

Cheap and chic
- Banys Orientals (see p168)
- Market Hotel (see p176)

Best for cocktails
- Hotel Arts (see p171)
- Hotel Axel (see p173)
- Hotel Murmuri (p174)

Rooms with a view
- Grand Hotel Central (see p168)
- Hotel Arts (see p171)

Recession beaters
- Hostal Gat Raval (see p169)
- Hostal Gat Xino (see p169)
- Hostal Girona (see p173)

Best for a dip
- Grand Hotel Central (see p168)
- Hotel Arts (see p171)
- Pullmann Skipper (p171)

ESSENTIALS

Casa Camper p169

understated. Natural materials and rustic finishes stand in stylish contrast to lavish satins, sharp design and high-tech perks (hi-fis, plasma-screen TVs). There's a lush rooftop garden.

Hotel Petit Palace Opera Garden

C/Boquería 10 (93 302 00 92, www.hthoteles.com). Metro Liceu. **€€€**.
The rooms are white and futuristic, with a different zingy colour on each floor and opera scores printed on the walls above the beds. Lamps and chairs lend a 1960s air, so pack your kinky boots and groovy flares to enjoy your stay to the full. Some bathrooms have massage showers, others jacuzzi baths. Only breakfast is served in the chic dining room. There's a little-known public garden at the back; a real luxury in this densely packed area.

Pensió Alamar

C/Comtessa de Sobradiel 1, 1º-2ª (93 302 50 12, www.pensioalamar.com). Metro Jaume I or Liceu. **€**.
A basic, but tasteful family-run *hostal*. Beds are new and excellent quality, and windows are double-glazed to keep noise to a minimum. The downside is that 12 rooms share two bathrooms. There are discounts for longer stays, and larger rooms for families. Single travellers are made welcome, with no supplement for occupying a double, and guests can do their laundry and cook in a well-equipped kitchen.

Pensión Hostal Mari-Luz

C/Palau 4 (93 317 34 63, www. pensionmariluz.com). Metro Jaume I or Liceu. **€**.
The entrance and staircase of this 18th-century stone building are imposing, but you then have to climb several flights of stairs to reach the Mari-Luz. The effort is well worth it – stripped wood doors and old floor tiles add character to the otherwise plain but quiet rooms, some of which face a plant-filled inner courtyard. There are dorms as well as double and triple rooms.

All aboard

With real-estate prices going through the roof, global crisis notwithstanding, hoteliers are increasingly looking out to sea. Sweden has its Salt & Sill, Dubai has the retired QE2, and never one to be outdone, Barcelona too has its very own super-duper 'yacht hotel'.

The **Sunborn Barcelona** docked in the Port Fòrum in the summer of 2009, and is the second such project for Finnish-owned Sunborn International (the first is in Finland, the next is scheduled for London). It's been granted a 25-year licence in Barcelona, the hope being that it will attract well-heeled pleasure-seekers to the Distrito 22@, a futuristic neighbourhood of skyscrapers and technology businesses that has so far failed to excite the leisure traveller.

That could all change, however, as this imposing vessel takes its place among the gin palaces and pleasure craft of the newly built quayside. Fuelled by solar energy provided by the extraordinary photovoltaic pergola that dominates the complex, the Sunborn is built over six floors, each with 180 suites, boasting private terraces and vast picture windows on to the big blue, sleek wooden floors and lots of pearl-coloured leather. An infinity pool will crown the rooftop, along with a spa and sports facilities, and a Michelin-starred chef is currently being sought to head up the main restaurant, all at the cool cost of €152 million.

■ www.sunborninternational.com

Hostal Gat Xino

Born & Sant Pere

Banys Orientals

C/Argenteria 37 (93 268 84 60,
www.hotelbanysorientals.com). Metro
Jaume I. €€.

Banys Orientals is one of the best deals to be found in Barcelona. It exudes cool, from its location at the heart of the Born to the stylish shades-of-grey minimalism of its rooms, and nice touches such as complimentary mineral water on the landings. The main debit is the small size of some of the double rooms.

Chic&basic

C/Princesa 50 (93 295 46 52,
www.chicandbasic.com). Metro Arc de
Triomf or Jaume I. €€.

This first floor *hostal* takes white-on-white to extremes, though not entirely unsuccessfully. Rooms come with white cotton linen, white floors, white walls, mirrored cornicing and glassed-in shower cabinets in the middle. Elsewhere the playful vibe continues with a chill-out room furnished with fairytale sofas and pouffes; it also has tea- and coffee-making facilities and a fridge.

Ciutat Barcelona

C/Princesa 35 (93 269 74 75,
www.ciutatbarcelona.com). Metro
Jaume I. €€.

The Ciutat Barcelona is a jolly, primary-coloured affair, offering a refreshing contrast to the chocolate and charcoal shades of most of Barca's smart hotels. Retro shapes prevail in the furnishings and decoration, and rooms are very small but reasonably comfortable. The big draw, however, is a swanky wood-decked roof terrace complete with shaded tables and a decent-sized plunge pool.

Grand Hotel Central

Via Laietana 30 (93 295 79 00,
www.grandhotelcentral.com). Metro
Jaume I. €€€.

Another of the recent wave of Barcelona hotels to adhere to the unwritten design protocol that grey is the new black. The Central's shadowy, Hitchcockian corridors open up on to sleekly appointed rooms that come with flatscreen televisions, DVD players and Korres toiletries. But the real charm of the hotel lies on the roof, in the shape of a vertiginous infinity pool.

Pensió 2000

C/Sant Pere Més Alt 6, 1° (93 310 74 66, www.pensio2000.com). Metro Urquinaona. €.

Pensió 2000 is a good-value *pensión* located opposite the Palau de la Música. Only two of the rooms are en suite, but the shared facilities are kept clean. The large rooms make it suitable for holidaying families.

Raval

Barceló Raval

Rambla del Raval 17-21 (93 320 14 90, 902 101 001, www.barceloraval.com). Metro Liceu.

This bleeding-edge, cylindrical building dominates the Rambla del Raval and promises to become something of an icon of the *barrio*. The smart roof terrace has 360° views (key buildings are labelled from a viewing platform) and a plunge pool. Rooms are starkly modern, with a technology port for all your multimedia needs and a Nespresso machine.

Casa Camper

C/Elisabets 11 (93 342 62 80, www.casacamper.com). Metro Catalunya. €€€.

Devised by the Mallorcan footwear giant, this quirky concept-fest has as one of its USPs a bedroom-living room arrangement so that you get two spaces for the price of one. Less cleverly, the living rooms are situated across the corridor from the bedrooms, so to enjoy the cinema-sized TV and hammock, pack respectable pyjamas or risk the dash of shame. There are no minibars, but you can take free snacks from the café.

Hostal Gat Raval

C/Joaquín Costa 44, 2° (93 481 66 70, www.gataccommodation.com). Metro Universitat. €.

Smart, clean and funky with small, reasonably bright rooms, each boasting a work by a local artist. Some rooms have balconies. The downsides are that nearly all the bathrooms are communal (though very clean) and there is no lift. The same owners run the nearby **Hostal Gat Xino** (93 324 88 33), which has a similar cheap and chic vibe.

Hotel Ciutat Vella

C/Tallers 66 (93 481 37 99, www.hotelciutatvella.com). Metro Catalunya or Universitat. €€.

This is a fun and funky option when the budget's tight. Rooms and decor are done simply in white with splashes of pillarbox red. There's Wi-Fi and a hearty breakfast served in a lounge downstairs, and best of all a fabulously kitsch Astroturf rooftop terrace with hot tub.

Hotel Curious p171

ESSENTIALS

Hotel Claris p174

Hotel Curious

*C/Carme 25 (93 301 44 84, www.hotel
curious.com). Metro Liceu.* €€.
Curious is an unusual new addition to
the Raval with a more art-based
approach to design. The rather funky
mauve-hued lobby is in total contrast
to more monotone bedrooms, which
have giant black and white prints
depicting Barcelona *barrios*.

Hotel España

NEW *C/Sant Pau 9-11 (93 550 00 00,
www.hotelespanya.com). Metro Liceu.* €€.
See box, p172.

Hotel Mesón Castilla

*C/Valldonzella 5 (93 318 21 82,
www.mesoncastilla.com). Metro
Universitat.* €€.
For a change from modern design,
check into this hotel, which opened in
1952. Communal areas are full of
antiques, while rooms have tiled floors
and are decorated with hand-painted
furniture. The best rooms have terraces.

Hotel Sant Agustí

*Plaça Sant Agustí 3 (93 318 16 58,
www.hotelsa.com). Metro Liceu.* €€.
With its sandstone walls and huge,
arched windows that look out on to the
plaça, not to mention the pink-marble
lobby filled with forest-green furniture,
this imposing hotel is the oldest in
town. Previously the Convent of St
Augustine, the building was converted
into a hotel in 1840. Rooms are spacious and comfortable, but there's no
soundproofing. Good buffet breakfast.

Barceloneta & the Ports

Hotel Arts

*C/Marina 19-21 (93 221 10 00,
www.hotelartsbarcelona.com). Metro
Ciutadella-Vila Olímpica.* €€€€.
The 44-storey, Ritz-Carlton-run Arts
scores top marks for service. Bang &
Olufsen CD players, interactive TV, sea

and city views and a 'Club' floor for
VIPs are just some of the perks. Avant-
garde flower displays make the lobby a
pleasant place to hang out. A beachfront
pool overlooks Gehry's *Fish* sculpture,
and a range of bars and restaurants
cater to every taste.

Pullmann Skipper

*Avda Litoral 10 (93 221 65 65,
www.pullmanhotels.com). Metro
Ciutadella.* €€€.
Situated near the Port Olímpic, the
Skipper is a swish, American-style five-
star reeling in long-weekenders with
some good package deals. It's good on
outdoor space with a large heated pool,
hammocks on the lawns and a full-
service spa. Additional treats include a
lazy Sunday brunch, luxury rooftop
pool and bar, and the AB Skipper yacht,
which guests can charter for private use.

W Hotel

*Plaça de la Rosa dels Vents 1 (93 295
28 00, www.whotels.com/barcelona).
Metro Barceloneta, then bus 17.*
€€€€.
Barcelona's answer to Dubai's Burj Al
Arab opened its doors in 2009 to a clam-
our of protest from local residents who
feel it disrupts the view of the horizon.
No one can deny it's a handsome building, however, and the lobby and terraces are masterpieces of design, as is
the restaurant and tapas bar, overseen
by masterchef Carles Abellan. Rooms
are relatively simply done out, the better to appreciate the incredible views of
the sea or city (request your preference
when booking).

Montjuïc & Poble Sec

Hostal BCN Port

*Avda Paral·lel 15 (93 324 95 00,
www.hostalbcnport.com). Metro
Drassanes or Paral·lel.* €.
A smart *hostal* near the ferry port, the
BCN Port has rooms that are furnished
in a chic contemporary style with not
a hint of the kitsch decor prevalent in

Viva the España!

One of the city's iconic hotels is restored to its former glory.

Though it's an exciting addition to the accommodation scene, it would be wrong – by about 150 years – to call the España a new hotel. First opened in 1859, it has had several heydays (and subsequent falls from grace).

In 1892, the wealthy Miguel Salvador bought the property and then spent lavishly on refurbishments, introducing the just-invented electricity and employing the leading artists of the day, among them some of the giants of Modernisme. You take your buffet breakfast in the Mermaid Salon, surrounded by breathtaking ceramic sea-life murals, designed by Ramon Casas, and sip cocktails in front of an elaborate turn-of-the-century fireplace by Eusebi Arnau, another of the sought-after names of the turn of the last century.

With a buzzing bar and foyer, it's no museum, but it's nonetheless a privilege to be able to stop and stare, relishing the details: the depictions of tiny sea creatures; the women painted on the walls of the interior patio bidding you '*Bon dia*' (good morning) and '*Bona nit*' (good night) as you enter and leave; the elegant sgraffiti on the staircase and in the light-filled atrium.

The hotel re-opened in late 2010 after a full restoration and update of some areas (contemporary designs have been used, too, notably in the Pati de les Monges internal quadrangle – though those gold balls rising from the courtyard are inspired by the breath of Modernista mermaids – and comfortably stylish taupe and brown rooms). The fabulously ornate restaurant has been taken over by triple Michelin-starred chef Martín Berasategui, though his control from the mothership in San Sebastián is mostly nominal.

Insider tip: ask for a room on the fourth floor: far enough up to give some distance from the occasional street noise (you're just Raval-side of La Rambla) and with slightly higher ceilings.
■ Hotel España (see p171).

more traditional budget places. All the rooms have en-suite bathrooms, as well as televisions and air-conditioning.

Eixample

Casanova BCN Hotel
Gran Via de les Corts Catalanes 559 (93 396 48 00, www.casanovabcn hotel.com). Metro Universitat or Urgell. **€€€.**
A smart hotel where each room has its own Nespresso machine, suites have two bathrooms, giant candles are scattered through the lounge areas and there's a small spa. Plans for a rooftop pool have been put on hold, but there's a Med-Mex restaurant, and DJs play in the bar on Friday and Saturday nights.

Hostal L'Antic Espai
Gran Via de les Corts Catalanes 660, pral (93 304 19 45, www.antice spai.com). Metro Passeig de Gràcia or Urquinaona. **€€.**
A real find for lovers of character. Each room is rammed with antiques, be it an ornately carved wooden bedhead, a teardrop chandelier, a faux Louis XV dresser or a silken throw. All have en-suite bathrooms and 21st-century gadgetry such as flatscreen TVs and free Wi-Fi, some have balconies, and there's a patio with silk flowers.

Hostal Eden
C/Balmes 55, pral 1ª (93 452 66 20, www.hostaleden.net). Metro Passeig de Gràcia or Universitat. **€.**
Located on three floors of a Modernista building, this warm and relaxed *hostal* with friendly, helpful staff offers free internet access and has a sunny patio with a shower for cooling off. The best rooms have marble bathrooms with corner baths, and Nos.114 and 115, at the rear, are quiet and have large windows overlooking the patio.

Hostal Girona
C/Girona 24, 1º (93 265 02 59, www. hostalgirona.com). Metro Urquinaona. **€.**

A gem of a *hostal*, filled with antiques, chandeliers and oriental rugs. The rooms may be on the simple side, but all have charm, with tall windows and tiled floors. It's worth splashing out on rooms in the refurbished wing with ensuite bathrooms, although some in the old wing have ensuite showers. Brighter, outward-facing rooms have small balconies overlooking C/Girona or bigger balconies on to a huge and quiet patio.

Hostal Goya
C/Pau Claris 74, 1º (93 302 25 65, www.hostalgoya.com). Metro Urquinaona. **€€.**
Located in a typical Eixample building with fabulous tiled floors, the bedrooms are done out in chocolates and creams, with comfortable beds, chunky duvets and cushions; the bathrooms are equally luxurious. The best rooms either give on to the street or the terrace at the back. Guests leaving the city in the evening can still use a bathroom to shower and change before they go.

Hostal San Remo
C/Ausiàs Marc 19, 1º-2ª (93 302 19 89, www.hostalsanremo.com). Metro Urquinaona. **€.**
Staying in this bright, neat and peaceful apartment feels a bit like staying with an amenable relative. The friendly owner, Rosa, and her dog live on site and take good care of their guests. All seven rooms have air-conditioning and shiny bedspreads; five out of seven have ensuite bathrooms, and most of them have a little balcony and double glazing.

Hotel Axel
C/Aribau 33 (93 323 93 93, www.axel hotels.com). Metro Universitat. **€€€.**
Housed in a Modernista building, with multi-coloured tiles in the lobby and bright rooms with bleached floors. The mostly gay, good-looking staff sport T-shirts with the logo 'heterofriendly', and everyone is made welcome. King-size beds come as standard, as does free mineral water and erotic artworks. 'Superior'

rooms have hydro-massage baths and stained-glass gallery balconies. The Sky Bar on the rooftop is where it all happens, with a little pool, jacuzzi, sun deck, sauna and steam room.

Hotel Claris

C/Pau Claris 150 (93 487 62 62, www.derbyhotels.com). Metro Passeig de Gràcia. €€€.
Antiques and contemporary design merge behind the neo-classical exterior of the Hotel Claris, which contains the largest private collection of Egyptian art in Spain. Some bedrooms are on the small side, while others are duplex, but all have Chesterfield sofas and plenty of art. The rooftop pool is just about big enough to swim in, with plenty of loungers, and a cocktail bar and DJ.

Hotel Constanza

C/Bruc 33 (93 270 19 10, www.hotel constanza.com). Metro Urquinaona. €€.
This quiet and pleasant boutique hotel continues to please. The theme is oriental, with Japanese silk screens, orchid and pebble prints and sleek teak furniture creating an atmosphere of Zen-like calm. The best rooms are at the back, some with smart walled-in terraces, and it has comfortable single rooms. There's a good buffet breakfast.

Hotel Granados 83

C/Enric Granados 83 (93 492 96 70, www.derbyhotels.com). Metro Diagonal. €€€.
The original ironwork structure of this former hospital lends an unexpectedly industrial feel to the Granados 83. The bare-bricked rooms include duplex and triplex versions, some with their own terraces and plunge pools. For mortals in the standard rooms, there is a rooftop pool and sun deck.

Hotel Majestic

Passeig de Gràcia 68 (93 488 17 17, www.hotelmajestic.es). Metro Passeig de Gràcia. €€€€.
Behind a neo-classical façade lies a panoply of perks, such as a service that allows you to print a selection of international newspapers. Non-guests can enjoy the high life in the rooftop pool and gym, which offer wonderful views out over the city. Rooms are suitably opulent, decorated with classical flair. The Drolma restaurant is excellent, if pricey.

Hotel Murmuri

Rambla Catalunya 104 (93 550 06 00, www.murmuri.com). Metro Diagonal. €€€€.
Murmuri has an effortless chic about it – creamy tones with gilt trim and

sculpted flower arrangements lend a cool, calm atmosphere, attracting a well-heeled, grown-up crowd, and there's a lively lobby for drinks and a slick Thai restaurant. Bedrooms are spacious and airy. For a sophisticated shopping weekend at the heart of the designer quarter, few places beat it.

Hotel Omm

C/Rosselló 265 (93 445 40 00, www. hotelomm.es). Metro Diagonal. €€€.
Bedrooms are light and bright, as opposed to the black on black corridors, and enjoy what may be the city's comfiest beds and double bathrooms. The restaurant boasts a Michelin star, but there's also a healthy bistro alternative, as well as an extensive bar. A trendy club occupies the perfectly soundproofed basement, and a bar and pool area perches on the roof with views straight over Gaudí's La Pedrera next door.

Hotel Pulitzer

C/Bergara 8 (93 481 67 67, www.hotel pulitzer.es). Metro Catalunya. €€€.
A discreet façade reveals an impressive lobby that's stuffed with comfortable white leather sofas, a reading area and a swanky bar and restaurant. The rooftop terrace is a fabulous spot for a cocktail, with squishy loungers, scented candles, tropical plants and views across the city. The rooms themselves are not big, but they are neatly decorated and come with cool grey marble, fluffy pillows and leather trim.

Hotel Soho

Gran Via de les Corts Catalanes 543-545 (93 552 96 10, www.nn hotels.com). Metro Urgell. €€€.
A duplex-height lobby filled with the light of numerous glass installations leads into a comfortable business space with library, desks, sofas, a small terrace and free internet. There's a cocktail bar and plunge pool on the roof. The large bedrooms have been done out in tasteful olive greens and wood, with gargantuan beds, LCD-screen TVs and glass bathrooms by Philippe Starck. The best have spacious terraces.

Mandarin Oriental

Passeig de Gràcia 38-40 (93 151 88 88, www.mandarinoriental.com/barcelona). Metro Passeig de Gràcia. €€€€.
Top designer Patricia Urquiola's high-design Mandarin Oriental oozes old-style glamour with a contemporary twist. Originally a bank, life in the hotel centres around the old trading floor – now a 'Mediterrasian' bistro – and the slick Bankers Bar, peopled by Catalan

Room-mate Emma p176

ESSENTIALS

TV celebs downing designer cocktails. Rooms are as plush as you could hope for, big on bespoke Urquiola pieces like 'Fat' sofas, cylindrical bathtubs and 'Caboche' chandeliers.

Market Hotel

Passatge Sant Antoni Abat 10 (93 325 12 05, www.markethotel.com.es). Metro Sant Antoni. €€.
The people who brought the wildly successful Quinze Nits chain of restaurants to Barcelona have gone on to apply their low-budget, high-design approach to this hotel. The monochrome rooms, though not huge, are comfortable and stylish for the price and downstairs is a handsome and keenly priced restaurant, typical of the group.

Room-mate Emma

C/Rosselló 205 (93 238 5606, www.room-matehotels.com). Metro Diagonal. €€.
The arrival of 'Emma' is a boon for the design-conscious and cash-strapped. The hotel reflects a fictional personality, as do all in the chain, in this case a graphic designer with aspirations to creating the next space hotel. The hotel's undulating ceilings, walls studded with sequins and mood lighting add va-va-voom. Rooms are small – if you value space, check into the suite with a private terrace and hot tub – but the pay-off is bouncy beds, power showers and a proper breakfast served until noon.

the5rooms

C/Pau Claris 72 (93 342 78 80, www.thefiverooms.com). Metro Catalunya or Urquinaona. €€€.
A chic and comfortable B&B in a handsome building, where the delightful Jessica Delgado encourages guests to feel at home. Books and magazines are dotted around the stylish sitting areas and bedrooms, and breakfast is served at any time of day. There are now two apartments in the neighbouring building and plans to add more rooms (and, presumably, a new name).

Villa Emilia

C/Calàbria 115-117 (93 252 52 85, www.hotelvillaemilia.com). Metro Rocafort. €€€.
There's not much to discover in the immediate vicinity but Emilia compensates with the glam Zinc Bar in the lobby, complete with black chandeliers, red velvet sofas and quality tapas. The pièce de résistance, however, is the open-air lounge on the rooftop, with sofas, candles, a well-stocked bar and a buzzer for service. The rooms are decent with large comfortable beds, and aim for a good night's sleep rather than design awards.

Casa Fuster

Passeig de Gràcia 132 (93 255 30 00, www.hotelcasafuster.com). Metro Diagonal. €€€€.
When the Fuster opened, many complained that this historic Modernista building should have been preserved as a public space. The famed on-site Café Viennese answers that demand somewhat, though when a cup of tea costs €15 you won't find many locals here. Service is spot on; rooms, while rather small, feel regal in their muted tones, and there are fresh flowers daily. The rooftop pool has a jacuzzi and great views, while the gourmet restaurant has an insider feel.

Barcelona Urbany

Avda Meridiana 97, Clot (93 245 84 14, www.barcelonaurbany.com). Metro Clot. €.
Forget the institutional youth hostels of old, with their mouldy showers and threadbare towels – the Urbany has brought about a paradigm shift in the market. For as little as €12 you can lie in a clean and comfortable dorm bed surfing the net, watch DVDs in a common room, swim in the pool or take a jacuzzi. Oh, and breakfast is included.

Getting Around

Arriving & leaving

By air

Aeroport de Barcelona

902 40 47 04, www.aena.es.
Barcelona's airport is at El Prat, south-west of the city. There are now two main terminals: the new Terminal 1 (known as T1), and Terminal 2 (T2). The latter comprises the old terminals formerly called A, B and C, and now called T2A, T2B and T2C. Tourist information desks and currency exchanges are found in both terminals.

Aerobús

The airport bus (information 010, www.aerobusbcn.com) runs two routes from Plaça Catalunya: bus A1 for T1 and A2 for T2. Buses to the airport go from Plaça Catalunya (in front of El Corte Inglés), stopping at Sants station and Plaça Espanya. Buses run every 8-10mins, leaving the airport from 6am-1am and returning from Plaça Catalunya 5.30am-12.30am. The trip takes 35-45mins; a single is €5.30, a return €9.15. At night the N17 runs every 20 mins between the airport (from 10pm) and Plaça Catalunya (from 11pm), with several stops on the way, including Plaça d'Espanya and Plaça Universitat. The last departure is at 4.50am. Journey time is 45 mins.

Airport trains

The long overhead walkway between terminals 2A and 2B leads to the train station. The Cercanías train (R2 Nord) leaves the airport at 08 and 38 mins past the hour (except the first train, which leaves at 5.42am) until 11.38pm, stopping at Barcelona Sants and Passeig de Gràcia. Trains to the airport leave Barcelona Sants at 09 and 39 mins past the hour (except the first train, which leaves at 5.35am), until 11.09pm daily (7mins earlier from Passeig de Gràcia, departing at 02 and 28 mins past the hour). The journey takes 18-25mins and costs €1.60 one way (no return tickets). Tickets are only valid for two hours after purchase (902 32 03 20, www.renfe.es/cercanias). The T-10 Zone 1 metro pass is also valid.

Taxis from the airport

The basic taxi fare from the airport to central Barcelona should be around €20-€26, including a €3.10 airport supplement. Fares are about 15 per cent higher after 8pm and at weekends. There is a €1 supplement for each large piece of luggage placed in the car boot. All licensed cab drivers use the ranks outside the terminals.

By bus

Most long-distance coaches (both national and international) stop or terminate at **Estació d'Autobusos Barcelona-Nord** (C/Alí Bei 80, 902 26 06 06, www.barcelonanord.com). Some international Eurolines services (information 93 367 44 00, www.eurolines.es) begin and end journeys at Sants.

By train

Most long-distance services operated by the Spanish state railway company **RENFE** run from Barcelona-Sants station, easily reached by metro. A few services from the French border or south to Tarragona stop at the

Estació de França in the Born, near the Barceloneta metro, but it's otherwise sparsely served. Many trains stop at Passeig de Gràcia or Plaça Catalunya, which can be the handiest for the city centre.

RENFE

902 320 320, www.renfe.es.
Open 00.15am-11.50pm daily.
RENFE tickets can be bought online, at train stations, travel agents or reserved over the phone and delivered to an address or hotel for a small extra fee. They have some English-speaking phone operators.

Public transport

Although it's run by different organisations, Barcelona public transport is highly integrated, with the same tickets valid for up to four changes of transport on bus, tram, local train and metro lines as long as you do it within 75 minutes. The **metro** is generally the quickest and easiest way of getting around the city. All metro lines operate from 5am to midnight Monday to Thursday, Sunday and public holidays; 5am to 2am Friday, and all through Saturday night. Buses run throughout the night and to areas not covered by the metro system. Local buses and the metro are run by the city transport authority (**TMB**). Two underground train lines connect with the metro but are run by Catalan government railways, the **FGC**. One runs north from Plaça Catalunya; the other runs west from Plaça Espanya to Cornellà. The two main tram routes are of limited use to visitors.

FGC information

Vestibule, Plaça Catalunya FGC station (93 205 15 15, www.fgc.net).
Open 7am-9pm Mon-Fri.
Other locations FGC Plaça d'Espanya (open 9am-2pm, 4-7pm Mon-Fri).

TMB information

Main vestibule, Universitat metro station, Eixample (93 318 70 74, www.tmb.net). **Open** 8am-8pm Mon-Fri.
Other locations vestibule, Metro Sants Estació & Sagrada Familia (both 7am-9pm Mon-Fri; Sants also opens 9am-7pm Sat, 9am-2pm Sun); vestibule, Metro Diagonal (8am-8pm Mon-Fri).

Buses

Many city bus routes originate in or pass through the city centre, at Plaça Catalunya, Plaça Universitat and Plaça Urquinaona. However, they often run along different parallel streets, due to the city's one-way system. Not all stops are labelled and street signs are not always easy to locate. Most routes run 6am-10.30pm daily except Sundays. There's usually a bus every 10-15mins, but they're less frequent before 8am, after 9pm and on Saturdays. On Sundays, buses are less frequent still; a few do not run at all.

Board at the front and disembark through the middle or rear doors. Only single tickets can be bought from the driver; if you have a *targeta,* insert it into the machine behind the driver as you board.

Fares and tickets

Travel in the Barcelona urban area has a flat fare of €1.45 per journey, but multi-journey tickets or *targetes* are better value. The basic ten-trip *targeta* is the **T-10** (Catalan *Te-Deu,* Spanish *Te-Diez,* €8.25), which can be shared by any number of people travelling simultaneously; the ticket is validated in the machines on the metro, train or bus once per person per journey. The T-10 offers access to all five of the city's main transport systems (local RENFE and FGC trains within the main metropolitan area, the metro, tram and buses). To transfer, insert your card into a machine a second time; unless 75 minutes have elapsed since your last journey, another unit will not be deducted. Single tickets don't allow free transfers.

You can buy T-10s at newsstands and Servi-Caixa cashpoints as well as metro and train stations, but not on buses.

Trams

Lines T1, T2 and T3 go from Plaça Francesc Macià, Zona Alta, to the outskirts of the city. The fourth line is more useful to visitors and runs from Ciutadella-Vila Olímpica (also a metro stop), via Glòries and the Fòrum.

All trams are fully accessible for wheelchair-users and are part of the integrated TMB *targeta* system: simply insert the ticket into the machine as you board. You can buy integrated tickets and single tickets from the machines at tram stops.

Tram information
Trambaix (902 19 32 75, www.tram bcn.com). **Open** *July, Aug* Mon-Fri 8am-3pm. *Sept-June* 9am-2pm, 4-7pm Mon-Thur; 9am-2pm Fri.

Taxis

It's usually easy to find one of the 10,500 black and yellow taxis. There are ranks at railway and bus stations, in main squares and throughout the city, but taxis can also be hailed on the street when they show a green light on the roof and a sign saying '*lliure/libre*' (free) behind the windscreen. Information on taxi fares, ranks and regulations can be found at www.emt-amb.com.

Fares
Current rates and supplements are shown inside cabs on a sticker on the rear side window (in English).

The basic fare for a taxi hailed in the street is €2, which is what the meter should register when you set off. The basic rates (90¢/km) apply 8am-8pm Mon-Fri; at other times, including public holidays, the rate is €1.15/km.

There are supplements for luggage (€1), for the airport (€3.10), Sants train station (€2.10), and the port (€2.10), and for nights such as New Year's Eve (€3.10), as well as a waiting charge. Taxi drivers are not required to carry more than €20 in change; few accept credit cards. There is a €2 supplement from midnight to 6am on Friday, Saturday and Sunday. And if a public holiday falls on one of these days, there's an additional €3.10 supplement.

Radio cabs
These companies take bookings 24 hours daily. Phone cabs start the meter when a call is answered but, by the time it picks you up, it should not display more than €3.40 during weekdays and €4.20 at night, at weekends or public holidays.
Barnataxi *93 322 22 22*.
Fono-Taxi *93 300 11 00*.
Ràdio Taxi *'033' 93 303 30 33*.
Servi-Taxi *93 330 03 00*.
Taxi Groc *93 358 11 11*.
Taxi Miramar *93 433 10 20*.

Driving
Car & motorbike hire

Car hire is relatively pricey, but it's a competitive market so shop around. Check carefully what's included: ideally, you want unlimited mileage, 16% VAT (IVA) included and full insurance cover (*seguro todo riesgo*) rather than the third-party minimum (*seguro obligatorio*). You'll need a credit card as a guarantee. Most companies require you to have

ESSENTIALS

had a licence for at least a year; many also enforce a minimum age limit.

Europcar *93 491 48 22, reservations 902 10 50 30, www.europcar.com.*

Motissimo *93 490 84 01, www.motissimo.es.*

Pepecar *807 41 42 43, www.pepecar.com.*

Vanguard *93 439 38 80, www.vanguardrent.com.*

Parking

Parking is fiendishly complicated, and municipal police are quick to hand out tickets or tow away cars. In some parts of the old city, access is limited to residents for much of the day. In some Old City streets, time-controlled bollards pop up, meaning your car may get stuck. Wherever you are, don't park in front of doors signed '*Gual Permanent*', indicating an entry with 24-hour right of access.

Pay and display areas

The Àrea Verda contains zones only for use of residents (most of the Old City and centre of Gràcia – look out for 'Àrea residents' signs). Elsewhere in central Barcelona, non-residents pay €2.42/hr with a 1hr, 2hr or 3hr maximum stay (check the meter).

If you overstay by no more than an hour, you can cancel the fine by paying an extra €6; to do so, press *Anul·lar denùncia* on the machine, insert €6, then press Ticket. Some machines accept cards (AmEx, MC, V); none accept notes or give change. For information, check www.bcn.cat/areaverda or call 010.

Car parks

Car parks ('*parkings*') are signalled by a white 'P' on a blue sign. SABA (Plaça Catalunya, Plaça Urquinaona, Rambla Catalunya, Avda Catedral, airport and elsewhere; 93 230 56 00,

902 28 30 80, www.saba.es) costs around €2.75/hr, while SMASSA car parks (Plaça Catalunya 23, C/Hospital 25-29, Avda Francesc Cambó 10, Passeig de Gràcia 60, and elsewhere; www.bsmsa.cat/mobilitat) cost €2.30-€2.80/hr.

Towed vehicles

If the police have towed your car, they should leave a triangular sticker on the pavement where it stood. The sticker should let you know to which pound it's been taken. If not, call 901 513 151; staff generally don't speak English. Recovering your vehicle within 4hrs costs €150.70, with each extra hour costing €1.96, or €19.50 per day. You'll also have to pay a fine to the police, which varies. You'll need your passport and documentation, or the rental contract, to prove ownership.

Petrol

Most *gasolineres* (petrol stations) have unleaded (*sense plom/sin plomo*), regular (super) and diesel (gas-oil). Petrol is cheaper in Spain than it is in most northern European countries.

Cycling

There's a network of bike lanes (*carrils bici*) along major avenues and by the seafront; local authorities are keen to promote cycling. However, weekday traffic can be risky, despite legislation that states that drivers must slow down near cyclists. No more than two bikes may ride side by side. Cycling information can be found at www.bcn.cat/bicicleta.

Un Cotxe Menys

C/Esparteria 3, Born (93 268 21 05, www.bicicletabarcelona.com). Metro Barceloneta. **Open** 10am-7pm daily.

Resources A-Z

For information on travelling to Spain from within the European Union, including details of visa regulations and healthcare provision, see the EU's travel website: http://europe.eu/travel.

Accident & emergency

The following lines are available 24 hours a day.

Emergency services *112*. Police, fire or ambulance.
Ambulance/Ambulància *061*. In a medical emergency, go to the casualty department (*Urgències*) of any of the main public hospitals. All are open 24 hours daily.
Centre d'Urgències Perecamps *Avda Drassanes 13-15, Raval (93 441 06 00). Metro Drassanes or Paral·lel.*
Hospital Clínic *C/Villarroel 170, Eixample (93 227 54 00). Metro Hospital Clínic.*
Hospital del Mar *Passeig Marítim 25-29, Barceloneta (93 248 30 00). Metro Ciutadella-Vila Olímpica.*
Hospital Dos de Maig *C/Dos de Maig 301, Eixample (93 507 27 00). Metro Sant Pau-Dos de Maig.*
Hospital de Sant Pau *C/Sant Quintí 89, Eixample (93 291 90 00). Metro Sant Pau-Dos de Maig.*

Pharmacies

Pharmacies (*farmàcies/farmacias*) are signalled by green and red neon crosses. Most are open 9am-1.30pm and 4.30-8pm weekdays, and 9am-1.30pm on Saturdays. About a dozen operate around the clock, while more have late opening hours; some of the most central are listed below. The full list of chemists that stay open late and overnight is posted daily outside every pharmacy and given in the newspapers. You

can also call 010 or 098. At night, duty pharmacies often appear closed – just knock on the shutters.
Farmàcia Alvarez *Passeig de Gràcia 26, Eixample (93 302 11 24). Metro Passeig de Gràcia.* **Open** 8am-10.30pm Mon-Thur; 8am-midnight Fri; 9am-midnight Sat.
Farmàcia Cervera *C/Muntaner 254, Eixample (93 200 09 96). Metro Diagonal/FGC Gràcia.* **Open** 24hrs daily.
Farmàcia Clapés *La Rambla 98, Barri Gòtic (93 301 28 43). Metro Liceu.* **Open** 24hrs daily.
Farmàcia Vilar *Vestíbule, Estació de Sants, Sants (93 490 92 07). Metro Sants Estació.* **Open** 7am-10.30pm Mon-Fri; 8am-10.30pm Sat, Sun.

Consulates

Australian Consulate *Avda Diagonal 458, 3º, Eixample (93 490 90 13, www.spain.embassy.gov.au). Metro Diagonal.* **Open** 10am-noon Mon-Fri. Closed Aug.
British Consulate *Avda Diagonal 477, 13º, Eixample (93 366 62 00, www.ukinspain.com). Metro Hospital Clínic.* **Open** 8.30am-1.30pm Mon-Fri (telephone hours 8am-4pm).
Canadian Consulate *Plaça Catalunya 9, 1º (93 412 72 36, www.canada international.gc.ca). Metro Catalunya.* **Open** 9am-12.30pm Mon-Fri.
Irish Consulate *Gran Via Carles III 94, 10º, Les Corts (93 491 50 21). Metro Maria Cristina.* **Open** 10am-1pm Mon-Fri.
New Zealand Consulate *Travessera de Gràcia 64, 2º, Gràcia (93 209 03 99). Metro Diagonal.* **Open** 9am-2pm, 4-7pm Mon-Fri.
US Consulate *Passeig Reina Elisenda 23, Sarrià (93 280 22 27, www.embusa.es). FGC Reina Elisenda.* **Open** 9am-1pm Mon-Fri.

Credit card loss

Each of these lines has English-speaking staff and is open 24 hours a day.
American Express *902 37 56 37.*
Diners Club *902 40 11 12.*
MasterCard *900 97 12 31.*
Visa *900 99 11 24.*

Customs

Customs declarations are not usually necessary if you arrive in Spain from another EU country and are carrying only legal goods for personal use. The amounts given below are guidelines only:

■ 800 cigarettes, 400 small cigars, 200 cigars or 1kg loose tobacco.
■ 10 litres of spirits (over 22% alcohol), 90 litres of wine or 110 litres of beer.

From a non-EU country or the Canary Islands, you can bring:

■ 200 cigarettes, 100 small cigars, 50 regular cigars or 250g (8.82oz) of tobacco.
■ 1 litre of spirits (over 22% alcohol) or 2 litres of wine or beer.
■ 50g (1.76oz) of perfume.
■ 500g coffee; 100g tea.

Visitors can also bring up to €6,000 in cash into the country without having to declare it. Non-EU residents are able to reclaim VAT (IVA) on some purchases when they leave.

Disabled travellers

The website www.accessible barcelona.com is a good resource for disabled travellers.

Institut Municipal de Persones amb Discapacitat

C/Valencia 344, Eixample (93 413 27 75, www.bcn.cat/accessible). Metro Girona. **Open** *9am-2pm Mon-Fri.*

The city's organisation for the disabled has information on access to venues and can provide a map with wheelchair-friendly itineraries. Call in advance to make an appointment.

Transport

Access for disabled people to local transport still leaves quite a lot to be desired. For wheelchair-users, buses and taxis are usually the best bets. For transport information, call TMB (93 318 70 74) or 010. Transport maps, which can be picked up from transport information offices and metro stations, indicate wheelchair access points and adapted bus routes. For a list of accessible metro stations and bus lines, check www.tmb.cat and click on 'Transport for everyone'.

Electricity

The standard current in Spain is 220V. Plugs are of the type that has two round pins. You'll need a plug adaptor to use British-bought electrical devices. If you have US (110V) equipment, you will need a transformer as well as an adaptor.

Estancs/estancos

Government-run tobacco shops, known as an *estanc/estanco* (at times, just *'tabac'*) and identified by a brown and yellow sign, are important city institutions. Along with tobacco, they also supply postage stamps and envelopes, public transport *targetes* and phonecards.

Internet

There are internet centres all over Barcelona, and the city council has undertaken to bring free Wi-Fi access to 200 public spaces by 2011.

Alsur Café

C/Sant Pere Més Alt 4, Sant Pere (93 310 12 86, www.alsurcafe.com). Metro Urquinaona. **Open** 10am-1am Mon-Thur; 10am-3am Fri, Sat; 10am-1.30am Sun. No credit cards.

Bornet Internet Café

C/Barra de Ferro 3, Born (93 268 15 07, www.bornet-bcn.com). Metro Jaume I. **Open** 10am-11pm Mon-Fri; noon-11pm Sat, Sun.
There are ten terminals in this small café and six more for laptops. One hour is €2.80.

Opening times

Most shops open from 9/10am to 1/2pm, and then 4/5pm to 8/9pm, Monday to Saturday. Many smaller businesses don't reopen on Saturday afternoons. All-day opening is becoming more common, especially for larger establishments.

Markets open at 7/8am; most stalls shut by 2pm, but many open on Fridays and Saturdays until 8pm.

Note that in summer, many of Barcelona's shops and restaurants shut for all or part of August. Many museums close one day each week, usually Mondays.

Police

If you're robbed or attacked, report the incident as soon as possible at the nearest police station (*comisaría*), or dial 112. The most convenient is the 24hr Guàrdia Urbana station (La Rambla 43, 092 or 93 256 24 30), which often has English-speaking officers on duty; they may eventually transfer you to the Mossos d'Esquadra (C/Nou de la Rambla 76, 088 or 93 306 23 00) to formally report the crime.

To do this, you'll need to make an official statement (*denuncia*). It's highly improbable that you will recover your property, but you need the *denuncia* to make an insurance claim. You can also make this statement over the phone or online (902 10 21 12, www.policia.es; except for crimes involving physical violence, or if the perpetrator has been identified). You'll still have to go to the *comisaría* within 72 hours to sign the *denuncia*, but you'll skip some queues.

Post

Letters and postcards weighing up to 20g cost 35¢ within Spain; 65¢ to the rest of Europe; 80¢ to the rest of the world – though anything in a large or non-rectangular envelope costs more. Prices normally rise on 1 Jan. It's easiest to buy stamps at *estancs* (see p182). Mail sent abroad is slow: 5-6 working days in Europe, 8-10 to the USA. Postboxes in the street are yellow, sometimes with a white or blue horn insignia. Postal information is available at www.correos.es or on 902 197 197.

Correu Central

Plaça Antonio López, Barri Gòtic (93 486 80 50). Metro Barceloneta or Jaume I. **Open** 8.30am-9.30pm Mon-Fri; 8.30am-2pm Sat.
Other locations Ronda Universitat 23, Eixample; C/Aragó 282, Eixample (both 8.30am-8.30pm Mon-Fri, 9.30am-1pm Sat).

Smoking

Since January 2011, smoking has been banned in enclosed public areas. Most hotels have non-smoking rooms or floors; although if you ask for a non-smoking room, some hotels may just give you a room that has had the ashtray removed.Most hotels have non-smoking rooms or floors, although if you ask for a non-smoking room, some hotels may just give you a

ESSENTIALS

room that has had the ashtrays removed. Smoking bans in cinemas, theatres and on trains are generally respected, though smoking in banks, offices and on station platforms is still quite common.

Telephones

Normal Spanish phone numbers have nine digits; the area code (93 in the province of Barcelona) must be dialled with all calls, both local and long-distance. Spanish mobile numbers always begin with 6. Numbers starting 900 are freephone lines, while other 90 numbers are special-rate services.

International & long-distance calls

To make an international call, dial 00 and then the country code, followed by the area code (omitting the first zero in UK numbers), and then the number you wish to call. Country codes are as follows: Australia 61; Canada 1; Irish Republic 353; New Zealand 64; South Africa 27; United Kingdom 44; USA 1. To phone Spain from abroad, you should dial the international access code, followed by 34, followed by the required number.

Public phones

The most common type of payphone accepts coins (5¢ up), phonecards and credit cards. There is a multilingual digital display (press 'L' to change language) and written instructions in English and other languages. Calls to directory enquiries on 11818 are free from payphones, but you'll usually have to insert a coin to make the call (it will be returned when you hang up). Telefónica phonecards (*targetes telefònica/tarjetas telefónica*) are sold at newsstands and *estancs*

(see p182). Other cards sold at phone centres, shops and newsstands give cheaper rates on all but local calls. This latter type of card contains a toll-free number to call from any phone.

Tickets

FNAC (see p135) has an efficient ticket desk on its ground floor: it sells tickets to theme parks and sights, but it's especially good for contemporary music concerts and events (it's also one of the main outlets for Sónar tickets). Concert tickets for smaller venues are often sold in record shops and at the venues themselves; check posters for further details. For information on getting tickets to the football, see p151.

ServiCaixa – La Caixa

902 332 211, www.servicaixa.com.
Use the special ServiCaixa ATMs (most larger branches of La Caixa have them), dial 902 33 22 11 or check the website to purchase tickets for cinemas, concerts, plays, museums, amusement parks and Barça games. You'll need the card with which you made the payment when you collect the tickets.

Telentrada – Caixa Catalunya

902 101 212, www.telentrada.com.
Through Tel-entrada you can purchase tickets for theatre performances, cinemas (including the IMAX), concerts, museums and sights over the phone, online or over the counter at any branch of the Caixa Catalunya savings bank. Tickets can be collected from Caixa Catalunya ATMs or the tourist office at Plaça Catalunya (see p185).

Time

Spain is one hour ahead of London, six hours ahead of New York, eight hours behind Sydney and ten hours behind Wellington. In all EU countries clocks move forward one hour on the last weekend of March and back on the last weekend of October.

Tipping

There are no fixed rules for tipping, but locals generally don't tip much. It's fair to leave 5-10 per cent in restaurants, but don't feel you have to if the service has been bad. People sometimes leave a little change in bars: not expected, but appreciated. In taxis, tipping is not standard, but many people will round up to the nearest euro. It's usual to tip hotel porters for carrying your bags.

Tourist information

Centre d'Informació de la Virreina

Palau de la Virreina, La Rambla 99, Barri Gòtic (93 316 10 00,www.bcn. cat/cultura). Metro Liceu. **Open** 10am-8.30pm daily (information office and ticket sales).
The information office of the city's culture department, with details of shows, exhibitions and special events.

Oficines d'Informació Turística

Plaça Catalunya, Eixample (info 93 285 38 34, bookings 93 285 38 33, www. bcn.cat, www.barcelonaturisme.com). Metro Catalunya. **Open** *Office* 9am-9pm daily. *Call centre* 9am-8pm Mon-Fri.
The main office of the city tourist board is underground on the Corte Inglés side of the square: look for big red signs with 'i' in white. It has information, money exchange, a shop and a hotel booking service, and sells phonecards, tickets for shows, sights and public transport.
Other locations C/Ciutat 2, Barri Gòtic; C/Sardenya (located opposite the Sagrada Familia), Eixample; Plaça Portal Pau (located opposite Monument a Colom), Port Vell; Sants station; La Rambla 115; corner of Plaça d'Espanya and Avda Maria Cristina; airport.

Palau Robert

Passeig de Gràcia 107, Eixample (93 238 80 91, www.gencat.net/probert). Metro Diagonal. **Open** 10am-7pm Mon-Sat; 10am-2.30pm Sun.
The Generalitat's lavishly equipped centre has maps and other essentials for the whole of Catalonia.

010 phoneline

Open 24hrs daily.
This city-run information line is aimed mainly at locals, but it manages to do an impeccable job of answering all kinds of queries. There are sometimes English-speaking operators.

Visas

EU nationals and citizens of the US, Canada, Australia and New Zealand do not need visas for stays of up to three months. For EU citizens a passport or national ID card valid for travel abroad is sufficient; non-EU citizens must have full passports.

What's on

The main papers all have daily 'what's on' events listings, with entertainment supplements on Fridays (most run TV schedules on Saturdays). For monthly listings, see *Barcelona Metropolitan* and freesheets such as *Mondo Sonoro* and *AB* (these can be found in bars and music shops).

Guía del Ocio

A weekly listings magazine available at any kiosk. Its listings aren't always 100% up-to-date or accurate but it is a useful starting point. It's also online at www.guiadelociobcn.es.

Time Out Barcelona

A comprehensive weekly listings magazine, in Catalan (www.timeout.cat).

ESSENTIALS

Catalan Vocabulary

Catalan phonetics are significantly different from those of Spanish, with a wider range of vowel sounds and soft consonants. Catalans use the familiar (*tu*) rather than the polite (*vosté*) second-person forms very freely, but for convenience verbs are given here in the polite form.

Useful expressions

hello *hola*; good morning *bon dia*; good afternoon *bona tarda*; good evening/night *bona nit*; goodbye *adéu*; please *sisplau*; very good/OK *molt bé*; thank you (very much) *(moltes) gràcies*; you're welcome *de res*; do you speak English? *parla anglés?*; I'm sorry, I don't speak Catalan *ho sento, no parlo català*; I don't understand *no ho entenc*; what's your name? *com es diu?*; Sir/Mr *senyor (sr)*; Madam/Mrs *senyora (sra)*; Miss *senyoreta (srta)*; excuse me/sorry *perdoni/disculpi*; excuse me, please *escolti* (literally, 'listen to me'); OK/fine *val/d'acord*; how much is it? *quant val?*; why? *perqué?*; when? *quan?*; who? *qui?*; what? *qué?*; where? *on?*; how? *com?*; where is...? *on és...?*; who is it? *qui és?*; is/are there any...? *hi ha...?/n'hi ha de...?*; very *molt*; and *i* or *o*; with *amb*; without *sense*; enough *prou* open *obert*; closed *tancat*; entrance *entrada*; exit *sortida*; I would like *vull*; how many would you like? *quants en vol?*; I like *m'agrada*; I don't like *no m'agrada*; good *bo/bona*; bad *dolent/a*; well/badly *bé/malament*; small *petit/a*; big *gran*; expensive *car/a*; cheap *barat/a*; hot (food, drink) *calent/a*; cold *fred/a*; something *alguna cosa*; nothing *res*; more *més*; less *menys*; more or less *més o menys*; toilets *els banys/els serveis/els lavabos*

Getting around

a ticket *un bitllet*; return *de anada i tornada*; left *esquerra*; right *dreta*; here *aquí*; there *allí*; straight on *tot recte*; at the corner *a la cantonada*; as far as *fins a*; towards *cap a*; near *a prop*; far *lluny*; is it far? *és lluny?*

Time

now *ara*; later *més tard*; yesterday *ahir*; today *avui*; tomorrow *demà*; morning *el matí*; midday *migdia*; afternoon *la tarda*; evening *el vespre*; night *la nit*; late night (roughly, from 1-6am) *la matinada*; at what time...? *a quina hora...?*; in an hour *en una hora*; at 2 *a les dues*; at 8pm *a les vuit del vespre*; at 1.30 *a dos quarts de dues*; at 5.15 *a un quart de sis/a las cinc i quart*; at 22.30 *a vint-i-dos-trenta*

Numbers

0 *zero*; 1 *u, un, una*; 2 *dos, dues*; 3 *tres*; 4 *quatre*; 5 *cinc*; 6 *sis*; 7 *set*; 8 *vuit*; 9 *nou*; 10 *deu*; 11 *onze*; 12 *dotze*; 13 *tretze*; 14 *catorze*; 15 *quinze*; 16 *setze*; 17 *disset*; 18 *divuit*; 19 *dinou*; 20 *vint*; 21 *vint-i-u*; 22 *vint-i-dos, vint-i-dues*; 30 *trenta*; 40 *quaranta*; 50 *cinquanta*; 60 *seixanta*; 70 *setanta*; 80 *vuitanta*; 90 *noranta*; 100 *cent*; 200 *dos-cents, dues-centes*; 1,000 *mil*

Days & months

Monday *dilluns*; Tuesday *dimarts*; Wednesday *dimecres*; Thursday *dijous*; Friday *divendres*; Saturday *dissabte*; Sunday *diumenge*; January *gener*; February *febrer*; March *març*; April *abril*; May *maig*; June *juny*; July *juliol*; August *agost*; September *setembre*; October *octubre*; November *novembre*; December *desembre*

Spanish Vocabulary

Although many locals prefer to speak Catalan, everyone in the city can speak Spanish. The Spanish familiar form for 'you' (*tú*) is used very freely, but it's safer to use the more formal *usted* with older people and strangers (verbs below are given in the *usted* form).

Useful expressions

hello *hola*; good morning *buenos días*; good afternoon, good evening *buenas tardes*; good evening (after dark); good night *buenas noches*; goodbye *adiós*; please *por favor*; very good/OK *muy bien*; thank you (very much) *(muchas) gracias*; you're welcome *de nada*; do you speak English? *¿habla inglés?*; I don't speak Spanish *no hablo castellano*; I don't understand *no lo entiendo*; OK/fine *vale*; what's your name? *¿cómo se llama?*; Sir/Mr *señor (sr)*; Madam/Mrs *señora (sra)*; Miss *señorita (srta)*; excuse me/sorry *perdón*; excuse me, please *oiga* (to attract someone's attention, politely; literally, 'hear me'); where is...? *¿dónde está...?*; why? *¿por qué?*; when? *¿cuándo?*; who? *¿quién?*; what? *¿qué?*; where? *¿dónde?*; how? *¿cómo?*; who is it? *¿quién es?*; is/are there any...? *¿hay...?*; very *muy*; and *y*; or *o*; with *con*; without *sin*; enough *bastante*; open *abierto*; closed *cerrado*; entrance *entrada*; exit *salida*; I would like *quiero*; how many would you like? *¿cuántos quiere?*; how much is it *¿cuánto es?*; I like *me gusta*; I don't like *no me gusta*; good *bueno/a*; bad *malo/a*; well/badly *bien/mal*; small *pequeño/a*; big *gran, grande*; expensive *caro/a*; cheap *barato/a*; hot (food, drink) *caliente*; cold *frío/a*; something *algo*; nothing *nada*; more/less *más/menos*; more or less *más o menos*; toilets *los baños/los servicios/los lavabos*

Getting around

a ticket *un billete*; return *de ida y vuelta*; the next stop *la próxima parada*; left *izquierda*; right *derecha*; here *aquí*; there *allí*; straight on *todo recto*; to the end of the street *al final de la calle*; as far as *hasta*; towards *hacia*; near *cerca*; far *lejos*

Time

now *ahora*; later *más tarde*; yesterday *ayer*; today *hoy*; tomorrow *mañana*; morning *la mañana*; midday *mediodía*; afternoon/evening *la tarde*; night *la noche*; late night (roughly 1-6am) *la madrugada*; at what time...? *¿a qué hora...?*; at 2 *a las dos*; at 8pm *a las ocho de la tarde*; at 1.30 *a la una y media*; at 5.15 *a las cinco y cuarto*; in an hour *en una hora*

Numbers

0 *cero*; 1 *un, uno, una*; 2 *dos*; 3 *tres*; 4 *cuatro*; 5 *cinco*; 6 *seis*; 7 *siete*; 8 *ocho*; 9 *nueve*; 10 *diez*; 11 *once*; 12 *doce*; 13 *trece*; 14 *catorce*; 15 *quince*; 16 *dieciséis*; 17 *diecisiete*; 18 *dieciocho*; 19 *diecinueve*; 20 *veinte*; 21 *veintiuno*; 22 *veintidós*; 30 *treinta*; 40 *cuarenta*; 50 *cincuenta*; 60 *sesenta*; 70 *setenta*; 80 *ochenta*; 90 *noventa*; 100 *cien*; 200 *doscientos*; 1,000 *mil*

Days & months

Monday *lunes*; Tuesday *martes*; Wednesday *miércoles*; Thursday *jueves*; Friday *viernes*; Saturday *sábado*; Sunday *domingo* January *enero*; February *febrero*; March *marzo*; April *abril*; May *mayo*; June *junio*; July *julio*; August *agosto*; September *septiembre*; October *octubre*; November *noviembre*; December *diciembre*

Menu Glossary

Basics

Catalan	Spanish	English
una cullera	una cuchara	a spoon
una forquilla	un tenedor	a fork
un ganivet	un cuchillo	a knife
una ampolla de	una botella de	a bottle of
vi negre	vino tinto	red wine
vi rosat	vino rosado	rosé
vi blanc	vino blanco	white wine
una altra	otra	another (one)
més	más	more
pa	pan	bread
oli d'oliva	aceite de oliva	olive oil
sal i pebre	sal y pimienta	salt and pepper
amanida	ensalada	salad
truita	tortilla	omelette

(note: **truita** refers to either an omelette or a trout.)

la nota	la cuenta	the bill
un cendrer	un cenicero	ashtray
bon profit	aproveche	enjoy your meal
sóc...	soy...	I'm a...
vegetarià/ana		
vegetariano/a	vegetariano/a	vegetarian
diabètic/a	diabético/a	diabetic

Cooking terms

Catalan	Spanish	English
a la brasa	a la brasa	chargrilled
a la graella/ planx	a la plancha	grilled on a hot metal plate
a la romana	a la romana	fried in batter
al forn	al horno	baked
al vapor	al vapor	steamed
fregit	frito	fried
rostit	asado	roast
ben fet	bien hecho	well done
a punt	medio hecho	medium
poc fet	poco hecho	rare

Carn/Carne/Meat

Catalan	Spanish	English
bou	buey	beef
cabrit	cabrito	kid
conill	conejo	rabbit
embotits	embotidos	cold cuts
fetge	hígado	liver
garrí	cochinillo	suckling pig
llebre	liebre	hare
llengua	lengua	tongue
llom	lomo	loin (usually pork)
pernil	jamón	dry-cured
serrà	serrano	ham
pernil dolç	jamón york	cooked ham
peus de porc	manos de cerdo	pigs' trotters
porc	cerdo	pork
porc senglar	jabalí	wild boar
vedella	ternera	veal
xai/be	cordero	lamb

Aviram/Aves/Poultry

Catalan	Spanish	English
ànec	pato	duck
gall dindi	pavo	turkey
guatlla	codorniz	quail
oca	oca	goose
ous	huevos	eggs
perdiu	perdiz	partridge
colomí	pichón	pigeon
pintada	gallina de Guinea	guinea fowl
pollastre	pollo	chicken

Peix/Pescado/Fish

Catalan	Spanish	English
anxoves	anchoas	anchovies
bacallà	bacalao	salt cod

besuc	*besugo*	sea bream
caballa	*verat*	mackerel
calamarsos	*calamares*	squid
llenguado	*lenguado*	sole
llobarro	*lubina*	sea bass
lluç	*merluza*	hake
moll	*salmonete*	red mullet
musclos	*mejillones*	mussels
pop	*pulpo*	octopus
rap	*rape*	monkfish
rèmol	*rodaballo*	turbot
salmó	*salmón*	salmon
sardines	*sardinas*	sardines
sípia	*sepia*	squid
tonyina	*atún*	tuna
truita	*trucha*	trout

(note: *truita* can also mean omelette.)

Marisc/Mariscos/ Shellfish

Catalan	Spanish	English
calamarsos	*calamares*	squid
cloïsses	*almejas*	clams
cranc	*cangrejo*	crab
escamarlans	*cigalas*	crayfish
escopinyes	*berberechos*	cockles
espardenyes	*espardeñas*	sea cucumbers
gambes	*gambas*	prawns
llagosta	*langosta*	spiny lobster
llagostins	*langostinos*	langoustines
llamàntol	*bogavante*	lobster
musclos	*mejillones*	mussels
navalles	*navajas*	razor clams
percebes	*percebes*	barnacles
pop	*pulpo*	octopus
sípia	*sepia*	squid
tallarines	*tallarinas*	wedge clams

Verdures/Legumbre/ Vegetables

Catalan	Spanish	English
albergínia	*berenjena*	aubergine
all	*ajo*	garlic
alvocat	*aguacate*	avocado
bolets	*setas*	wild mushrooms
carbassons	*calabacines*	courgette
carxofes	*alcachofas*	artichokes
ceba	*cebolla*	onion
cigrons	*garbanzos*	chickpeas
col	*col*	cabbage
enciam	*lechuga*	lettuce
endivies	*endivias*	chicory
espinacs	*espinacas*	spinach
mongetes blanques	*judías blancas*	haricot beans
mongetes verdes	*judías verdes*	French beans
pastanaga	*zanahoria*	carrot
patates	*patatas*	potatoes
pebrots	*pimientos*	peppers
pèsols	*guisantes*	peas
porros	*puerros*	leek
tomàquets	*tomates*	tomatoes
xampinyons	*champiñones*	mushrooms

Postres/Postres/ Desserts

Catalan	Spanish	English
flam	*flan*	crème caramel
formatge	*queso*	cheese
gelat	*helado*	ice-cream
música	*música*	dried fruit and nuts with muscatel
pastís	*pastel*	cake
tarta	*tarta*	tart

Fruïta/Fruta/Fruit

Catalan	Spanish	English
figues	*higos*	figs
gerds	*frambuesas*	raspberries
maduixes	*fresas*	strawberries
pera	*pera*	pear
pinya	*piña*	pineapple
plàtan	*plátano*	banana
poma	*manzana*	apple
préssec	*melocotón*	peach
prunes	*ciruelas*	plums
raïm	*uvas*	grapes
taronja	*naranja*	orange

ESSENTIALS

Index

MARISCCO

Plaça Reial,8 • 934124536
Corsega 272 • 932922816
www.mariscco.com

In the heart of the Barrio Gotic, on Plaça Reial you'll find the restaurant **Mariscco Reial** (formerly Taxidermista).

The restaurant used to be the Grand Café Espanyol, then later the Natural Science museum with a workshop for taxidermy. A place frequented by worldwide lovers and producers of art and culture such as Joan Miró, Ava Gardner, Mario Cabré and Salvador Dalí.

Respecting the original architecture, **Mariscco Reial** offers the opportunity to eat in a spacious interior with high ceilings and beautiful eclectic spaces.

Mariscco Reial has private dining rooms as well as a beautiful large

terrace under one of the arcades of the Plaça Reial, open all year in a cosmopolitan atmosphere. **Mariscco Reial** welcomes its guests with a counter full of fresh

local seafood and their Mediterranean cuisine uses only top quality ingredients.

Among the house specialties are lobster soup with rice or rice soup with prawns — cooked to perfection. The ample wine cellar allows you to choose from an extensive wine list.

ESSENTIALS